A G[uide to]

Literary Sites
of the South

A Guide to

Literary Sites

of the South

Ella Robinson

VISION V PRESS

ON THE COVER

The Archibald Rutledge Home in McClellanville, South Carolina, is part of the Hampton Plantation State Park. Archibald Rutledge was the first poet laureate of South Carolina.

THE AUTHOR

Ella Robinson is a freelance writer from Pleasant Grove, Alabama. A graduate of Samford University with a major in English, she has had 22 years of experience in editing and writing.

Vision Press
P.O. Box 1106
3230 Mystic Lake Way
Northport, Alabama 35476

Library of Congress Cataloguing-in-Publication Data

Robinson, Ella, 1954-
   A guide to literary sites of the South / Ella Robinson.
        p.   cm.
   ISBN 1-885219-08-3
   1. Literary landmarks—Southern States—Guidebooks. 2. American literature—Southern States—History and criticism.
   3. Authors, American—Southern States—Homes and haunts.
   4. Southern States—Intellectual life. 5. Southern States—In literature. I. Title.
   PS144.S67R63 1998

97-32236
CIP

Printed in the United States of America

1525228

Acknowledgments

For their help on this book, thanks must go to the following:

Joanne Sloan and Cheryl Wray, Vision Press; Margaret Armbrester, Samuel Ullman Museum; Amanda Chenault, Bayou Folk Museum; Katherine M. Smith and A. Neticals, Edgar Allan Poe Museum; Marion S. Chambon, Beauregard-Keyes House; Valerie R. Rivers, Marjorie Kinnan Rawlings State Historic Site; Sylvia Robards and Linda Larson, Ernest Hemingway House Museum; Kitty Oliver and the Middle Georgia Historic Society, Inc., Sidney Lanier Cottage; Nancy Towe, Margaret Mitchell House; Andrea Davis, University of Mississippi; Victoria Taylor Hawkins, Baltimore City Life Muscums; Warren R. Weber and Carol McBryant, Carl Sandburg Home; Ted Mitchell, Thomas Wolfe Memorial; Jerry Guntharp and Al Norris III, Scott & Zelda Fitzgerald Museum; Karen M. Kelly and Carole Mumford, Joel Chandler Harris Association, Inc.; Jed DeKalb, Tennessee State Photographic Services; Jeanne Hochmuth, Weems-Botts Museum; Frances Roberts and Ivy Barber, Weeden House; Jeane Moore, Robert Penn Warren Birthplace Committee; D'Andrea Coleman, National Park Service, U.S. Department of the Interior, Booker T. Washington Home; Alice Williams, Hampton Plantation State Park; Margaret Taylor, Pearl S. Buck Birthplace Museum; Kathy McCoy, Monroe County Heritage Museums; Robert E. Jones, Flannery O'Connor Childhood Home; Linda Evans and Gayle Fripp, Greensboro Historical Museum; Jim Pate, Southern History, Birmingham Public Library; Norwood A. Kerr, Alabama Department of Archives and History; Angela Nelson, Tuscaloosa Public Library; Andrea Watson, W. S. Hoole Special Collections Library; Susan Moody, Helen Keller Library; Katharine Suttell, Atlanta-Fulton Public Library; Jean Landon, Washington Memorial Library; Wilber A. Richards, Ina Dillard Russell Library; Gerald Roberts, Berea College Library; Kate Black, University of Kentucky Library; A. L. Harmon, Murray State University; Averil J. Kadis,

A Guide to Literary Sites of the South

Enoch Pratt Library; Karen Patterson, William Alexander Percy Memorial Library; Lisa Speer, University of Mississippi; Lebby B. Lanert, Greensboro Public Library; Ann Wright, Pack Memorial Library; Patricia Glass Bennett, Charleston Library Society; Bill Fagelson, University of Texas at Austin; Anne L. Cook, Texas Department of Transportation; Steven E. Smith, Texas A&M University; Elizabeth Mozelle, Richmond Public Library; Margaret C. Cook, College of William and Mary; Katy White and Rosemary Jones, Friends of Libraries, U.S.A.

To
Daniel Robinson

"From that house there has come so much life
that it ought never to die or fall into ruin....
For me that house was a gateway to America."
Pearl S. Buck

Contents

Introduction

Why This Book?

When I first thought of writing this book, I went to Montgomery, Alabama, and toured the F. Scott & Zelda Fitzgerald Museum. It was a warm summer day with the sun streaming through the parlor windows. I stood looking at a picture Zelda had painted. The pinks, lavenders, and greens washed together to form a delicate ballerina. Suddenly, the screen door at the back of the house creaked, then slammed. I thought about Scott holding Scotty, their daughter, in his arms. For just a moment I believed I heard the little girl's giggles and Scott's heavy footfalls.

Soon I was immersed in the stories this book would tell and found myself walking through the rooms of other writers' homes across the South. In all these homes, I experienced much of what I had experienced at that Fitzgerald home.

At William Faulkner's beloved Rowan Oak in Oxford, Mississippi, I could almost see the author sitting at his desk, contemplating the next lines of his next novel; then I could visualize him roaming the flower garden and sitting under a shady tree, searching for inspiration.

In bustling Atlanta, I found myself transported to the days when Joel Chandler Harris welcomed people into his home, the Wren's Nest. Echos resound of Harris' welcoming words and the laughter of children as they were told a new Uncle Remus tale from the author's own mouth.

I want you to experience such sensations as you read this book. I hope that you will be able to visualize the beauty of the writers' homes and other sites, and that you will be amazed by a new bit of information you learn about an author you thought you already knew everything about. And I hope, too, that you will be able to use this book as a travel guide and experience these sensations firsthand and up-close-and-personal.

How to Use This Book

This book was written with the traveler in mind. It offers detailed information about home sites open to the public and short profiles of the authors who lived in these homes. It also provides information about other sites associated with Southern writers (such as historical markers, festivals, and burial sites) and accompanying profiles of those writers.

Although this book is not meant as a definitive literary resource, it will provide the reader with a little history and a lot of trivia. It tells who gave his last penny to a swimming pool and who established the first public library in Richmond, Virginia. It tells about the Alabama author whose book was banned during the Civil War and the author who was labeled a heretic by her schoolmates. Profiles focus on authors who loved the South—and a few who didn't.

Not all the authors featured in this book can be called Southern writers. Many people define a Southern author as one who writes about the South. However, this book also focuses on authors who have *lived* in the South—understandably so because this book is at its heart a journey to writers and their homes. Ernest Hemingway and Carl Sandburg, for example, were both born in Illinois and wrote about topics beyond the Mason-Dixon line; however, they both found a home in the South and wrote prolifically while living here. Tennessee Williams was born in the South, but he spent most of his life away from it. However, the influence of Southern culture is evident in all of his works.

The time line that runs through this book spans 200 years. For example, Mason Locke Weems, who began his writing career in the late 1700s, is included. (His home in Dumfries, Virginia, is open for public tours.) There are profiles of many authors who wrote during the Civil War and the Reconstruction period.

You will find a vast array of other sites to visit aside from the obvious writers' homes. In addition to the featured 26 home sites, the book also includes information about 62 other sites of interest (monuments, markers, etc.,) 54 burial sites, and 19 festivals. In all, the guide includes 13 states and profiles 113 authors.

This book equips you to go on a literary tour of the South. In traveling, though, realize that there are several tactics you can use to make your traveling easier. First, note that hours, admission fees, addresses, and telephone numbers are listed for each house and museum. When planning a vacation or day tour, it is advisable to call or write to the home ahead of time to assure that the house will be open and inquire about changes in the admission fee. Class tours and large groups should always call to make reservations at least one month in advance.

Also notice that a number of festivals are mentioned throughout the book; these are always a good stop on a vacation. Since various circumstances can affect whether a festival is held from year to year, please contact the festival promoters for the most current information before making plans to attend. Addresses and/or telephone numbers are provided for each festival listed.

Reading about and visiting Southern authors' homes and other historic sites gives one a new perspective about the person and his or her work. After learning about the living conditions, personal acquaintances, and political influences of an author, a reader can better understand an author's writings.

As visitors walk the same path an author walked, see a pipe and typewriter waiting for their owner to return, or hear the creak of a screen door, it is hard to convince them that they didn't hear the voice or see a shadow of an author who lived and wrote many years ago.

Enjoy this trek down the paths of Southern literature and enjoy your days on the road.

A Guide to Literary Sites of the South

Alabama

F. Scott Fitzgerald
Zelda Fitzgerald
Helen Keller
Samuel Ullman
Booker T. Washington
Maria Howard Weeden
Truman Capote
Nelle Harper Lee
William March Campbell
Samuel Mintern Peck
Abram Joseph Ryan
Augusta Jane Evans Wilson
Hudson Strode

F. Scott & Zelda Fitzgerald Museum

919 Felder Avenue
Montgomery, Alabama 36106

Hours: Wednesday through Friday, 10 a.m.-2 p.m.;
Saturday & Sunday, 1-5 p.m.
Admission: Donation
Telephone: (334) 264-4222

Scott and Zelda Fitzgerald rented this house in October 1931 and lived here with their daughter, Scotty, until April 1932. It is the only museum in the world dedicated to the memory of the Fitzgeralds.

Built in 1909, the home has 10,000 square feet of living space. Much of it now is used for apartments, with only the first floor being open to the public.

A tour guide welcomes visitors and is available for questions. An optional 30-minute documentary of the Fitzgeralds is well worth the time.

Among the items on display are two marble-topped tables from Zelda's child-hood home in Montgomery (which is no longer standing), several of her paintings, and many photographs and letters.

Scott worked on his novel *Tender Is the Night* while living here, and Zelda began her only published novel, *Save Me the Waltz*, while living in the house.

Zelda suffered a nervous breakdown in the spring of 1932 and was moved from this house to Highland Hospital in Asheville, North Carolina. Feeling the strain of the Depression, Scott moved from the house to Hollywood to work as a screen-writer.

After Scott's death in 1940, Zelda lived with her mother on Sayre Street in Montgomery (that home is privately owned and not open to the public) with the exception of several periods in a mental hospital in North Carolina.

F. Scott Fitzgerald
(1896-1940)

The writing voice of the Jazz Age

Home—*Montgomery, Alabama*
Special Collections—*Indiana University, Lilly Library, Bloomington, Indiana; Minnesota Historical Library, St. Paul, Minnesota; University of Nevada, Reno, Nevada; Princeton University, Rare Books and Special Collections, Princeton, New Jersey*
Festival—*Fitzfest, Montgomery, Alabama, in June (annual event)*
Burial Site—*St. Mary's Catholic Cemetery, Rockville, Maryland*

A tall, attractive man, F. Scott Fitzgerald enjoyed being in the center of the 1920s social scene. Wild parties, disillusionment, sensationalism, defiance of convention, and personal ambitions—these were the elements of his novels as well as the realities of his lifestyle. His writing reflected the flamboyance of the era and identified him with the jet set.

Born in St. Paul, Minnesota, in 1896, he grew up in a society-conscious home. Although his parents were not wealthy, they lived a fashionable lifestyle and encouraged their son to associate with the elite. He studied at Princeton University where he became well known as a writer for the student drama society. Although he established himself as a member of the popular crowd, he remained aware of a difference between himself and the rich. The special magic of the wealthy became a reoccurring theme in his writing.

His first short story, "The Mystery of Raymond Mortgage," was published when he was 13. *The Girl from Lazy J*, his first play, was performed in St. Paul when he was 15.

In 1917 he accepted a commission in the U.S. Army and the next year was stationed at Camp Sheridan in Montgomery, Alabama. While at a dance at the Montgomery Country Club, he met and fell in love with Zelda Sayre. They kept in touch throughout his tour of duty, and at his discharge from the army he vowed to earn enough money to persuade Zelda to marry him. He then set out to rewrite the novel that he had completed while serving in the army. *This Side of Paradise* became an enormous success and enabled him to ask Zelda for her hand in marriage.

As a writer, Fitzgerald established himself as the voice of young men and women of the Jazz Age. He wrote short stories quickly and sold them to the most popular magazines of the day. In 1925, his greatest accomplishment—*The Great Gatsby*—was published. Although the novel is now hailed as one of the best of the twentieth century, it didn't achieve popular or financial success. Critics have cited the publication of *The Great Gatsby* as the beginning of his decline in popularity.

He and Zelda made a sensational pair. For almost ten years they lived a party life, giving and attending elaborate gatherings, traveling, drinking, and spending carelessly. Zelda suffered a nervous breakdown in 1930, the beginning of what turned into a lifetime of treatment in and out of sanitariums. The Depression and frivolous living took a toll on the Fitzgeralds, and Zelda's medical bills caused them an even greater debt. To earn money, Scott moved to Hollywood to work as a screenwriter.

He died of a heart attack on December 21, 1940, in California, while writing *The Last Tycoon.*

Zelda Sayre Fitzgerald
(1900-1948)

She had a voice all her own

Home—*Montgomery, Alabama*
Memorial—*Montgomery Museum of Fine Arts, Montgomery, Alabama*
Festival—*Fitzfest, Montgomery, Alabama, in June (annual event)*
Special Collection—*Princeton University, Rare Books and Special Collections, Princeton, New Jersey*
Burial Site—*St. Mary's Catholic Cemetery, Rockville, Maryland*

Petite, brown haired Zelda Sayre made her mark as a lively, mischievous Southern belle. She tantalized boys by dancing on table tops and appeared at a school commencement exercise with her stockings rolled to her knees. However, bouts of depression interfered with her fun-loving spirit. Both extreme emotions are reflected in her short stories and her only novel, *Save Me the Waltz.*

Born on July 24, 1900, in Montgomery, Alabama, she attended public schools, focusing on friends and fun and little on academics. She met the handsome Lt. Scott Fitzgerald at a dance at the Montgomery Country Club in 1918. Fitzgerald was stationed for a short time at an army base near Montgomery. Zelda was dazzled by his flamboyance. They kept in touch throughout his time in service, and shortly after his discharge they married. They had one daughter, Scotty.

Zelda's married life grew into a whirlwind of adventure—traveling the United States and Europe, attending parties, and throwing parties of her own. The Fitzgeralds became the definition of the Jazz Age. During this time Zelda concentrated on painting and ballet, while living in her husband's shadow. As Scott became more and more popular, she became more and more depressed. Growing restless and seeking to create an identity for herself, she turned to writing.

With Scott's assistance she wrote several short stories that were published in periodicals under Scott's name or with a joint byline. As a result of these articles centered on youth and the Jazz Age, *College Humor* magazine asked Scott to write a series of articles geared for the teenage market. He had no interest in writing for teenagers and negotiated a deal for Zelda to write the articles that would carry a joint byline as a marketing advantage.

While living in Paris in 1929-30, Zelda wrote short stories such as "The Original Follies Girls," "The Southern Girl," and "The Girls with Talent."

Although she had become an accomplished writer, she could not shake the association with Scott. Her story, "A Millionaire's Girl," seemed so well written that *Saturday Evening Post* assumed that Scott had written it, and the magazine published it under his name.

In her quest to achieve success of her own, Zelda became physically and psychologically exhausted. In 1930, she suffered a nervous breakdown, the first of three during her lifetime.

As a step to recovery, she turned even more to writing—composing letters to Scott, working on short stories such as "Miss Ella" and "A Couple of Nuts" and her novel, *Save Me the Waltz*. Critics have said that her writing grew to a point where Scott viewed her as a rival. However, publishers and readers never gave her or her writing the recognition it deserved.

In 1932, after her second breakdown, she entered a Baltimore sanitarium. She spent the rest of her life in and out of mental hospitals. During the periods when she was released from treatment, Zelda lived with her mother in Montgomery.

She died on March 10, 1948, in a fire at Highland Hospital in Asheville, North Carolina.

Ivy Green

Helen Keller Birthplace
300 West North Commons
Tuscumbia, Alabama 35674

Hours:
Monday through Saturday, 8:30 a.m.-4 p.m.; Sunday, 1-4 p.m.
Closed Easter, Labor Day, Thanksgiving Day, and December 24-26
Admission: Adults, $3; Ages 6 to 11, $1; Under 6, free
Telephone: (205) 383-4066

Helen Keller's grandfather built this white frame home in 1820, six decades before Helen's birth. Its architecture is unique, including ornamental embellishments and a bay window. Each of its large square rooms has a fireplace.

Her cradle and the table where she disrupted so many family meals are on display. Much of the furniture in the home belonged to the Kellers, but some period pieces and some of the wall and table decorations were donated by local residents.

At 19 months old, Helen was stricken with a fever which left her blind and deaf. Her parents sought the professional assistance of Anne Sullivan, a young teacher, who became Helen's constant companion at Ivy Green and throughout her life. Keller's experiences at Ivy Green led her to a career in writing and speaking on the behalf of the handicapped. She lived most of her adult life in Connecticut.

Many tourists take time to walk in the gardens of Ivy Green. Here they find the famous water pump where Helen understood her first word—*water*.

Helen Keller
(1880-1908)

A champion of the disabled

Home—*Ivy Green, Tuscumbia, Alabama (houses special collection of books and letters)*
Library—*Helen Keller Library, Tuscumbia, Alabama (doesn't house special collection)*
Play—The Miracle Worker, *Tuscumbia, Alabama (performed annually during June and July)*
Special Collections—*Francis Bacon Library, Claremont, California; American Foundation for the Blind, McMigel Memorial Library, New York, New York*

A champion of social reform for the treatment of the handicapped, Helen Keller spent most of her life deaf and blind. Through hard work and the life-long support of her friend Anne Sullivan, she became a speaker and writer, producing speeches and magazine articles that made a difference for people with all handicaps, especially the deaf and blind.

At 19 months old, she lost her hearing and sight due to a high fever. She grew to be an unmanageable child, confused and angered by her dark world. She explained, "Sometimes I stood between two persons who were conversing and touched their lips. . . . I moved my lips and gesticulated frantically without result. This made me so angry at times that I kicked and screamed until I was exhausted." When she was six, her father wrote to the Perkins Institute for the Blind in Boston requesting a teacher.

A young graduate, Anne Sullivan, arrived in Tuscumbia on March 3, 1887. Having had her eyesight partially restored, Sullivan understood Helen better than anyone ever had. Using a combination of firmness, determination, and love, Sullivan worked each day with Helen. Once Helen realized that everything had a name, she made great progress. English was only a beginning; she learned to speak French and German as well. She studied math, science, and literature at Wright-Humason School for the Deaf and Cambridge School for Young Ladies. In 1904 she graduated from Radcliffe College with honors.

Using public speaking and writing as her forums, she became an advocate for the handicapped. Through articles in the *Kansas City Star* and *Ladies' Home Journal*, she spoke openly about blindness in newborns. She became a reporter for the United Press International in 1913 and contributed numerous articles, poems, and essays to various periodicals, including *Atlantic Monthly, Youth's Companion, McClure's,* and *Century.* She also spent much of her time lecturing on behalf of the handicapped throughout the world.

Anne Sullivan's husband, John Albert Macy, who was a literary critic and editor, encouraged Keller to compile the series of articles that she wrote for the *Ladies' Home Journal* while attending Radcliffe into book form. The result of this endeavor, *The Story of My Life* (1903), remains a popular book almost a hundred years after its first publication. Keller took critics off guard with her book *Midstream: My Later Life* (1929). Her inclusion of images of sight and sound amazed critics and readers alike. Scholars have commented that such vivid images would be noteworthy of a writer without handicaps.

Her other publications include *The Song of the Stone Wall,* a book of poetry, (1910); *My Religion* (1927); *Let Us Have Faith* (1940); and *Helen Keller, Her Socialist Years: Writings and Speeches* (1967).

She died on June 1, 1968, in Westport, Connecticut. Her remains lie at St. Joseph's Chapel in the National Cathedral in Washington, D.C.

Samuel Ullman Museum

2150 15th Avenue South
Birmingham, Alabama 35205

Hours: By appointment only
Admission: Free
Telephone: (205) 934-5634
For tour information write to: UAB Center for International Programs,
318 Hill University Center, 1400 University Boulevard,
Birmingham, AL 35294-1150.

This two-story frame home located on Birmingham's Southside was built in 1908. It has 11 rooms; however, only the first floor is open for tours.

Period items and original furniture decorate the home. Some of Samuel Ullman's possessions are on display, including his rosewood bed and several chairs. Also on display are the poet's inkwell, books, and some silver serving pieces.

Ullman moved here in 1906 to live with his daughter Leah Newfield and her family. The side stairway provided Ullman with a private entrance to his room. Here he wrote many of his poems and letters. He enjoyed baby-sitting with his grand-children and matching table-game strategies with his son-in-law.

He wrote his famous poem, "Youth," while he lived in this house. The poem is said to have touched the hearts and minds of many people, including General Douglas MacArthur. It is still viewed as a credo for success by many Japanese busi-nessmen.

The home was established as a museum through the efforts and contributions of citizens and corporations in Japan and the United States. The house is used for retreats, seminars, and receptions. With prior arrangements, the public may sched-ule use of the museum.

A collection of Ullman's poems and papers is also housed here.

Samuel Ullman
(1840-1924)

His poem inspired millions

Home—Samuel Ullman Museum, Birmingham, Alabama
The Ullman Building—University of Alabama in Birmingham,
Birmingham, Alabama (used for college classes)
Special Collection—Birmingham Public Library, Birmingham, Alabama
Burial Site—Jewish Cemetery, Birmingham, Alabama

Labeled the "Phantom Poet," Samuel Ullman is better known in Japan than in the United States. A civic, religious, and educational leader, he spent much of his retirement years writing poetry and letters. His most popular poem, "Youth," continues to inspire millions of people.

Born on April 13, 1840, in Hechingen, Germany, he was the first child of Jacob and Lena Ullman. Soon after his birth, the family moved to France. Ten years and four children later, the family immigrated to the United States, making their home in Port Gibson, Mississippi.

Ullman attended the local schools, and at age 13 he began working in his father's butcher shop, making daily meat deliveries before school. In 1856, he left Port Gibson to attend school in Louisville, Kentucky. He returned to Port Gibson two years later and became his father's "first assistant." Although he never attended college, learning came easily and quickly to him, and he devoted himself to lifelong self-education. Later in life, he joked about people calling him "Doctor" Ullman.

He served in the Mississippi militia during the Civil War. For several months, he was assigned to the Regimental Band, and later records show that he served under the command of Stonewall Jackson. After the war, he moved to Natchez,

Mississippi, where he married Emma Mayer in 1867; they had eight children.

For almost 20 years Ullman lived in Natchez, establishing himself as a devoted husband and father, interim lay rabbi, businessman, civic leader, and proponent of public education. In 1884, he and his family joined the thousands of others who were attracted to Birmingham, Alabama. The 13-year-old city promised exciting economic opportunities. First opening the Ullman Hardware Store, he soon found ways to serve his new community. He was appointed to serve on the first Birmingham Board of Education, where he helped establish and monitor administrative procedures. He and his family became active in Birmingham's Jewish community, with Ullman serving as president and as lay rabbi of Temple Emanu-El. Before his retirement in 1908, he also worked as an insurance agent.

Throughout his life, he wrote long letters and put his thoughts to paper, usually in poetic form. However, most of his poetry was written after his retirement. He wrote his most popular poem, "Youth," in 1918, at the age of 78. Declaring that youth is a state of mind, not a time of life, he empowers the reader to "catch waves of optimism" and the hope of dying "young at eighty."

A copy of "Youth" is said to have hung in General Douglas MacArthur's offices in Manila and in Tokyo. "Youth" was published in the North American edition of *Reader's Digest* in 1945 and in the Japanese edition in 1946. It was through this publication that many Japanese soldiers returning home from the Pacific after World War II read the optimistic poem.

The poem spread into Japanese culture. Even today businessmen quote the poem, hang it in their offices, and share it with friends and associates. For example, in 1990, reporters and employees gathered in Pittsburgh, Pennsylvania, to hear the plans for the future of the National Steel Corporation. The corporation's new chairman, Kokichi Hagiwara, began the meeting by reading his business plan—"Youth" by Samuel Ullman.

After his retirement, Ullman regularly wrote letters to the editors of local newspapers, entertaining letters to friends and family, and poetry. His letters were informative and backed with intelligent insight, and his poetry was reflective and emotional. He wrote about Judaism, his wife, the brotherhood of man, life, death, and everyday experiences.

His poems were honest and full of justice, compassion, and devotion to God. His sense of time and place was that of a Southern writer. He often employed rural settings and descriptions in his poetry. *From the Summit of Years, Four Score* (1920) is a collection of all of his poems. The volume was prepared by his family in honor of his 80th birthday.

Ullman died on March 21, 1924, in Birmingham, Alabama.

The Oaks

Booker T. Washington's Family Home
1212 Old Montgomery Road
Tuskegee, Alabama 36083

Hours: Open daily, 9-11 a.m. and 1-4 p.m., with guided tours on the hour.
Closed on Thanksgiving, Christmas, and New Year's Day
Admission: Free
Telephone: (334) 727-3200
(Note: Tour groups must schedule at least one month in advance.)

This beautiful Victorian brick home was built entirely by Tuskegee Institute students and faculty in 1899. The paid student and faculty workers followed the plans designed by Robert Robinson Taylor, the first African American to graduate from Massachusetts Institute of Technology (MIT) in Boston, Massachusetts. The workers made the bricks using the soil from the Institute land to construct the home. It is one of the few surviving structures of the era designed and built by African Americans.

At the time of its construction, the home and the adjoining property had been purchased by Booker T. Washington. It didn't become a part of Tuskegee Institute until many years later.

Because Washington loved his home, he lamented about having to spend so much time away from it and his family. Speaking engagements and other work-related obligations required him to be on the road almost half of each year.

On the first floor, above the picture molding, are frieze murals which were painted in 1908 by E. W. Borman, a European artist. In the parlor and dining room are a piano and table games, set and ready to play. The Washingtons enjoyed spending the evenings in the parlor, telling stories about ancestors and talking about the events of the day. Many nights Portia, Washington's daughter, entertained the family by playing the piano.

The second floor is where Washington made his office. Here he mixed functional furniture with elaborate, hand-carved furniture from the Orient.

While visiting in the area, many tourists drive through the Tuskegee National Forest along U.S. 80. At the picnic area, Taska, is a replica of the old log cabin where Washington was born.

Note: Washington was born on a plantation in Hardy, Virginia. The plantation has been restored and is open to the public. See Virginia homes section.

Booker Taliaferro Washington
(1856-1915)

Pioneer author and educator

Home—*The Oaks, Tuskegee Institute, Tuskegee, Alabama*
Birthplace Replica—*Tuskegee National Forest, Tuskegee, Alabama*
National Monument—*Hardy, Virginia*
Monument—*State Capitol grounds, Charleston, West Virginia*
Special Collections—*Library of Congress, Manuscript Division,*
Washington, D.C.; Harvard University Library, Cambridge, Massachusetts
Burial Site—*Tuskegee Institute Cemetery, Tuskegee Institute, Tuskegee,*
Alabama

Writing was an avocation for Booker T. Washington; however, his autobiography *Up from Slavery* (1901) became widely read and admired. He wrote 11 books, several of which he co-authored. Most of his writing was autobiographical, and all of it was written to help edify African Americans.

He was born into slavery on April 5, 1856, near Roanoke, Virginia. After emancipation he moved with his family to West Virginia where he worked in the salt and coal mines. Washington attended Hampton Institute from 1872 until he graduated in 1875. He briefly considered careers in law and the ministry; however, he could not suppress his passion for learning and his desire to share his knowledge. Deciding to pursue a teaching career, he accepted a teaching position in Malden, West Virginia. In 1878 he attended Wayland Seminary, and in 1879 he returned to Hampton, this time as a teacher.

Washington married three times—to Fanny N. Smith in 1882, to Olivia Davidson in 1885, and to Margaret James Murry in 1892. He had three children.

In 1881 Washington moved to Tuskegee, Alabama, and began the Tuskegee

Normal and Industrial Institute. He spent the rest of his life building this college and offering African Americans a new way of life through industrial education.

A highly respected educator throughout the nation, Washington commanded equal admiration in the political arena of the late 1880s and early 1900s. His address at the Cotton States Exposition in Atlanta in 1895 established him as the leader of African Americans. Presidents, as well as business and industry leaders, turned to him for advice.

Washington's more noted books include *The Future of the American Negro* (1899), *The Story of My Life and Work* (1900), *Working with the Hands* (1904), and *My Larger Education* (1911).

Washington died on November 14, 1915, at Tuskegee Institute.

Weeden House Museum

300 Gates Avenue, SE
Huntsville, Alabama 35801

Hours: March-December—Tuesday-Sunday, 1-4 p.m.
Admission: Adults, $3; Children under 12, $1
Telephone: (205) 536-7718

This home is the birthplace of Alabama poet and artist Maria Howard Weeden. Built in 1819—27 years before Wecden's birth—this elegant home sits on the western edge of Huntsville's Twickenham Historic District. It is the only home in the District that is open regularly for public tours.

The leaded-glass fanlight above the front door is a dazzling feature noted by many tourists. The striking hand-crafted window is not uncommon to nineteenth-century homes of this grandeur. Inside is a graceful spiral staircase, hand-carved Federal mantels, and ornate woodwork. Walls and mantels are painted in authentic early nineteenth-century colors. Some of the furnishings on display belonged to the Weeden family.

Union troops captured this beautiful home to use as a headquarters during the Civil War, forcing Weeden and her family to take refuge further south. After the war the Weedens returned to their home to find it and the community devastated by Union troops. Weeden began teaching art classes in her home and writing stories and poems for the Presbyterian paper, the *Christian Observer*, to supplement the family's income and to rebuild the lifestyle the war had destroyed.

In the museum are four published volumes of her poetry, each containing her own illustrations. Many of Weeden's paintings are on display in the home, including portraits of her neighbors and friends.

Maria Howard Weeden
(1847-1905)

Artist and Poet

Home—*Huntsville, Alabama*
Bronze plaque and photograph—*Alabama Women's Hall of Fame*
Museum—*A. Howard Bean Hall, Judson College, Marion, Alabama*
Burial Site—*Maple Cemetery, Huntsville, Alabama*

A "born artist," Maria Howard Weeden resorted to writing her own verse when she couldn't find the words that suited her artistry. Living in the precarious time prior to the Civil War, she drew pictures of local African Americans—people she simply called friends. Many of her poems reflected the relationship between whites and African Americans during the later 1800s.

Born in Huntsville in 1846, six months after her father's death, Weeden showed at an early age an unusual aptitude for painting. Records indicate that she took art lessons from a local portrait painter before she was ten. As an attentive and talented student, she practiced often. Flowers and people became her specialty.

During the Civil War, the Union army found her house, because of its size and location, to be ideally suited for its Huntsville headquarters. With the house taken over by the soldiers, the family was forced to move to Tuskegee, where one of Weeden's older sisters lived. After the war, the family returned to their home and found it in need of repair and their budget severely depleted. At age 18, Weeden began supporting her family's income by teaching art classes and making greeting cards and gift books.

The frail, shy woman could be found almost any day of the week sitting in a large upstairs room of her home in front of an easel. Her high-necked blouses and long flowing skirts were her work uniform while painting for herself and while gently instructing young art students.

Her greeting cards and gift books demanded verse to go along with their illustrations. When she couldn't find verse she liked, she wrote her own. Soon she became preoccupied with "illuminating poems," because of the "literary flavor" the task provided. When William O. Allison, a land speculator from New Jersey, visited Huntsville, Weeden's talent overwhelmed him. He arranged, with her permission, to take her paintings and poetry to New York and have them published in book form. This book, *Shadows on the Wall*, brought her nationwide acclaim. Her illustrations of old slaves, people whom she knew, and poetry that had a simple, direct quality offered a tribute to the respect found between former master and former slave.

Doubleday, McClure and Company published another edition of her poetry in 1899 titled *Bandanna Ballads*. Joel Chandler Harris, author of the Uncle Remus tales, honored Weeden by writing the introduction to this book. She wrote two more volumes of poetry, *Songs of the Old South* and *Old Voices*.

She died on April 12, 1905, in Huntsville, Alabama. On March 5, 1998, she was inducted into the Alabama Women's Hall of Fame.

Other Alabama
Writers
and Sites

Truman Capote

(1924-1984)

Bestselling author of *In Cold Blood*

Monument —*Monroeville, Alabama*
Special Collections—*Monroe County Heritage Museum, Monroeville, Alabama; Library of Congress, Manuscript Division, Washington, D.C.; University of Nevada, Reno, Nevada*

Considered one of the twentieth century's most flamboyant and lyrical writers, Truman Capote began writing when he was ten. Even at an earlier age he carried a notebook in his pocket to capture descriptions of images and events. He became a self-proclaimed "fanatic on rhythm and language."

Truman Streckfus Persons was born on September 30, 1924, in New Orleans, Louisiana. In 1928, after his parents' divorce, he moved to Monroeville, Alabama, to live with relatives. An active and sometimes mischievous child, he enjoyed dreaming up adventures and getting his friends—which included Nelle Harper Lee—to act out the details. He lived for seven years in Monroeville, stockpiling characters, adventures, and experiences that he would later incorporate in his short stories.

In 1935 Truman moved to New York to live with his mother and her new husband, Joe Capote. Instead of attending public schools as he had in Monroeville, he went to various private schools. At age 17, he accepted a position with the *New Yorker*, first as a mail clerk and then as a feature writer. Two years later he moved to New Orleans.

He devoted himself completely to writing. Once when asked what he wanted to do in life, he responded without hesitation, "Write and read." His first major publication came in 1945 when the magazine *Mademoiselle* published "Miriam." It won the O. Henry Award the next year. Three years later *Other Voices, Other Rooms* (1948) was published. This first novel made him at 23 an overnight success.

His early short stories were introspective and autobiographical. He wrote detailed descriptions with a crisp and precise style, allowing him to paint stories that entertained a growing audience. Two volumes—*A Tree of Night and Other Stories* (1948) and *Breakfast at Tiffany's* (1958)—contain many of these early stories.

In 1951 *The Glass Harp* was published. In this novel Capote explored the conflicting worlds of dreamers and realists with humor. Through the course of the book, a young orphan boy's relatives become tree dwellers in an attempt to escape reality.

Capote's experiences while traveling abroad were the inspiration for two collections of works. *Local Color*, published in 1950, was a compilation of essays and stories recounting his experiences in Europe. While traveling in Russia with a touring company of *Porgy and Bess*, he wrote essays that made up the volume *The Muses are Heard* (1956).

In 1959, he began work on what has become one of his most memorable works, *In Cold Blood* (1965). After six years of research into the mass-murder of a Kansas farm family, he produced what he called a "nonfiction novel." With its publication, he became a media celebrity, one of the most sought after personalities for talk shows as well as New York and Hollywood parties.

He wrote little after the publication of *In Cold Blood*. He spent ten years working on his next novel, *Answered Prayers,* which remained unfinished at his death. While he was still working on the manuscript, *Esquire* published several excerpts containing unflattering portrayals of some celebrities that Capote knew. The excerpts were not well received by readers or the celebrities. Crushed by the criticism, Capote had no desire to continue writing.

He died on August 25, 1984, in Los Angeles, California. His remains lie at Westwood Memorial Park.

Nelle Harper Lee
(1926-)

Author of *To Kill a Mockingbird*

Monument—Legal Milestone Monument to fictional lawyer, Atticus Finch, Monroeville, Alabama
*Play—*To Kill a Mockingbird, *annual performance in May in Monroeville, Alabama*
Special Collection—Monroe County Heritage Museum, Monroeville, Alabama
*Pulitzer Prize—*To Kill a Mockingbird

A master of symbolism, Nelle Harper Lee has published only one novel—*To Kill a Mockingbird*. Exploring the social conflict that grew out of the maturing South, she drew upon childhood memories and characterizations for this Pulitzer Prize-winning novel.

Born on April 28, 1926, in Monroeville, Alabama, Lee attended Monroeville public schools; Huntingdon College in Montgomery, Alabama; the University of Alabama, where she studied law; and Oxford University.

At age seven, she became interested in writing and soon created short stories and essays. When she attended the University of Alabama, her stories, editorials, and reviews were regularly published in campus newspapers and magazines. In 1950 she moved to New York City to pursue a writing career. She accepted a position with Eastern Airlines and British Overseas Airways to support herself while writing, but she soon resigned from her position and concentrated on writing full time.

In 1960, she published *To Kill a Mockingbird*, a novel set in south Alabama and employing characters patterned after her childhood family and friends. For this novel, she received a Pulitzer Prize in 1961, the Alabama Library Association Award, and the Brotherhood Award of the National Conference of Christians and Jews. In 1962, she received the *Bestsellers* Paperback of the Year award.

On the surface, *To Kill a Mockingbird* seems to be a child's simple tale of the 1930s South. However, readers find the narrative to be a complex commentary on the themes of ignorance vs. knowledge, cowardice vs. heroism, guilt vs. innocence, and prejudice vs. tolerance. The novel has been translated into ten languages and adapted for a motion picture.

Since the publication of *To Kill a Mockingbird*, Lee has continued to write, but little has been published. Once when asked about her writing, she said that she begins writing at noon and works until early evening, completing only a page or two each day. In 1961 she published two short essays in national magazines. "Love—In Other Words" was published in the April 15, 1961, issue of *Vogue*, and "Christmas to Me" appeared in the December 1961 issue of *McCall's*.

She lives in New York City.

William March [Campbell]
(1893-1954)

Master portrayer of Southerners

***Special Collection**—W. S. Hoole Special Collections Library, University of Alabama, Tuscaloosa*
***Burial Site**—Evergreen Cemetery, Tuscaloosa, Alabama*

Wrilliam March wrote about people—people in war times, people living in small Southern towns, and people involved in missionary life in the South Seas. His insightful works addressed both the charming and unbecoming characteristics of humanity.

Born William March Campbell on September 18, 1893, in Mobile, Alabama, he wrote and gained notoriety as William March. Sporadically attending local public schools, March went to work in a lumbermill at age 14. He enrolled at Valparaiso University in Indiana in 1913 where he studied for two years before going on to study law at the University of Alabama. However, financial responsibilities caused him to drop out of school before receiving a law degree. In 1917 he joined the U.S. Marine Corps, where he received the Navy Cross, the Distinguished Service Cross, and the Croix de Guerre with Palm during World War I.

From 1918 to 1938 he worked as a businessman for the Waterman Steamship Company in New York. During that time, he published four books: *Company K* (1933); *Come in at the Door* (1934); *The Little Wife and Other Stories* (1935); and *The Tallons* (1936). In 1938, at the age of 45, he retired from the steamship company. He remained in New York and continued his writing until 1953 when he bought a home in New Orleans.

Critics have said that throughout March's writing career, he could not write a dull page. After retirement, he wrote *Some Like Them Short* (1939), *The Looking Glass* (1943), *Trial Balance* (1945), *October Island* (1952), and *The Bad Seed* (1954). *A William March Omnibus* (1956) and *99 Fables* (1960) were published posthumously.

He died on May 15, 1954, in New Orleans, Louisiana.

Samuel Mintern Peck
(1854-1938)

Alabama's First Poet Laureate

Special Collection—*W. S. Hoole Special Collections Library, University of Alabama, Tuscaloosa*
Burial Site—*Greenwood Cemetery, Tuscaloosa*

Alabama's first poet laureate, Samuel Mintern Peck used verse to reflect on his childhood. "The Grapevine Swing," which illustrated the joy of growing up in Alabama, was widely read and praised.

Born on November 4, 1854, in Tuscaloosa, Alabama, he attended the University of Alabama, Bellevue Hospital Medical College in New York, and Columbia University. He also studied for several years in Paris. At the urging of his parents, he received a medical degree in 1879; however, he never opened a practice. Instead, he became a literature and languages scholar touring the United States and Europe. During his travels, he maintained a permanent residence in Tuscaloosa.

He published poems regularly in magazines such as the New York *Evening Post*, *Youth's Companion*, *Independent*, and *Century*. He also published poetry in various northern and southern newspapers.

In the 1890s he turned to writing short stories about Alabama and the people he knew. These stories were widely accepted by editors of popular magazines and admired by Peck's already faithful readers. Many of these short stories are found in *Alabama Sketches*, published in 1902. He also wrote four unpublished novels.

He died on May 3, 1930, in Tuscaloosa, Alabama.

Abram Joseph Ryan
(1838-1886)

Poet-Priest of the Confederacy

Marker—*Bishop's House, Mobile, Alabama*
Marker—*St. Boniface Friary, Louisville, Kentucky*
Statue—*Ryan Park, Mobile, Alabama*
Monument—*The Poet's Monument, Augusta, Georgia*
Burial Site—*Roman Catholic Cemetery, Mobile*

Known as the "Poet of the Confederacy" and the "Poet of the Lost Cause," Father Abram Joseph Ryan mused about his writing saying, "[the poems were] written at random,—off and on, here, there, anywhere,—just as the mood came, with little of study and less of art, and always in a hurry."

Ryan was born on February 5, 1838, in Hagerstown, Maryland. He was ordained a priest in 1860 after having studied at the Seminary of St. Mary's of the Barrens in Perryville, Missouri; the Christian Brothers Cathedral School in St. Louis; and at Niagara University in New York. Although turned down for assignment as a commissioned military chaplain, he joined the Confederacy as a freelance chaplain. In this capacity he ministered to the smallpox victims at Gratiot Prison in New Orleans. During this time in New Orleans, he also edited the *Star*, a Catholic weekly publication.

"In Memory of My Brother" and "In Memoriam" were among his earliest poems. Both were written in tribute to his brother, a Confederate soldier, who was killed in action. His poetry became popular after the war when he published such poems as "The Conquered Banner," "The Sword of Robert E. Lee," and the "March of the Deathless Dead." His followers labeled him "The Poet-Priest of the Confederacy."

After his work at Gratiot Prison, he served as curate of St. Patrick's in Augusta, Georgia. There he edited the *Pacificator* and later the *Banner of the South*. From Georgia, he moved on to serve in churches in Mississippi, Tennessee, and finally Alabama.

From 1870 to 1877, he served at the Cathedral of the Immaculate Conception, and in 1877 he became pastor of St. Mary's Church, both in Mobile, Alabama. He retired to the Convent of St. Bonifacius in Louisville, Kentucky, in 1883.

He died on April 22, 1886, in Louisville, Kentucky.

Hudson Strode
(1892-1976)

Travel writer, biographer, critic, professor

Special Collection—W. S. Hoole Special Collections Library, University of Alabama, Tuscaloosa, Alabama
Burial Site—Cremated ashes were scattered at the Hudson Strode estate in Tuscaloosa, Alabama

Best known for his three-volume biographical series of Jefferson Davis, Hudson Strode also wrote plays, short stories, and a variety of accounts of his travels in foreign countries. He was a lecturer, literary critic, writer, sometimes actor, and a knight. (In 1961, King Gustaf Adolf of Sweden honored him with the title of Knight of the Royal Order of the North Star.) His most influential role, though, was probably that of a creative writing professor at the University of Alabama. Students in his writing classes are said to have produced over 55 novels, 101 short stories, and countless articles. Many of his students have received critical acclaim for their works.

He was born on October 31, 1892, in Cairo, Illinois. He lived the first several years of his life in Illinois, Colorado, Kentucky, and Mississippi. In December 1904, at the age of 12, he moved with his mother and step-father (his father died when Strode was four years old) to Demopolis, Alabama, where he attended local public schools. In 1909, he enrolled in the University of Alabama where he received an AB degree in 1913. He went on to receive a master's degree from Columbia University in New York in 1914 and to do special studies work at Harvard University in 1916. On December 20, 1924, he married Therese Cory.

While in New York from 1913-1916, he worked in and around the theater, making friends and learning the trade. However, when time came to choose a career, he opted for teaching, accepting a position as English instructor at Syracuse University in Syracuse, New York. In 1916 he received an offer of a position as associate professor at the University of Alabama, Tuscaloosa. His responsibilities would include teaching Shakespeare—an opportunity he couldn't turn down. For almost 60 years, he retained a relationship with the University of Alabama. He taught English, speech, and creative writing and sponsored the drama club. Even in his retirement years he taught, supported, and encouraged literature and writing students.

He began his own writing career while living in New York. He wrote book and drama reviews for the Syracuse *Post-Standard*. While attending Columbia University and while teaching at Syracuse University, he wrote his first short stories—"Number 29," published in *McClures*, and "The Imperial Battle," published in *Forum*. Throughout his life he published book reviews, poems, essays, and short stories in magazines such as *New Republic*, *Harper's Bazaar*, and *The American Mercury*.

A born adventurer, he enjoyed traveling in the United States and abroad. In 1922, he took a year off from teaching and traveled throughout Europe. While there he wrote and sold several short accounts of his adventures. In 1932, while recuperating from a respiratory illness in the warm climate of Bermuda, he published *The Story of Bermuda*. His other travel books include *Finland Forever* (1941), *The Timeless Mexico* (1944), *Pageant of Cuba* (1946), and *Sweden: Model for a World* (1949).

His recognition as a biographer came from his three-volume account of the life of Confederate president Jefferson Davis. *Jefferson Davis: American Patriot*, the first volume, was published in 1955. Critics enjoyed Strode's fresh writing style and his treatment of historical material. The second volume, *Confederate President* (1959), received similar reviews, and he was honored for "righting historical misconceptions."

Tragic Hero (1964), the third volume of the biography series, wasn't as well received. Critics called the account of Davis' defeat and return to private life biased and sympathetic. However, all seem to agree that Strode's three-volume series is an excellent narrative and contains accurate information that hasn't been recorded as successfully elsewhere.

In 1975, *The Eleventh House: Memoirs* was published. In his final book, Strode entertained readers with many fascinating episodes from his life, recounting meetings with friends and associates including Eugene O'Neill, Julia Peterkin, H. L. Mencken, Stark Young, and Ernest Hemingway.

Strode died on September 22, 1976, in Tuscaloosa, Alabama.

Augusta Jane Evans Wilson

(1835-1909)

A novelist of moral and political convictions

Markers—*Mobile, Alabama, and Columbus, Georgia*
Special Collection—*W. S. Hoole Special Collections Library, University of Alabama, Tuscaloosa, Alabama*
Burial Site—*Magnolia Cemetery, Mobile, Alabama*

A staunch supporter of the Confederacy, Augusta Jane Evans Wilson wrote sentimental novels featuring strict morals. Her mission was to use her writing to teach the highest principles of Christianity.

She was born on May 8, 1835, in Augusta, Georgia. At the age of 14, she moved with her family to Mobile, Alabama, where she lived for the rest of her life. In 1868, when she was 33, she married Lorenzo Madison Wilson, a Mobile businessman.

Inez: a Tale of the Alamo, her first novel, was published in 1855, when she was 20 years old. Within three years she had written a second novel, *Beulah.* However, *Macaria, or Altars of Sacrifice*, published in 1864, became her most controversial novel. She used this novel as a forum for her political opinions. She wrote about her support for the Confederacy so strongly that military leaders called her book propaganda. Yankee troops in Tennessee were forbidden to read or have the novel in their possession.

During her lifetime, she wrote many novels and amassed quite a following despite her use of complex language and obscure references. Her most memorable novel, *St. Elmo* (1866), quickly became the subject of parody; Charles H. Webb wrote *St. Twel'mo*, in which the heroine is said to have swallowed an unabridged dictionary. Wilson's other novels include *Vashti* (1869), *At the Mercy of Tiberius* (1887), and *Devota* (1907).

She died on May 9, 1909, in Mobile, Alabama.

Florida

Ernest Hemingway
Marjorie Kinnan Rawlings
Rex Ellingwood Beach
Edward William Bok
Paul Green
Zora Neale Hurston
Tennessee Williams
James Weldon Johnson

Ernest Hemingway Home and Museum

907 Whitehead Street
Key West, Florida 33040

Hours: Daily, 9 a.m.-5 p.m.
Admission: Adults, $6.50; Children, ages 6-12, $4.00
Telephone: (305) 294-1136

Ernest Hemingway, his wife Pauline, and his two sons (one son from his previous marriage) moved into this Spanish Colonial house in 1931. Lush gardens of exotic plants and trees surround this lovely two-story home built of rock hewn from the grounds. Hemingway owned this home until his death in 1961.

The Hemingways were the first in Key West to have a pool built at their home. It is fed by two salt water wells. Hemingway often joked about the expense of the pool. He pressed a penny into the patio cement surrounding the pool and claimed it took his "last penny."

He converted the loft of the poolhouse into a writing alcove. Most mornings he awoke before the rest of his family, walked a catwalk to the loft, and wrote until noon or later.

While living in Key West, Hemingway wrote many of his novels including *Death in the Afternoon* (1932), *Green Hills of Africa* (1935), *The Fifth Column* (1938), *For Whom the Bell Tolls* (1940), and *To Have and Have Not* (1937). He also wrote many short stories here, including "The Short Happy Life of Francis Macomber" and "The Snows of Killmanjaro."

Ernest Hemingway
(1899-1961)

Disciplined writer of direct, terse prose

Southern Home—Key West, Florida
Festival—Key West, Florida, in July (annual event)
*Special Collections—Azusa Pacific College, Azusa, California;
Claremont College, Claremont, California; University of California, San
Diego, California; Stanford University, Stanford, California; University of
Delaware, Newark, Delaware; Boise State University, Boise, Idaho;
Newberry Library, Chicago, Illinois; Northwestern University Library,
Evanston, Illinois; Knox College, Galesburg, Illinois; Oak Park Public
Library, Oak Park, Illinois; Indiana University, Lilly Library,
Bloomington, Indiana; John F. Kennedy Library, Boston, Massachusetts;
Washington University Libraries, St. Louis, Missouri; University of
Nevada, Reno, Nevada; Princeton University Libraries, Princeton, New
Jersey; University of Texas Libraries, Austin, Texas; University of Virginia,
Alderman Library, Charlottesville, Virginia*
Pulitzer Prize—The Old Man and the Sea, 1953
Nobel Prize for Literature—1954

A sportsman, a world traveler, and a rugged out-
doorsman—Ernest Hemingway was also a disci-
plined writer. He once said, "I decided that I
would write one story about each thing that I
knew about. I was trying to do this all the
time I was writing, and it was good and
severe discipline."

Born on July 21, 1899, in Oak Park, Illinois, Hemingway began writing while attending Oak Park High School. He worked
on the school newspaper and published stories in the literary magazine. After graduating
from high school, he volunteered for military
service, hoping to be stationed in Europe. However, he was turned down because he had injured

one of his eyes while boxing in high school.

In 1918 he joined a Red Cross ambulance corps and went to the Italian front. He spent only a brief time in Italy due to a severe wound that took several months to heal. After a time of recovery back in Illinois, he worked for a newspaper and wrote poetry and short stories. He spent his spare time in gymnasiums, boxing and watching others box. There he developed a fascination with man's willingness to put himself in danger.

In 1921 he went to Europe on assignment as a roving reporter for the Toronto *Star*. While in Paris, he met other Americans searching for artistic inspiration. Among them was Gertrude Stein who shared with him her belief in writing using simple language, rhythm, and repetition. He sought her advice and took several stories to her for critique. However, in later years, he credited his economic use of words to his journalism background rather than any of Stein's influence. Although his first book was *In Our Time* (1925), a collection of short stories, his novel, *The Sun Also Rises* (1926), was the book that launched his career. With each succeeding book, his popularity grew. Critics called him the original hero of his stories.

In the 1930s, he returned to Europe to cover the Spanish Civil War. He wove his experiences there into the plot of *For Whom the Bell Tolls* (1941). In 1952 *The Old Man and the Sea* was published, and in 1953 it earned him a Pulitzer Prize. This short novel continues to be the subject of many scholarly studies. In this novel, as in many of his tales, Hemingway focused on the universal themes of courage and endurance, setting nature against a man who is willing to place himself in danger. The year after he won the Pulitzer he received the Nobel Prize for Literature.

A Moveable Feast (1964), his autobiographical account of his days in Paris, is considered by many scholars to be his best work.

He committed suicide on July 2, 1961, in Ketchum, Idaho. He is buried there in Ketchum Cemetery.

Marjorie Kinnan Rawlings State Historical Site

Route 3, Box 92
Hawthorne, Florida 32640
(on South County Road 325 in Cross Creek)

Hours: House—Open October 1 though July 31.
Farm—Year-round, 9 a.m.-5 p.m. daily.
General Public—Thursday-Sunday: 10 a.m., 11 a.m., and each hour from 1-4
p.m. School Groups—Tuesdays and Wednesdays: 10 a.m. to 11:30 a.m.
Reservations must be made at least one month in advance.
Admission: Adults, $2; Children, $1; Children under 6, free
(Fees are being evaluated and may be changed soon.)
Telephone: (904) 466-3672

Marjorie Kinnan Rawlings and her husband, Charles, moved to this inspiring retreat in Cross Creek, Florida, in 1928. The eight-room house was built during the 1880s of native cypress and heart pine. Actually three separate structures connected by a bathroom, screened porches, and verandahs, this house—surrounded by nature—gave Rawlings the quiet atmosphere she needed for writing. She often spent eight to twelve hours a day on the verandah where she wrote and watched "the comings and goings of birds to the feed basket in a crepe myrtle bush."

The house contains most of Rawlings' original furnishings including the Hitchcock dining room set, numerous paintings and prints, and her handmade writing table. Scrapbooks of family photographs and articles related to Rawlings' writing are available for tourists to view.

While there, visitors can enjoy a stroll through the yard, citrus groves, and gardens. Many chickens, mallard ducks, and a big yellow house cat are there ready to entertain children as well as adults. Tourists who aren't able to schedule a tour of the home can enjoy their visits exploring the grounds and peeking through the windows and doors of the old cracker-style house.

After Marjorie and Charles Rawlings divorced in 1933, she lived alone at Cross Creek until 1941 when she married Norton S. Baskin and moved to St. Augustine. She continued to use the Cross Creek farmhouse as a writing retreat until her death in 1953.

While living in Cross Creek, she wrote her most famous novel, *The Yearling*, using the nearby Ocala National Forest for the setting. Other novels such as *South Moon Under*, *Golden Apples*, *When the Whippoorwill*, *Cross Creek* (which tells of her life while living in this house), *Cross Creek Cookery*, *The Sojourner*, and *Secret River* are spiced with the scenery and local color of Cross Creek.

Marjorie Kinnan Rawlings
(1896-1953)

Pulitzer-Prize winner for *The Yearling*

Home—*Marjorie Kinnan Rawlings Historic Site, Hawthorne, Florida*
Special Collection—*University of Florida, Gainesville, Florida*
Burial Site—*Island Grove, Florida*
Pulitzer Prize—The Yearling, *1939*

Although Marjorie Rawlings had a strong-willed and outspoken nature, many of her neighbors in Cross Creek, Florida, found her to be a sensitive and compassionate person. While living on her farm, she acquired a love of the outdoors and its treasures, a trait that reveals itself in much of her writing.

Rawlings was born on August 8, 1896, in Washington, D.C. After attending the University of Wisconsin, she accepted a position as a reporter and feature writer in Louisville, Kentucky, and later in Rochester, New York. The hectic pace of big city life and staff writing led her to seek out the quiet, almost secluded, lifestyle of north-central Florida. She and her husband, Charles, moved to Cross Creek in 1928. Here she found an untouched portion of the American frontier which inspired her to write stories based on nature and its beauty.

Capturing the beauty of Florida and the personality of her neighbors, she gained a loyal following for her stories. By listening intently and analyzing local speech patterns, she created a series of humorous short stories using the local dialect. She wrote about her neighbors whom she respected and admired. Most of the people of Cross Creek accepted the tales as the compliments they were intended. Through these stories readers across the nation learned about Cross Creek, Florida.

Rawlings enjoyed entertaining her neighbors. She admitted to receiving as much satisfaction from preparing a perfect dinner for a few friends as from turning out a perfect paragraph in her writing. Through visiting with and coming to know her neighbors, she had rich associations from which to draw when building characters such as those found in her Pulitzer Prize-winning novel, *The Yearling* (1938).

Set in the Big Scrub, a community almost 30 miles from Cross Creek, the characters in *The Yearling* are based on a family whom Rawlings met and with whom she spent a considerable amount of time. This novel is considered her most unified work. She built the plot and characters in her mind for five years before actually putting words on paper.

Her autobiographical book, *Cross Creek* (1942), contained personal stories and glimpses of local color that offended one neighbor. Soon after its publication, Rawlings faced a libel suit. However, because so many of her neighbors refused to testify against her, the suit was reduced to invasion of privacy.

Marjorie and Charles divorced in 1933, leaving Marjorie alone at Cross Creek. In addition to her writing, she managed the farm and developed an even deeper love for nature and the wild animals that shared the land. Eight years later, in 1941, she married Norton S. Baskin and moved with him to St. Augustine. She made regular trips to her farm in Cross Creek to write and visit with friends and neighbors. At the time of her death, Rawlings was working on a biography of Ellen Glasgow.

She died on December 14, 1953, at her beach home near St. Augustine.

Other Florida
Writers
and Sites

Rex Ellingwood Beach
(1877-1949)

Author who wrote about the Klondike Gold Rush

Marker—*Girl Scout Log House, Sebring, Florida*
Special Collection—*Rollins College, Olin Library Archives, Winter Park, Florida*
Burial Site—*Rollins College Campus, Winter Park, Florida*

Noted for his tales of Alaska, Rex Beach sought adventure for himself and for his writing topics. While attending law school, he heard about the gold rush in the Klondike. The promise of adventure and quick fortune appealed to him more than dull classroom studies. In Alaska, he found his "fortune" in writing about the gold rush rather than participating in it.

Born on September 1, 1877, in Atwood, Michigan, he grew up in Tampa, Florida. Because his father, a fruit farmer, believed that the Florida climate would be more favorable for his crops, he moved the family to Tampa when Rex was a baby. Rex attended public schools and entered Rollins College in Winter Park, Florida, in 1891. After his graduation in 1896, he enrolled in law school in Chicago. Soon discovering he preferred a stadium to a courtroom, he joined the Chicago Athletic Association to play football. When he transferred to the swim team in 1897, he broke the indoor record for water polo.

In 1899 he returned to law school; however, stories of prospecting for gold in Alaska tempted his adventurous spirit. He left in 1900 to join the gold rush. While in Alaska, he first became a zinc miner and then decided to try his hand at writing about the people and activity around him. His first novel, *Pardners* (1905), received little attention. *The Spoilers* (1906), however, quickly became a bestseller.

Alaskan Adventures is a collection of three of his stories about the Alaskan region: "The Spoilers," "The Barrier," and "The Silver Horde."

In his later writing he turned to other locations such as the Canal Zone in *The Ne'er-do-well* (1911), New York in *The Auction Block* (1914), and his home state of Florida in *Wild Pastures* (1935).

He committed suicide on December 7, 1949, in Sebring, Florida.

Bok Tower Gardens

Edward Bok Memorial
1151 Tower Boulevard
Lake Wales, FL 33853

Hours: 8:00 a.m. to 5:00 p.m.,
Sunday through Saturday
Admission: Adults, $4; Children, $1; Under 5, free
Telephone: (941) 676-1408

Edward William Bok, editor of *Ladies' Home Journal* for 30 years, created the 157-acre garden as his tribute to the American people. An immigrant from The Netherlands, he remained grateful for the way Americans accepted him.

A pink and gray Georgia marble and St. Augustine coquina stone bell tower is the visual centerpiece of this park. The tower contains a 57-bell carillon. Recitals are heard daily at 3 p.m.; clock music begins at 10 a.m. and is played at half-hour intervals.

Edward William Bok
(1863-1930)

Influential editor of *Ladies Home Journal*

Monument—*Bok Tower Gardens, Lake Wales, Florida*
Burial Site—*Bok Tower Gardens, Lake Wales, Florida*
Pulitzer Prize—The Americanization of Edward Bok, *1920*

One of America's most successful editors, Edward William Bok served as editor of *Ladies' Home Journal* for 30 years, influencing women's attitudes toward themselves, their families, and their communities. His became the first magazine in the United States to reach a circulation of one million subscribers. Noted for encouraging his readers to accept civic responsibility, he used his magazine to promote traditional American values and discourage women's participation in politics.

Bok was born on October 9, 1863, in Helder, The Netherlands. When he was seven, his family moved to New York City. He found life in America difficult with children calling him names and making fun of his broken English. His family depended on him to scavenge wood and coal to heat their home and to provide a meager income by collecting tin cans, cleaning shop windows, and delivering newspapers.

Bok began his writing career while still in grammar school. He convinced the editor of the *Brooklyn Eagle* that people would subscribe to the newspaper if they could read about themselves. With the help of his classmates, he reported regularly on the social activities of the people who lived in his community. At age 12, he dropped out of public school and accepted a position as an office boy for the Western Union Telegraph Company.

In his spare time, he read encyclopedias, searching for information about successful people. He began corresponding with people such as James A. Garfield, Ulysses S. Grant, and William Wadsworth Longfellow. At age 18, Bok set out to personally meet Oliver Wendell Holmes, Louisa May Alcott, and Ralph Waldo Emerson. This obsession with celebrities led to his career as an editor. When Joseph P. Knapp of the American Lithograph Company offered to pay him for writing short biographies of famous Americans, he realized he could earn more money if he paid some of his friends to write the biographies while he edited their work.

After working for Henry Holt and Company and *Scribner's Magazine*, he established the Bok Syndicate Press in 1886, attracting 137 subscriber newspapers. His ambition impressed Cyrus H. K. Curtis, publisher of *Ladies' Home Journal,* so much that he offered the 26-year-old a position as editor of the monthly women's magazine.

As editor, Bok created a magazine that had an intimate personal voice. He kept himself attuned to the readers, asking them what they wanted in the magazine and responding to their suggestions. The October 1919 issue, the last issue under his full editorial control, sold more than two million copies and carried more than one million dollars in advertisements.

Although he retired as magazine editor, he continued to write, producing *The Americanization of Edward Bok* (1920), for which he received a Pulitzer Prize; *America, Give Me a Chance!* (1926); and many other widely read books. He spent most of his retirement years in Lake Wales, Florida, where he created a tribute to the American people—the Bok Tower Gardens.

He died on January 9, 1930, in Lake Wales, Florida.

Paul Green
(1894-1981)

Festival—Cross and Sword *(drama written by Green), St. Augustine, Florida (annual performance)*

(Please see biography in North Carolina chapter.)

Zora Neale Hurston
(1903-1960)

Distinguished novelist in the Harlem Renascence

Museum—*Zora Neale Hurston National Museum of Fine Arts, Eatonville, Florida*
Festival—*Zora Neale Hurston Festival of the Arts and Humanities, Eatonville, Florida (annual event)*
Burial Site—*Garden of the Heavenly Rest, Fort Pierce, Florida*

Zora Neale Hurston's use of language and voice set her work apart from other African-American writers of her era. Acclaimed as one of the most notable writers during the Harlem Renascence, she distinguished herself during this literary and cultural movement of the 1920s by employing authentic Southern mannerism and speech in her writing. Often other writers of the period chose to distort and romanticize those characteristics.

Born on January 7, 1903, in Eatonville, Florida, she was the seventh of eight children. Her father, John Hurston, was mayor of Eatonville for three terms. When Zora Neale was nine years old, her mother died, leaving her to live with various relatives and friends until she went to work as a maid at age 14. Soon after, she accepted a position as wardrobe girl for the Gilbert and Sullivan theatrical troupe.

She attended Morgan Academy (now Morgan State University) in Baltimore, Maryland; Howard University in Washington, D.C.; and Barnard College in New York, where she earned a bachelor's degree in 1928.

In 1921, the Howard University student literary magazine published her first short story, "John Redding Goes to Sea." Three years later, *Opportunity: A Journal of Negro Life*, a publication founded by the National Urban League and the NAACP (National Association for the Advancement of Colored People), published "Drenched in Light."

In 1925, she moved to Harlem to join the artistic and intellectual community of other African-American writers. Here she wrote the play, *Color Struck,* which won second prize in the 1926 writing contest sponsored by *Opportunity* magazine.

Her style of writing and her sense of self gave her a special talent for recording African-American folklore. For several years, she studied the folklore in Florida and Louisiana. *Mules and Men* (1935) was the result of this extensive research.

Jonah's Gourd Vine, a novel based on the lives of Hurston's parents, was published in 1934. Her second novel, *Their Eyes Were Watching God* (1937), is considered by some critics to be a stronger narrative, employing various literary devices and expanding the vision of the central character.

Her other novels include *Tell My Horse* (1938), *Moses, Man of the Mountain* (1939), *Dust Track on a Road* (1942), and *Seraph on the Suwanee* (1948). During her writing career, she received several awards and honors including both a Rosenwald and Guggenheim fellowship.

She has influenced many African-American writers by her use of metaphor and rhyming speech in capturing African-American folkways and oral traditions.

She died on January 28, 1960, in Fort Pierce, Florida.

Tennessee [Thomas Lanier] Williams (1911-1988)

Memorial—*Tennessee Williams Fine Arts Building, Florida Key Community College, Key West, Florida*

(Please see biography in Mississippi chapter.)

James Weldon Johnson
(1871-1938)

African-American poet, musician, and dramatist

*Special Collections—Yale University, New Haven, Connecticut;
Wellesley College, Wellesley, Massachusetts*

An ambitious, energetic man, James Weldon Johnson had the ability to stir emotions with his writing. His quest to capture the rich oral tradition and folk heritage of African Americans in the South paved the way for folklorists such as Zora Neale Hurston. He experimented with repetition, rhythm, cadence, pauses, and other literary devices to portray the essence of black speech.

Born on June 17, 1871, in Jacksonville, Florida, Johnson attended public schools there and then Atlanta University in Georgia. He graduated in 1894 and accepted the position of teacher/principal at his former school in Jacksonville. In his spare time, he challenged himself by reading and studying law books and writing poetry. In 1896 he passed the Florida bar.

He is perhaps most noted for his poem "Lift Every Voice and Sing" (1900). His brother John wrote a musical score for the poem, and together they created the popular anthem that is still sung today. In 1901 they found their niche in New York. As a team, they wrote songs and musical productions for many popular African-American performers. They wrote music for plays, material for vaudeville, and created the basis for several minstrel shows.

In 1905 Johnson sought "meaningful work" and turned his focus to campaigning for Theodore Roosevelt. After the election, the President appointed him consulate to Venezuela and then to Nicaragua. He served in these positions for seven years, during which time he contributed poems to *Century, Atlantic Monthly, Harper's,* and *Crisis,* the official publication of the NAACP.

In 1912, while consul general to Nicaragua, he published his only novel, *The Autobiography of an Ex-Coloured Man.* First published anonymously, it was re-released under Johnson's name in 1927. The novel explored the difficulties of a gifted man of mixed racial heritage who battled the feelings of alienation caused by living in both the white and black world. Two years later, Johnson became a field secretary for the NAACP.

Some critics believe that Johnson's writing was inspired by black music and oratory. Some have said that throughout his writing career he searched for a way to capture the complex black lifestyle and speech patterns without resorting to clichés and stereotypes.

In December 1920, Johnson published "The Creation," a sermon in poetic black speech. Seven years later it was published, along with six other poetic sermons, in *God's Trombones: Seven Negro Sermons in Verse.*

His last collection of poetry, *St. Peter Relates an Incident of the Resurrection Day and Other Poems,* was published in 1935. This collection of 39 poems included the popular poem "Lift Every Voice and Sing."

In 1930 he accepted a teaching position at Fisk University in Nashville, Tennessee, which he held for eight years.

He was killed in an automobile accident on June 26, 1938. He is buried in Greenwood Cemetery in Brooklyn, New York.

Georgia

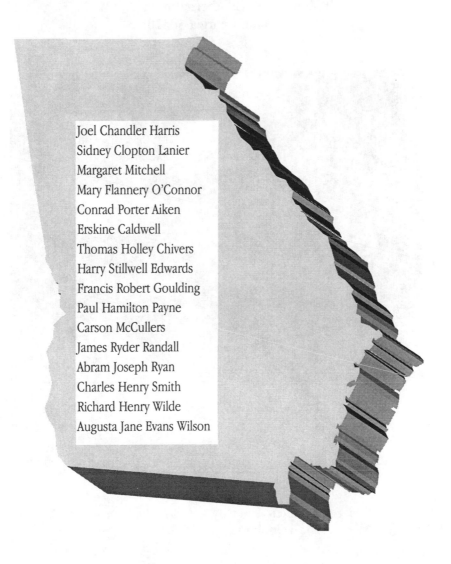

Joel Chandler Harris
Sidney Clopton Lanier
Margaret Mitchell
Mary Flannery O'Connor
Conrad Porter Aiken
Erskine Caldwell
Thomas Holley Chivers
Harry Stillwell Edwards
Francis Robert Goulding
Paul Hamilton Payne
Carson McCullers
James Ryder Randall
Abram Joseph Ryan
Charles Henry Smith
Richard Henry Wilde
Augusta Jane Evans Wilson

Wren's Nest

Joel Chandler Harris Home
1050 Ralph David Abernathy Blvd., SW
Atlanta, Georgia 30310

Hours:
Tuesday through Saturday, 10 a.m.-4 p.m.; Sunday, 1-4 p.m. Closed on
Mondays and major holidays
Admission:
Adults, $6; Senior citizens and teenagers, $4; Children, ages 4-12, $3
Telephone: (404) 753-7735

This comfortable Queen Anne home, now sitting in the hustle of Atlanta, was named by Joel Chandler Harris and his children for the family of birds that set up housekeeping in the family's mailbox. Best known for his Uncle Remus tales, Harris was one of the leading editorial writers of the *Atlanta Constitution* and a charter member of the American Folklore Society. He lived here with his family, which included nine children, from 1881 until his death in 1908.

The house began as a three-room structure with the dirt-floor kitchen located in the basement and accessible only from the outside. In 1884, after the sale of two books, Harris enlarged the house, adding an upstairs room intended for his study. However, he had become so accustomed to being near his family that the room quickly became a storage area. While living here, he wrote 30 books, many reflecting on life in rural Georgia.

Located in Atlanta's oldest neighborhood, the house contains authentic Victorian wallpaper, carpet, and curtains. The foundation is of native fieldstone, and the pine woodwork has been faux grained to look like oak. Children enjoy the many replicas of Brer Rabbit and other Harris characters.

Visitors can take a picnic lunch and eat in the large, grassy backyard. The museum shop is open during tour hours. On Saturdays from September to May and Tuesday through Saturday from mid-June to mid-August visitors can sit back and listen to a storyteller spin the yarns made popular by Harris. (A small extra fee is charged for the storytelling.)

During the Christmas season, the house is decorated with authentic Victorian decorations, and special storytellings are scheduled.

Joel Chandler Harris
(1848-1908)

Creator of the Uncle Remus tales

Home—Wren's Nest, Atlanta, Georgia
Markers—Eatonton, Georgia;
Statue of Brer Rabbit—Eatonton, Georgia
Museum—Uncle Remus Museum, Eatonton, Georgia
Festival—Joel Chandler Harris Birthday Celebration (annual event held the weekend nearest to December 9, also Christmas open house), Uncle Remus Museum
Special Collections—Emory University Library, Atlanta, Georgia; University of Virginia, Charlottesville, Virginia
                                Burial Site—Westview Cemetery, Atlanta, Georgia

A small, shy red-haired man, who spoke with a bad stammer—hardly the way readers of the Uncle Remus tales envision the writer who introduced African folk tales to the United States during the 1880s.

Joel Chandler Harris was born on December 9, 1848, near Eatonton, Georgia. The son of a single parent, he received little formal education; he became quite a reader, though, delving into literature.

When he was 14, Harris left home to work as a typesetter for the weekly newspaper, *The Countryman*. For four years, he was under the tutelage of Joseph Addison Turner, a respected plantation owner, writer, and editor. It was during these years that he learned the ways of plantation life and made friendships with plantation workers who were to later make him a popular writer.

When the Civil War brought inevitable financial destruction to *The Countryman*, he went on to accept editorial positions for newspapers in Georgia—Macon,

Forsyth, and Savannah—and New Orleans, Louisiana. He gained a reputation as an easy-going jester, a contradiction to his brooding nature and perplexing fear of strangers.

In 1872, while visiting Savannah, Georgia, he met Esther La Rose. They fell deeply in love and married on April 21, 1873. Theirs was a romance that lasted a lifetime. Together they created a warm and loving home for their nine children.

In 1876, Harris accepted a position as associate editor for the Atlanta *Constitution*. There he voiced his political opinions through a column narrated by a character named Uncle Remus, a composite of three or four men he knew in Eatonton. Using the African-American dialect Harris had learned during plantation days, Uncle Remus won national fame for Harris. Through the years Remus evolved into a wise old storyteller who reminisced about the "old times" of the plantation and offered wisdom and witticisms to an admiring public.

Uncle Remus: His Songs and His Sayings (1880), Harris' first book, is a compilation of the newspaper stories. It sold 10,000 copies in four months and created his reputation as an expert on the Old South. After having read the stories, Mark Twain was so impressed that he asked Harris to go on a lecture tour with him, an opportunity the shy Harris was quick to decline.

During his lifetime, he published more than 20 books, all focusing on the South and its people and often taking on an autobiographical tone. *On the Plantation* (1892) is set on the Turnwold plantation, and *Sister Jane: Her Friends and Acquaintances* (1896) romanticizes the issue of illegitimacy and mirrors his childhood memories.

Retiring from the *Constitution* in 1900, he continued writing and published several books. *Gabriel Tolliver: A Story of Reconstruction* (1902) was one of his most notable books and is his only major long work. In 1907 he edited *Uncle Remus Magazine*, a publication read by many admiring adults and children.

He received an honorary Doctor of Literature degree in 1902 from Emory College, and in 1905 he became a member of the American Academy of Arts and Letters. He had thousands of fans, many of whom visited this home. Two famous admirers, President Theodore Roosevelt and philanthropist Andrew Carnegie, each gave $5,000 to help establish the Wren's Nest as a museum in 1913.

Harris died in Atlanta on July 3, 1908.

Sidney Lanier Cottage

935 High Street
P. O. Box 13358
Macon, Georgia 31208-3358

Hours:
Monday through Friday, 9 a.m.-1 p.m. and 2-4 p.m.; Saturday,
9:30 a.m.-12:30 p.m.; Closed on holidays
Admission:
Adults, $3.00; Children under 12, 50¢; Students age 12 and over,
$1.00; Group rates also available
Telephone:(912) 743-3851

The birthplace of Sidney Clopton Lanier, this simple white clapboard cottage is furnished with authentic period pieces and accessories. Items on display include Lanier's silver alto flute, a tea service, books, a chair, his wife's wedding dress, and family photographs.

The cottage is an excellent location for a wedding, reception, dinner, party, or meeting. It is often reserved by the public for such special occasions. Special tours can also be arranged for school classes.

Several weeks after Lanier's birth, his family moved to Griffin, Georgia, where Lanier lived until he was six years old. In 1948, the family returned to Macon.

The Lanier home was one filled with love and respect for family. Here the Lanier children were encouraged to pursue intellectual and artistic interests. Lanier received a tiny yellow flute for Christmas when he was only a few years old. By age five, he was able to keep time as his mother played the piano. As he grew older, he spent many hours of free time studying music and poetry.

As a boy, he became as much at home in the woods of Macon as he was in his home. He enjoyed climbing trees and fishing, and it was here that he honed his skills as a flutist. He often took his handmade reed flute with him to the river bank or into the woods and experimented with sounds to imitate nature.

He left Macon at age 14 to attend Oglethorpe College in Midway, Georgia. He didn't return to Macon until the end of the Civil War, and then only for a short visit before moving to Alabama. In 1867, the year that his only novel, *Tiger-Lilies,* was published, he moved back to Macon and married Mary Day. The couple lived on Orange Street and later on Hardeman Avenue. (These homes no longer exist.)

While in Macon, many tourists enjoy visiting the small park across the street from the cottage that is named in honor of Lanier.

Sidney Clopton Lanier
(1842-1881)

Poet and advocate for the arts

Birthplace Home—Sidney Lanier Cottage, Macon, Georgia
Dorm Room—Oglethorpe University, Atlanta, Georgia
Monument—Poet's Monument, Augusta, Georgia
Special Collections—Alabama Department of Archives and History,
Montgomery, Alabama; Oglethorpe University Library, Atlanta, Georgia;
Johns Hopkins University, Baltimore, Maryland; Duke University,
Durham, North Carolina; University of Virginia, Charlottesville, Virginia
Burial Site—Greenmount Cemetery, Baltimore, Maryland

A man of culture and devotion to his country, Sidney Clopton Lanier spent much of his efforts campaigning for economic independence of the growing South. He encouraged Southerners to turn away from cotton, which he believed financially bound them to the industrialized North, and focus on the arts, which he thought would create a basis for a new sense of community.

Born on February 3, 1842, Lanier grew up surrounded by music, books, and pictures. He taught himself to play the flute and spent much of his adult life playing professionally. He attended private schools and went on to graduate at the top of his class at Olgethorpe College in 1860.

A year later, he enlisted in the Confederate Army. He and his brother, Clifford, served together as mounted scouts, stationed in Virginia from 1863 to 1864. Lanier transferred to North Carolina in 1864 and became a signal officer on a blockade runner. He was captured by Union troops and sent to a Federal prison in November of that year.

While imprisoned only three months, he contracted a serious illness, later diagnosed as tuberculosis. Thoughts of music and writing occupied his lonely days of imprisonment. Two years later in 1867 his only novel, *Tiger Lilies*, was published. He wrote this passionate war protest in only three weeks.

After his release from military prison, he held several positions which included a hotel clerk in Montgomery, Alabama, and a law clerk in his father's law practice. In 1867 he married Mary Day from Macon; they had four sons. Suffering ill health, he spent his spare time compiling literature textbooks.

Even with a family to support, he could not subdue his desire to create music and write poetry. From 1869 to 1871, he wrote a series of poems featuring the Georgia countryside and promoting personal integrity and hard work. He played flute in a symphony orchestra and wrote poems on the backs of envelopes. In 1875, Lanier's poem "Corn" was published in *Lippincott's Magazine*. He continued to write, producing poems and the book *Florida: Its Scenery, Climate, and History* (1875), the result of a stay in the state while seeking relief for his tuberculosis.

He began teaching English literature at Johns Hopkins University in 1879. During this time, he wrote *The Science of English Verse* (1880) and *The English Novel and the Principle of Its Development* (published posthumously in 1883).

He died on September 7, 1881, in Lynn, North Carolina.

Margaret Mitchell House

990 Peachtree Street
(located at the corner of 10th and Peachtree Streets)
Atlanta, Georgia 30309-3964

Hours:
Monday through Saturday, 9 a.m.-4 p.m. ; Sunday, 12-4 p.m.
Admission: Adults, $6.00; Senior citizens and students, $5.00;
Children 12 and under, $4.00
Museum Shop: Open Monday through Saturday, 9 a.m.-5 p.m.;
Sunday, 12-5 p.m.
Telephone:(404) 249-7012

Built in 1899, this rambling Tudor/Revival building was home first to Cornelius J. Sheehan, the owner of *Greer's Almanac*. It was located on Peachtree Street until the 1913 business boom. The owners didn't want their house overtaken by commercial encroachment, so they moved it several feet back on the lot and turned what was then the back of the house into the front.

In 1919, the house was converted into a three-story apartment building, and in 1925, it became the honeymoon home of John R. Marsh and Margaret Mitchell. Theirs was a one-bedroom, ground-floor apartment, so tiny and dark that Mitchell nicknamed it "The Dump."

While recuperating from arthritis, Mitchell occupied her time by writing and began the novel *Gone with the Wind* in 1926. The couple lived in this apartment for seven years. In 1932, they moved to another apartment a few blocks north on Peachtree Street.

Over the years, the house was neglected, and in 1977 it was boarded up. It has since suffered two fires, but it has been renovated to appear as it did when Mitchell and her husband lived there. The home is open for public tours and is available for weddings, meetings, and other special events when booked in advance.

Margaret Mitchell
(1900-1945)

Author of *Gone with the Wind*

Home—*Atlanta, Georgia*
Marker—*Near childhood home, 1401 Peachtree St., Atlanta, Georgia*
Memorabilia Collection—*Atlanta Historical Society, Atlanta, Georgia*
Special Collections—*Atlanta-Fulton Public Library, Atlanta, Georgia;*
Agnes Scott College, Decatur, Georgia; Boston University, Boston,
Massachusetts; Harvard University Library, Cambridge, Massachusetts
Burial Site—*Oakland Cemetery, Atlanta, Georgia*
Pulitzer Prize—Gone with the Wind, *1937*

Author of one of the greatest American novels, Margaret Mitchell wrote *Gone with the Wind* purely as amusement for herself. She had to be persuaded by a friend to let a publisher read it.

Born on November 8, 1900, in Atlanta, Georgia, Margaret Munnerlyn Mitchell was greatly influenced by her parents. Her mother was a prominent figure in Georgia's suffrage movement, and her father was, for a brief time, president of the Atlanta Historical Society. As a child she enjoyed reading and listening to tales of the Civil War and Reconstruction. She wrote short stories and plays and kept a notebook of story ideas.

While a freshman at Smith College in 1918, her formal education came to an abrupt halt when her mother died. She had to return home to care for her father and brother. Four years later, in 1922, she married Berrien K. Upshaw; their marriage lasted only a few months.

In 1923 she became a reporter for the Atlanta *Journal*. During this time, she wrote a novelette, *Ropa Carmagin*, featuring a Southern white girl in love with a mulatto man. This manuscript, along with two children's stories—"The Big Four" and "Little Sister"—are now lost.

In 1925 she married John Marsh, an Atlanta businessman. She was careful to retain her independence, and in formal situations preferred to be addressed as Miss Mitchell. Less than a year after their marriage, a series of injuries caused her to quit her job at the *Journal*. When her attempts to write short stories for national magazines proved unsuccessful, she occupied her days with writing a long novel—purely for her own amusement. She worked on *Gone With the Wind* for six years and was persuaded by a friend to show it to an editor at Macmillan's.

Gone With the Wind, her only published novel, was released in 1936. It sold a million copies during the first six months. It was made into a motion picture, received a Pulitzer Prize and the American Booksellers Association award, and was a bestseller in many foreign countries. Because of the story's popularity, Mitchell spent the rest of her life absorbed in activities surrounding *Gone With the Wind*. She was overwhelmed with letters, telephone calls, and requests for personal appearances.

In 1939 her alma mater, Smith College, presented her with an honorary master's degree.

Struck by a taxicab while crossing Peachtree Street with her husband, she died on August 11, 1945.

Flannery O'Connor Childhood Home

207 East Charlton Street
Savannah, Georgia 31401

Hours: Saturday, 1-4 p.m.; Sunday, 1-4 p.m.
Admission: Free (donations accepted)
Phone: Leave a message at (912) 233-6014

This charming three-story home was built in the early 1900s. Much of the building has been divided into apartments; however, the first floor is decorated in 1930s style and is open for tours. Many of the furnishings are period pieces, and some items belonged to the O'Connor family.

Flannery O'Connor lived in this spacious home from her birth in 1925 until 1938 when she moved with her family to Milledgeville, Georgia, to live with her grandmother. The bedrooms were on the second floor, and the third floor was used mostly for guests.

Tourists are welcome to enjoy the beautiful garden area in the back of the house. This is where playful young Flannery participated in such antics as teaching a chicken to walk backwards.

Each year, during the Georgia Heritage Celebration and on St. Patrick's Day, the home presents special readings from O'Connor's works. Other literary activities are sponsored annually from October to May by the Flannery O'Connor Home Foundation.

Mary Flannery O'Connor
(1925-1964)

Author of acclaimed moral short stories

Childhood Home—Savannah, Georgia
Annual Literary Activities (October-May)—Childhood Home,
Savannah
Special Collections—O'Connor Room, Ina Dillard Russell Library,
Georgia College, Milledgeville, Georgia (restricted use); University of
Maryland Library, College Park, Maryland; Washington University
Libraries, St. Louis, Missouri; University of Nevada, Reno, Nevada
Burial Site—Memory Hill Cemetery, Milledgeville, Georgia

Born to devout Roman Catholic parents, Flannery O'Connor reflected her profound Christian beliefs in her writing. She employed traditional Southern characters but delved into their sins of vanity and foolish accumulation of earthly possessions. Perhaps her greatest talent was casting contemporary characters to portray the emptiness of existence without Christ.

O'Connor was born on March 25, 1925, in Savannah, Georgia. She attended the Savannah parochial schools until 1938 when her father became seriously ill. The family then moved in with O'Connor's grandmother in Milledgeville, Georgia. Graduating from Georgia State College for Women (now Georgia College) as an artist and writer, she went on to the University of Iowa, where she earned a Master of Fine Arts degree in 1947. "The Geranium," her first published short story, resulted from her studies at the Writers Workshop of the University of Iowa. It appeared in the national magazine *Accent*.

Wise Blood, her first novel, was published in 1952 by Harcourt, Brace. In the years following, she wrote many popular short stories for magazines such as *Harper's*, the *Sewanee Review,* and *Kenyon Review*. Today she is perhaps best known for her first collection of stories, *A Good Man is Hard to Find* (1955).

Throughout the majority of her writing career, she suffered from the effects of lupus. However, she remained a serious writer, filling each of her works with religious morals. Her last collection of short stories, *Everything That Rises Must Converge*, was published a year after her death.

She died on August 3, 1964, in Milledgeville, Georgia.

Other Georgia
Writers
and Sites

Conrad Porter Aiken

(1889-1973)

Poet, children's author, novelist, critic

Marker—Oglethorpe Avenue, Savannah, Georgia
Special Collections—Huntington Library, San Marino, California;
Georgia Southern College Library, Statesboro, Georgia; Harvard
University Library, Cambridge, Massachusetts; Washington University, St.
Louis, Missouri; University of Nevada, Reno, Nevada; State University of
New York, Stoney Brook, New York; University of Saskatchewan Library,
Saskatoon, Canada
Burial Site—Bonaventure Cemetery, Savannah, Georgia
*Pulitzer Prize—*Selected Poems, *1930*

For more than 50 years, Conrad Porter Aiken wrote short stories, essays, children's books, novels, and literary criticism. He published more than 30 collections of poetry which emphasized self-knowledge and a search for personal identity.

Aiken was born on August 5, 1889, in Savannah, Georgia. When he was 11 years old, his parents died, leaving him to live with an aunt in New Bedford, Massachusetts. As a student at Middlesex School in Concord, Massachusetts, he wrote for and edited the school's magazine. In 1907 he entered Harvard University where he became friends with T. S. Eliot. He wrote for the Harvard *Advocate* and became the class poet. In 1912 he received a bachelor's degree from Harvard. He spent several years traveling abroad and living in England. He married three times and had three children.

He was a prolific writer. His early poems were published in nine volumes from 1914 to 1923. Among the collections are *Earth Triumphant* (1914); *Turns and Movies* (1916); *The Charnel Rose, Senlin: A Biography, and Other Poems* (1918); and *The Immortal Liar* (1921).

He moved to England in 1921, the same year that his first short story, "The Dark City," was published. The story received good reviews, and he went on to write "Strange Moonlight" in 1922. This was an autobiographical story, telling of his childhood in Savannah and led to his first novel, *Blue Voyage* (1927). This fantasy is almost a poem in prose form. It features a dramatist's voyage to England, his love for a girl, and his quest for self-knowledge.

In the late 1920s, Aiken's personal conflicts began to affect his family life and eventually resulted in divorce. However, this was perhaps his most productive period of writing. Many scholars consider his work during this time his most enduring and significant accomplishment. He received a Pulitzer Prize for *Selected Poems* in 1929.

He wrote four volumes of poems, known as "Preludes," during the early 1930s. These poems served as a way for him to examine the relationship of self to the world. From 1934 to 1936, he served as London correspondent for the *New Yorker*, using the pseudonym Samuel Jeake, Jr.

In 1939, when he returned to the United States, his poetry took on a new focus as he wrote about his life and experiences in New England. These poems were collected in books such as *And in the Human Heart* (1940), *The Soldier* (1944), *The Kid* (1947), and *Skylight One: Fifteen Poems* (1949).

The novel, *Conversation; or, Pilgrims' Progress*, was published in 1940. This autobiographical novel set in Cape Cod examines the conflicting roles in a man's life—that of being a husband, father, and artist. It was only three years earlier that Aiken had divorced and married for the third time.

He also excelled as a literary critic. In *Skepticisms* (1919) he wrote commentary on contemporary poets and their various works. He also wrote an introduction for an edition of Emily Dickinson's poems in 1924 which is said to have established her reputation.

During the 1950s and 1960s, his writing demonstrated a renewed affirmation of life. His poetry embraced themes relating to language and art, and he began publishing children's books. *Cats and Bats and Things with Wings* was published in 1965, followed by *Tom, Sue, and the Clock* in 1966, and *A Little Who's Zoo of Mild Animals* (published posthumously in 1977).

He continued to write poetry, fiction, and criticism until shortly before his death on August 17, 1973, in Savannah, Georgia.

Erskine Caldwell
(1902-1987)

Once known as the world's best-selling novelist

Memorabilia Collection—Atlanta Historical Society, Atlanta, Georgia
Special Collections—University of Delaware, Newark, Delaware;
University of Nevada, Reno, Nevada; Dartmouth College, Hanover, New

Hampshire; Syracuse University Library, Syracuse, New York; University of Virginia, Charlottesville, Virginia

An immensely popular writer, Erskine Caldwell had more than 100 short stories and novelettes rejected before publishing "The Georgia Cracker" in 1926. However, before the end of his career, he was reportedly the world's best-selling novelist. His powerful writing is perhaps best illustrated in *Tobacco Road* (1932), a disturbing novel of poverty and starvation set in rural Georgia.

Born on December 17, 1902, in Newnan, Georgia, he was the son of a Presbyterian preacher. He moved with his family to churches in Georgia and Tennessee during his childhood. He attended Erskine College in South Carolina, the University of Virginia, and the University of Pennsylvania. However, he never graduated from a college.

He married four times. His first marriage to Helen Lannegan resulted in three children. Second, he married the photographer Margaret Bourke-White, who shared the byline of several of his books. His third marriage to June Johnson resulted in one son. His last marriage was to Virginia Fletcher.

In 1925 he and his first bride moved to Maine, where they lived seven years. During this time, Caldwell worked odd jobs and pursued a writing career. Throughout his life, he wrote prolifically; however, his first short stories found publication only in "little" magazines. Editor Maxwell Perkins read some of Caldwell's early writing, and realizing his potential, Perkins agreed to publish his first novel, *American Earth* (1930), and then quickly negotiated a contract to publish *Tobacco Road* in 1932.

Caldwell's early career included a short stint with the Atlanta *Journal*, a brief time writing screenplays in Hollywood, and a period working as a foreign correspondent during the Spanish Civil War. In the early 1940s, he and his second wife, Margaret Bourke-White, traveled in China, Mongolia, and Russia. Together they published *Moscow Under Fire* (1942) and *Russia at War* (1942).

The couple divorced in 1942, and Caldwell married June Johnson. One year later, *Georgia Boy* was published. This collection of 14 stories narrated by a 12-year-old boy is often referred to as one of Caldwell's best books.

From 1944 to 1945, he published three more books. In 1946, *God's Little Acre* was released in mass-market paperback. Selling over one million copies in six months, the book made Caldwell's popularity skyrocket. By 1963, his paperbacks had sold 61 million copies, resulting in his being advertised for many years as the world's bestselling novelist.

Caldwell died on April 11, 1987, in Paradise Valley, Arizona.

Thomas Holley Chivers
(1809-1858)

Poet, dramatist, and friend of Poe

Marker—Washington, Georgia
Special Collection—Duke University, Durham, North Carolina

A poet and friend of Edgar Allan Poe, Holley Chivers was an unhappy man who found comfort in writing. Many fellow writers were critical of his works; however, he and Poe shared a mutual respect for each other's talent. He had a somber outlook on life and often wrote with a harsh viewpoint.

Chivers was born on October 18, 1809, in Washington, Georgia. He studied medicine and trained as a physician at Transylvania College, where he graduated in 1830. Since his father was a successful farmer, Thomas never felt pressure to earn a living; so he spent much of his time writing. As solstice for an unhappy marriage, he turned to poetry, which resulted in the collection, *The Path of Sorrow*, published in 1832.

Eventually, he abandoned his marriage and his career as a physician. He found happiness with writing and spent most of his time in New York writing poetry. He is credited with being the first poet to successfully imitate the language and rhythm of Southern blacks in poetry. Experimenting with vocabulary, meter, and sound, his poetry shows evidence of careful concentration and attention to detail.

He published his first drama, *Conrad and Eudora*, in 1834. Based on the true story of a Kentucky tragedy, the murder of Colonel Solomon Sharp became a popular story for many Southern storytellers. Even Poe wrote about the love triangle that ended in the death of the Civil War colonel. Although Chivers presented an incredibly accurate rendering of the story, his book was only a moderate success.

When he met Poe in 1840, they became casual friends, sharing letters and discussing literature. However, Poe's critique of Chivers' works branded Chivers as "one of the best and one of the worst poets in America."

The Lost Pleiad and Other Poems (1845) contains 68 poems written from 1836-1844. Most deal with love and death. With the publication of this volume, critics began to compare his poetry with that of Poe. The supernatural treatment in many of the poems caused great speculation and accusations of plagiarism.

The publication of *Enochs of Ruby* (1851) renewed the controversy among Chivers' fellow writers. Poems such as "Isadore," "To Allegra Florence in Heaven," and "The Vigil of Aiden," were plainly labeled as plagiarisms of Poe. Throughout the controversy, Poe never objected to Chivers' works. However, the accusations became so strong that William Gilmore Simms cautioned Chivers against using Poe's work as a model.

The negative comments did little to deter Chivers. Calling his critics "the Jackasses of America . . . who bray nonsense," he continued to write, producing 11 volumes of poetry and drama and a biography of Edgar Allan Poe titled *Chivers' Life of Poe* (1852). He also studied mysticism and occultism, producing the books *Virginalia* (1853) and *Search After Truth* (1848).

He died on December 18, 1858, in Decatur, Georgia.

Harry Stillwell Edwards
(1855-1938)

Novelist, poet, and author of short stories

Burial Site—Rosehill Cemetery, Macon, Georgia

Author of nearly 100 short stories, poems, and two novels, Harry Stillwell Edwards is noted for his realistic depiction of African Americans. His best known book is *Eneas Africanus* (1919), a compilation of stories featuring a character based on a real person.

Born on April 23, 1855, in Macon, Georgia, he wrote newspaper sketches throughout his school years. He graduated with a Bachelor of Laws degree from Mercer University and began a law practice while continuing to write for the Macon *Telegraph* and the Macon *Evening News*. Five years later, he married Mary Roxie Lane, a children's writer. It was only through her encouragement that he submitted his first short story, "Elder Brown's Backslide," to *Harper's Magazine*. His writing showed such an extraordinary grasp of the African-American lifestyle and dialect that many popular magazines were eager to publish his short stories.

He wrote two novels—*Sons and Fathers* (1896) and *The Marbeau Cousins* (1898). Some critics have labeled *Sons and Fathers* as the best mystery novel ever written by an American. *The Marbeau Cousins*, set in Holly Bluff, Georgia, the community where he grew up, was Edwards' favorite of the two.

He presented the legends and traditions of the South to an enthusiastic audience of admirers throughout the country. Many of his poems and short stories were published in magazines, but the majority of his writing was for newspapers. He had

a regular column in the Atlanta *Journal* titled "Coming Down My Creek."
He died on October 22, 1938, in Macon, Georgia.

Francis Robert Goulding
(1810-1887)

Bestselling author of juvenile novels

Burial Site—Presbyterian Cemetery, Roswell, Georgia

A Presbyterian minister, Francis Robert Goulding published *Robert and Harold or, The Young Marooners on the Florida Coast* in 1852. This juvenile novel was reprinted more than ten times in the United States and England and was translated into several foreign languages.

Born on September 28, 1810, in Midway, Georgia, he attended the University of Georgia and the Columbia Theological Seminary in South Carolina. He married Mary Howard in 1833; they had six children. After his first wife's death, he married Matilda Rees in 1855; they had two daughters.

He began his literary career in 1844 with the publication of the children's book, *Little Josephine*, which he wrote for the American Sunday School Union. In 1852 he published his most popular work, *Robert and Harold*. This Robinson Crusoe-like tale wove educational information about nature and medicine throughout an entertaining narrative. His books featured characters with high morals and respect for their parents.

During the Civil War, he published the *Soldiers Hymn Book* (1864) and served as a volunteer chaplain, ministering to Confederate soldiers. After the war he returned to writing juvenile fiction, creating a series of Indian adventures.

Sal-o-quah; or, Boy-Life Among the Cherokees (1870); *Nacoohee; or Boy-Life from Home* (1871); and *Sapelo; or, Child's Life in Tide Waters* (1888) traced the progress of children from home through school into adolescence. Childish pranks were emphasized, and children were often forced to live without adult supervision. However, the children always upheld their parents' values. Scholars have contrasted these tales with Twain's *Tom Sawyer* and *Huckleberry Finn*.

Goulding died on August 22, 1881, in Roswell, Georgia.

Paul Hamilton Hayne
(1830-1886)

Once called the "Poet Laureate of the South"

Monument—*The Poet's Monument, Augusta, Georgia*
Special Collections—*Duke University, Durham, North Carolina; College of Charleston Library, Charleston, South Carolina*
Burial Site—*Magnolia Cemetery, Augusta, Georgia*

Labeled the "Poet Laureate of the South," Paul Hamilton Hayne began writing at age nine and had his first poem published in the *Charleston Courier* when he was 15. Throughout his school years, his poetry appeared regularly in the *Southern Literary Messenger*, the *Southern Literary Gazette*, *Graham's Magazine*, and the *Home Journal*.

Hayne was born on January 1, 1830, in Charleston, South Carolina. After his father's death when Paul was two years old, he was reared by his mother and her brother Robert. He and his childhood friend, poet Henry Timrod, attended Christopher Cote's School, where Hayne was often punished for reading romances and poetry instead of doing his classwork. In 1850 he graduated from the College of Charleston where he studied law. He married Mary Middleton in 1852; they had one son.

Hayne accepted a position in 1852 as editor of the *Southern Literary Gazette*, leaving his law career behind and devoting the rest of his life to literature. In 1857 he founded *Russell's Magazine*. Through this publication, he tried to balance political views with high literary standards to reach audiences in the North and South. As with most literary magazines of the period, the Civil War forced *Russell's* out of business.

From 1855 to 1860, he published three collections of poetry. *Poems*, containing mostly juvenile verse, was published in 1855, followed by *Sonnets, and Other Poems* in 1857. *Avolio: A Legend of the Island of Cos* (1860) is said to contain Hayne's best pre-war verse.

During the war, he dedicated himself to writing and lecturing for the Confederacy. He regularly published verse and prose to encourage soldiers, uplift families, and honor the Southern cause. In 1865, having lost practically everything in the war, he moved to Augusta, Georgia. There he accepted the position of editor of the *Constitutionalist*, a position he kept for only three months due to his poor health.

Although usually first remembered for his historical poetry, he wrote many nature poems and long narratives. "In the Wheat Field," "On a Jar of Honey," and "Muscadines" bring to essence the Southern way of life. Many of his narratives are based on other literary works. "The Wife of Brittany" (1870), for example, is based on Chaucer's "Franklin's Tale." This poem in particular was praised by Longfellow, Whittier, and Lanier.

For the rest of Hayne's life, he worked as a freelance writer and editor, contributing to such publications as *Harper's Bazaar*, *Lippincott's*, and *Scribner's Monthly*. Some of his other works include *Legends and Lyrics* (1872), *The Mountain of the Lovers* (1875), and *Poems* (1882). His poetry during his last 20 years yielded him the title of "Poet Laureate of the South."

He died on July 6, 1886, near Atlanta, Georgia.

Carson McCullers
(1917-1967)

Author of *The Heart is a Lonely Hunter*

Marker—*Childhood Home, 1519 Starke Avenue, Columbus, Georgia*
Special Collections—*University of Miami, Miami, Florida; University of Nevada, Reno, Nevada; Duke University, Durham, North Carolina*

Repelled by the stories of her ancestors and the Civil War, Carson McCullers spent most of her adult life avoiding the South. However, she found the modern South useful as a symbolic setting in much of her fiction. She called on many of the distinctive elements of Southern life to convey themes in her works of anxiety and failure.

Carson McCullers was born Lula Carson Smith on February 19, 1917, in Columbus, Georgia. She attended the local schools and at age 17 was encouraged by her mother to study creative writing at Columbia University and New York University. In 1937 she married James Reeves McCullers, Jr., a native of Alabama.

Although she and her husband were both writers, her writing always came first. While on her honeymoon in Charlotte, North Carolina, she began writing her first novel, *The Heart Is a Lonely Hunter*. This novel of remarkable insight was published in 1940, when McCullers was 23 years old. After taking three years to complete her first novel, the second story came more quickly; she wrote *Reflections in a Golden Eye* (1941) in only two months.

With the publication of *The Heart Is a Lonely Hunter*, the couple moved to New York, vowing never to live in the South again. By the time *Reflections in a Golden Eye* was published, they had divorced; however, they remarried in 1945, after Reeves returned from a tour of overseas duty in World War II. Their second marriage was more volatile than the first, and Reeves committed suicide in 1953.

Although it is not McCullers' best work, *The Member of the Wedding*, published in 1946, has been called the one piece of her work that made her famous and financially secure. It was adapted for the stage in 1951 and the screen in 1952.

McCullers surrounded herself with a variety of creative people, such as George Davis, the editor of *Mademoiselle*, Gypsy Rose Lee, and poets Richard Wright and Chester Kallman. Among her many honors were two Guggenheim fellowships and membership in the National Institute of Arts and Letters. Magazines such as the *New Yorker*, *Vogue*, and *Redbook* regularly published her fiction and essays.

For more than ten years, between bouts of poor health, she worked on her last novel, *Clock Without Hands* (1961). After several strokes, a heart attack, and reoccurring respiratory disorders, she died on September 29, 1967, in Nyack, New York. She is buried in Oak Hill Cemetery in Nyack.

James Ryder Randall
(1839-1908)

Poet of "unofficial" anthem of the Confederacy

Monument—*Poet's Monument, Augusta, Georgia*
Special Collection—*Georgetown University, Washington, D.C.*
Burial Site—*Magnolia Cemetery, Augusta, Georgia*

Best known for his poem "Maryland, My Maryland," James Ryder Randall was labeled an exceptional poet while a college student at Georgetown College. He based most of his poetry on historical events.

He was born on January 1, 1839, in Baltimore, Maryland, with an interesting ancestry. His paternal ancestors had a town named after them during the 17th century—Randallstown, Maryland. And his great-great grandfather was René Leblanc, the Notary in Longfellow's "Evangeline." Randall attended Georgetown College; however, poor health kept him from finishing his final year there. He married and had eight children.

As a professor of English and classics at Poydras College in Pointe Coupee,

Louisiana, he continued to write historical poetry, a talent that he had gained a reputation for while in college. He wrote "Maryland, My Maryland," called the unofficial anthem of the Confederacy, after reading in the New Orleans *Delta* about the fighting between Maryland and Massachusetts troops. His other historical poems such as "Pelham," "There's Life in the Old Land Yet," and "At Arlington" are full of history and hope for a recovering South. After the war, Randall devoted himself to journalism. He edited two Augusta-based papers, the *Chronicle* and the *Constitutionalist*. Two of his collections of poetry were published after his death— *Maryland, My Maryland and Other Poems* (1908) and *The Poems of James Ryder Randall* (1910).

He died on January 14, 1908.

Abram Joseph Ryan
(1838-1886)

Monument—The Poet's Monument, Augusta, Georgia

(Please see biography in Alabama chapter.)

Charles Henry Smith
(1826-1908)

Author of famous newspaper essays

Marker—Gwinnett Courthouse Square, Lawrenceville, Georgia
Burial Site—Oak Hill Cemetery, Rome, Georgia

Charles Henry Smith was an influential Southerner who served as a lawyer, alderman, and mayor. During the Civil War, Smith was an officer in the Army of Northern Virginia and in the Forrest Artillery Company. Many people believe that his most powerful influence came in the form of the Bill Arp letters, a collection of more than 2,000 essays that he wrote between 1861 and 1903.

Smith was born on June 15, 1826, in Lawrenceville, Georgia. He attended the University of Georgia (then called Franklin College) in 1844. However, his father became ill and needed him to return home to manage the family store, causing him to leave his studies before completing a degree. He later passed the Georgia bar exam and became a lawyer representing the Georgia circuit court. He married Mary Octavia Hutchins in 1849; they had 13 children.

The Bill Arp essays were informal letters to the editor. They appeared first in the *Southern Confederacy* and the *Constitution*, both Atlanta newspapers. Then the essays were reprinted in an estimated 700 newspapers throughout the United States.

Bill Arp began as a strong, conservative Southerner, with poor grammar and spelling skills, who wanted to express the failures, hopes, and frustrations he felt while dealing with the Civil War and Reconstruction. Through the years, the topic of Arp's letters changed with the times, and Arp himself became more of an educated and literary Southern gentleman.

Smith wrote these popular essays until his death on August 24, 1903, in Cartersville, Georgia.

Richard Henry Wilde
(1789-1847)

Biographer and professor of Italian literature

Burial Site—Magnolia Cemetery, Augusta, Georgia

A successful lawyer, Richard Henry Wilde is most remembered for his study of Italian literature. He spent almost ten years in Florence, Italy, writing short biographies of Italian poets and translating their poems into English. He also wrote numerous original poems.

Born on September 24, 1789, in Dublin, Ireland, Wilde moved with his parents to Baltimore, Maryland, in 1797. When his father died in 1803, Wilde and his mother moved to Augusta, Georgia, where she opened a dress shop, and he attended the local schools. He passed the law exam and in 1811 became the attorney general of Georgia. Representing the state of Georgia, he spent several years in the United States Congress. He married Caroline Buckle in 1819; they had two sons.

In 1835 Wilde suffered political defeat and emotionally struggled with the death of his wife. He moved with his sister and two sons to Florence, Italy. There he occupied his time studying the native literature and beginning a biography of Dante.

In 1844 he returned to the United States, moving his family to New Orleans, where he opened a law office and later accepted a position as one of the first professors in the new Tulane law school. However, he contracted yellow fever and died September 10, 1847, just before classes began.

All the collections of his poetry—*Hesperia* (1867); *The Italian Lyric Poets* (1966); *and Poems, Fugitive and Occasional* (1966)—were published posthumously.

Augusta Jane Evans Wilson
(1835-1909)

Marker—*Columbus, Georgia*

(Please see biography in Alabama chapter.)

Kentucky

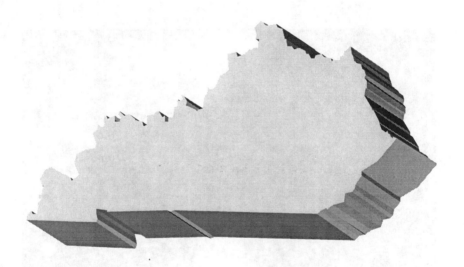

Robert Penn Warren
James Lane Allen
Irvin Shrewsbury Cobb
Elizabeth Madox Roberts
Abram Joseph Ryan
Jesse Stuart
John Patrick [Goggan]
James Still

Robert Penn Warren Birthplace

Third and Cherry Streets
P. O. Box 296
Guthrie, Kentucky 42234

Hours: Tuesday through Saturday, 11:30 a.m.-3:30 p.m.;
Sunday, 2-4 p.m.
Admission: Free
Telephone: (502) 483-2683

This red brick "railroad bungalow" was built in the late 1800s. Sitting on the edge of Guthrie's historic district, it was a part of the thriving railroad community, which claimed to be "the crossroads of railroads in America."

A prime example of turn-of-the-century architecture, the rooms feature original fireplaces and hardwood floors. Some of the period antiques which decorate the home belonged to the Warrens. Visitors are encouraged to take special note of the displays of Robert Penn Warren's books, photographs, and other memorabilia.

The home is available to the public for reading and research; the complete collection of Warren's works are available. (Here he published 10 novels, 16 volumes of poetry, many short stories, and plays.) There is also a meeting room available for scheduling lectures, films, and discussion groups.

Warren lived in Guthrie, Kentucky, for 16 years. He grew up hearing stories about local townspeople and their lifestyles. These early impressions are evident in Warren's works.

Robert Penn Warren
(1905-1989)

America's First Poet Laureate

Home—Guthrie, Kentucky
Special Collections—Yale University, New Haven, Connecticut; University of Kentucky, Lexington, Kentucky; University of Nevada, Reno, Nevada; Vanderbilt University, Nashville, Tennessee
Pulitzer Prizes—All the King's Men, 1947; Promises, 1958; Now and Then, 1979

The recipient of three Pulitzer Prizes and the only writer to have won a Pulitzer for both fiction and poetry, Robert Penn Warren had a diverse literary career. He wrote fiction, poetry, drama, criticism, biography, and textbooks in the fields of literature, journalism, and sociology. He, along with Cleanth Brooks, founded the *Southern Review*, one of the most distinguished literary quarterlies in America.

Born on April 24, 1905, in Guthrie, Kentucky, Warren attended Vanderbilt University in Nashville, Tennessee, where he studied under John Crowe Ransom, a noted English professor and poet. He also attended the University of California at Berkeley and Yale University before going as a Rhodes Scholar to Oxford, England. He married two times—first to Emma Brescia and then to Eleanor Clark. He had two children.

John Brown: The Making of a Martyr (1929) was his first published book. This unorthodox biography examines the social and political events that led to the development of the South. His first novel, *Night Rider* (1939), discussed the same themes as the John Brown biography—the ambiguity of truth, the corruption of the idealist, and the difficulty of self-knowledge. Literary scholars have acknowledged these reoccurring themes in most of his writing.

His greatest talent is said to have been his feel for narrative. His novels—*All the*

King's Men (1946), *World Enough and Time* (1950), and *Brother to Dragons* (1953)—are examples of his special handling of legends, ballads, and historical events.

All the King's Men, a fictionalization of the career of Louisiana politician Huey P. Long, earned Warren his first Pulitzer Prize. His next two Pulitzers honored poetry collections—*Promises* (1958) and *Now and Then* (1979). In 1986 he was named America's first poet laureate.

He died on September 15, 1989, in Stratton, Vermont, and is buried there.

Other Kentucky Writers and Sites

James Lane Allen

(1849-1925)

Author of bestselling Southern love stories

Special Collection—*University of Kentucky, Lexington, Kentucky*
Burial Site—*Lexington Cemetery, Lexington, Kentucky*

Beautiful descriptions of the Southern landscape set James Lane Allen's work apart from that of his fellow writers. His first major publication, *A Kentucky Cardinal* (1894), a poetic tale of frustrated love, was a bestseller for almost ten years.

Born near Lexington, Kentucky, on December 21, 1849, Allen attended public schools and worked his way through Kentucky University. After graduating with honors in 1872, he accepted a job teaching Latin in a local school. Later he moved to Richmond College in Richmond, Missouri, and then to Bethany College in West Virginia, teaching Latin in both colleges. In the evenings and on weekends, He wrote several successful articles and short stories for magazines such as *Harper's* and *Century*.

By 1893 he had left teaching to pursue a writing career. He lived in New York City and published his first book, *Flute and Violin* (1891), a compilation of his already published magazine stories. His novella, *A Kentucky Cardinal* (1894), described the landscape of the Kentucky he knew so well. The idyllic hero and the self-centered heroine captured a wide audience of readers for more than a decade. He is most noted for his novel, *The Choir Invisible* (1897), a love story filled with local color and moralistic sentiment.

In the 1900s his writing took on a more serious tone. He probed the minds of his characters and questioned the perseverance of religious faith. After *The Reign of Law* in 1900 and *The Mettle of the Pasture* in 1903, his writing became too obscure for readers and critics of his time. He continued to write but with little success until a few years before his death.

He died on February 18, 1925, in New York.

Irvin Shrewsbury Cobb

(1876-1944)

Creator of the popular Judge Priest

Special Collection—Murray State University, Murray, Kentucky
Burial Site—Oak Grove Cemetery, Paducah, Kentucky

A witty humorist, Irvin Cobb based many of his characters on the Kentuckians he knew best. He gained a loyal following with his Louisville *Evening Post* column, "Sour Mash." His most notable character was Judge Priest, a mint-julep-drinking veteran of the Civil War.

Born on June 23, 1876, in Paducah, Kentucky, Cobb learned about the Confederacy from his father, a veteran of the war. From an early age, he was attentive to the people around him, their actions and lifestyles forming the basis for much of his writing. He quit school to become a reporter for the Paducah *Daily News*, and later accepted staff positions with the Cincinnati *Post* and Louisville *Evening Post*. In 1900, He married Laura Spencer Baker. The next year he became the managing editor of the Paducah *News-Democrat*.

When he was 28, he moved to New York where he landed such assignments as reporting on the Russo-Japanese Peace Conference in New Hampshire. His imaginative coverage of such serious assignments resulted in his being hired as staff humorist for Joseph Pulitzer's New York *World*. There he began the column "Through Funny Glasses," which built for him a large, admiring audience.

He went on to write for the *Saturday Evening Post* and *Cosmopolitan*; later he moved to Hollywood to write screenplays and to act in several motion pictures.

Back Home (1912) was the first of his books to feature Judge Priest, the benevolent gentleman made popular in his *Saturday Evening Post* stories. In 1917, his writing took on a more serious tone as he approached the topic of propaganda; however, his humorous exaggeration made *Speaking of Prussians* (1917) and *The Glory of the Coming* (1918) popular with readers.

Tales of the macabre were another fascination for Cobb, and he was ingenious in his creation of them. Some critics of the time compared his ability to create terrifying stories almost equal to that of Edgar Allan Poe's. Most of his tales had a distinctive Southern tone. "The Belled Buzzard" (1912) was set in a swamp where a local squire lured a young peddler to his death. The most honored of his horror stories was "Snake Doctor" (1922) for which he won an O. Henry Award.

Although he lived through some difficult periods of history—the Civil War, the nation's transition, and two World Wars—he still managed to entertain through his writing. *Exit Laughing* (1941), an autobiography and his last book, was as humorous and easy to read as were his first columns published in local newspapers.

He died on March 10, 1944, in New York.

Elizabeth Madox Roberts
(1881-1941)

Poet and novelist

***Burial Site**—Cemetery Hill, Springfield, Kentucky*

Elizabeth Madox Roberts created characters and settings based on the small Southern town of Springfield, Kentucky. As a poet and novelist, she developed a keen sense of regional authenticity that gained for her an international reputation but yielded little financial success.

She was born on October 30, 1881, in Perryville, Kentucky. She moved with her family to nearby Springfield when she was three years old. She went to high school in Covington, Kentucky, and graduated from the University of Chicago in 1921. During her childhood, Roberts listened as her father, Simpson, discussed art and philosophy with family and friends. Her father's scholarly influence is apparent in her poetry and prose. Her works include *In the Great Steep's Garden* (1915), *Under the Tree* (1922), *The Time of Man* (1926), *Song in the Meadow* (1940), and *Not by Strange Gods* (1941).

She died on March 13, 1941, in Orlando, Florida.

Abram Joseph Ryan
(1838-1886)

***Historic marker**—St. Boniface Friary, Louisville, Kentucky*

(Please see biography in Alabama chapter.)

Jesse Stuart

(1907-1984)

The "Chronicler of Appalachia"

Special Collections—Indiana State University, Terre Haute, Indiana; Boyd County Public Library, Ashland, Kentucky; University of Kentucky; Lexington, Kentucky; Morehead State University, Morehead, Kentucky; Jesse Stuart Suite, Murray State University Library, Murray, Kentucky **Burial Site—***Plum Grove Cemetery, Greenup County, Kentucky*

Considered the best known and most widely read of the Appalachian writers, Jesse Stuart wrote of the land and people that he knew best. His local color tales of life—births, deaths, weddings, elections—have been published on five continents and in many languages.

Born on August 8, 1907, in W-Hollow, Greenup County, Kentucky, Stuart attended Lincoln Memorial University (Harrogate, Tennessee) where he earned a bachelor's degree in 1924. After serving as principal of Greenup County High School for two years, he attended Vanderbilt University and George Peabody College. He married Naomi Deane Noris in 1939.

Throughout his life, he was a teacher, lecturer, writer, and farmer. He successfully ran a 1,000-acre farm while pursuing a writing career. He easily assumed the role of an entertainer, reading his tales and poetry to any willing audience. A prolific writer, he won many awards, including a Guggenheim Fellowship in 1937 and a Fellowship of the Academy of American Poets in 1961.

He published his first book, *Harvest of Youth*, while principal of Greenup High School in 1930. During the next several years, while attending college, he wrote poetry and short fiction. His autobiographical work, *Beyond Dark Hills* (1938), began as a class project.

Taps for Private Tussie (1943), perhaps his most successful book, is a humorous look at the effects of World War II on the life of a Kentucky family. It drew a large audience, selling more than two million copies in two years.

In 1954 he was chosen as poet laureate of Kentucky. Fans and critics alike were fascinated by his poetry, leading to his honorary titles of "Chronicler of Appalachia" and the "American Robert Burns."

His love of the South and its people is evident in his writing. He used local settings, characters, and incidents for the basis of many of his books, stories, and poems. Stories of W-Hollow are collected in several volumes which include *Head O' W-Hollow* (1936), *Men of the Mountains* (1941), and *Thirty-Two Votes before Breakfast* (1974). He also honored the men and women of W-Hollow with poetry published in collections including *Man with a Bull-Tongue Plow* (1934)—a collection of 703 sonnets—and *Hold April* (1962).

Nonfiction accounts of various episodes in his life are collected in volumes such as *Beyond Dark Hills* (1938), *The Year of My Rebirth* (1956), and *To Teach, To Love* (1970). These books chronicle his growing-up years, recuperation from a heart attack, and teaching experiences.

By 1967, at the age of 60, he had published 26 books and 300 short stories. Before suffering disabling paralysis, he wrote another 10 books and almost 100 short stories. His last book, *The Kingdom Within*, was published in 1979.

He suffered several heart attacks and a stroke that left him in a coma for the last two years of his life. He died on February 17, 1984, in Ironton, Ohio.

John Patrick [Goggan]
(1906-1995)

Pulitzer Prize-winning dramatist

Special Collection*—*Boston University, Boston, Massachusetts
Pulitzer Prize*—The Teahouse of the August Moon, *1954

At the age of 19, after having spent several years drifting from one hobo camp to another, John Patrick Goggan found his way to San Francisco and, eventually, to a script-writing career. From 1929 to 1933, he wrote more than 1,100 scripts for the radio series "Cecil and Sally." With his first byline, he dropped his last name and from then on was known as John Patrick. Throughout his career, Patrick, who considered himself a craftsman first and an artist second, was most comfortable with the title of entertainer.

Born on May 17, 1905, in Louisville, Kentucky, Patrick was abandoned by his parents. He grew up in a variety of foster homes and boarding schools from Kentucky to Texas to New Orleans. In 1925 he moved to San Francisco and accepted his first job as a radio announcer. He later served as an ambulance driver in Egypt, Syria, and Southeast Asia during World War II. After his discharge, he attended Harvard University and Columbia University; however, he never received a degree.

Hell Freezes Over, his first play, was performed on Broadway in 1935. Poor attendance and bad reviews forced the play to close after only a few performances, and all scripts were destroyed. In 1938 he accepted a screenwriting job with Twentieth Century-Fox. In this position he successfully co-authored 19 film scripts.

He continued to write plays when he wasn't on an assignment with Twentieth Century-Fox. With his 1942 play, *The Willow and I*, he established himself as a master of mood and atmosphere. This psychological drama and highly emotional love story, set in the Deep South during the early 1900s, won him a large following.

Writing an entire script on scraps of paper, he created his first major success, *The Hasty Heart* (1945), while aboard ship returning from his military assignment in Southeast Asia. Knowing that officials confiscated, censored, and often destroyed anything written during World War II, he had a friend smuggle the script off the ship and mail it to him once they had both settled in the United States. From the success of this play, he was able to purchase a 65-acre farm in New York, which he appropriately named "Hasty Hill."

The Teahouse of the August Moon (1953), a satire on the U.S. military's attempt to create a democracy in Okinawa, won a Pulitzer Prize, a Tony Award, a Drama Critics' Circle Award, and a Theatre Club Award. It received great acclaim, especially in countries outside the U.S. Theaters goers enjoyed watching Americans poke fun at themselves. *Teahouse* was his most financially successful stage play.

In 1957 his play *Les Girls* won the Screenwriter's Guild Award. Two years later the screenplay *Some Came Running*, adapted from the novel by James Joyce, became the top-grossing film of the year. It received top billing in *Film Daily's* top ten films of 1959. Along with his successes, however, he also received criticism and bad reviews.

During the late 1970s and early 1980s, he concentrated on several plays including two companion pieces that each consisted of three one-act plays. *That's Not My Father!* and *That's Not My Mother* were both produced in 1980. In that same year, he released two other plays, *Opal's Million Dollar Duck* and the *Girls of the Garden Club*. His other plays include *The Magenta Moth* (1983), *It's a Dog's Life* (1984), *Sense and Nonesense* (1988), and *Cheating Cheaters* (1988).

Patrick died in 1995.

James Still

(1906-)

Poet and novelist of Appalachia

Special Collections—Berea College Library, Berea, Kentucky; Morehead State University, Morehead, Kentucky; University of Kentucky Library, Lexington, Kentucky

Southern Appalachia was the setting for most of James Still's fiction and poetry. A skillful linguist, he has received praise for his clean, spare style which many scholars believe elevates him from being a regional writer to one who has universal appeal. He received an O. Henry Memorial Prize, two Guggenheim fellowships, and an award from the Academy of Arts and Letters and the National Institute of Arts and Letters.

Born on July 16, 1906, in Lafayette, Alabama, Still attended Lincoln Memorial University (Harrogate, Tennessee), Vanderbilt University, and the University of Illinois. He accepted a teaching position at Hindman Settlement School and moved on to the English department of Morehead State University. From 1942 to 1945, he served in the U.S. Army Air Corps in Africa and the Middle East.

In 1937 he published his first novel, *Hounds on the Mountain*. With this novel and throughout his career, he focused on themes of honor, loyalty, self-reliance, and independence. His characters learned to endure and to respond to the world with humor.

Time magazine called *River of Earth* (1940)—a novel that is set in his familiar Appalachia—"a small masterpiece."

Still's writing often proved harsh for himself and his characters. He once admitted, "I left a character tilted back in a chair for two years because he quit talking to me." Always writing to please himself, he said if it pleased others along the way then that was good.

His other works include *On Troublesome Creek* (1941), *Way Down Yonder on Troublesome Creek* (1974), *Jack and the Wonder Beans* (1976), and *Pattern of Man* (1977).

Louisiana

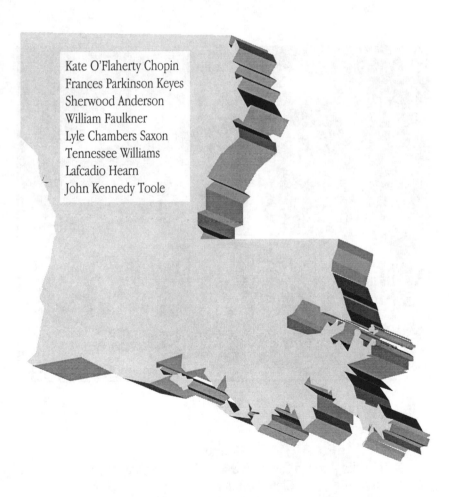

Kate O'Flaherty Chopin
Frances Parkinson Keyes
Sherwood Anderson
William Faulkner
Lyle Chambers Saxon
Tennessee Williams
Lafcadio Hearn
John Kennedy Toole

Bayou Folk Museum

Kate Chopin Home
P. O. Box 411
Cloutierville, Louisiana 71416

Hours:
Monday through Saturday, 9 a.m.-5 p.m.; Sunday, 1-5 p.m.;
Closed on major holidays
Admission: Adults, $5.00; Children, $2.50
Telephone: (318) 379-2233

This two-story plantation home, constructed of handmade brick, heart cypress, and pine, was built by slaves in 1809. The leaded glass windows, the upstairs wainscoting, and the French doors which open onto the balcony are original to the home. Handmade square nails and wooden pegs are visible in some areas of the building. Each floor has two fireplaces.

The property has three other buildings—a doctor's office, a blacksmith's shop, and a building that houses the restrooms. Two towering magnolias and a beautiful wrought-iron and brick fence are visible from the street. Many of the trees such as dogwoods, persimmons, and sweet olives grew on the property when Chopin lived there. She would have certainly had daylilies, irises, ivies, and mint growing outside her door, just as they do today.

Kate Chopin, her husband Oscar, and their five children moved to this village home in 1879. Oscar had inherited a portion of the nearby family plantation which included a large general store and several farms. When Oscar died in 1882, Kate ran the store and other property alone. A woman of considerable strength and determination, she supervised the cotton production and took care of the children. In 1884, at the urging of her mother, Chopin and her children left the plantation and returned to St. Louis.

While touring the home, visitors will find the first edition of *Bayou Folk* and various items that belonged to Chopin.

Kate O'Flaherty Chopin
(1851-1904)

Controversial feminist author

Home—*Cloutierville, Louisiana*
Special Collection—*University of Wisconsin, Madison, Wisconsin*

A modern woman living in a time of formality and strict social rules, Kate Chopin shocked her readers with her philosophy for the social awakening of women. In 1899 critics and the reading public attacked her novel, *The Awakening*, calling it an immoral book. Today, however, it is heralded as a great work of art.

Born on February 8, 1851, in St. Louis, Missouri, Kate O'Flaherty rebelled against authority and strict rules in her early school days. She challenged authority in the convent schools in St. Louis, reading books of her own choice and writing imaginative poems and short essays. In 1870 she married Oscar Chopin, a Louisiana cotton broker and banker. They had six children.

In 1879, the Chopins moved to Louisiana, where Oscar had inherited a portion of the family plantation. However, Kate, the rebel from Missouri, never quite fit in with the Louisiana aristocracy. She dressed differently, smoked cigarettes, and took long walks through the streets of New Orleans instead of attending to her housework. Perhaps the worst offense of all, though, was that she often publicly met and talked with people of all classes.

For four years, Oscar managed the large general store and small farms that he had inherited while Kate raised their children and challenged the social standards for women. After Oscar's death in 1883, she cared for the children and managed the property alone for a year before moving to St. Louis in 1884 to live near her mother. Unfortunately, her mother died suddenly, causing Chopin to sink into a deep depression. To alleviate her pain, she turned to writing professionally.

From 1889 to 1902, she published short stories featuring Louisiana Creoles and Acadian characters in magazines such as *Atlantic Monthly*, *Vogue*, *Saturday Evening Post*, and *Youth's Companion*. She published her first novel, *At Fault*, in 1890. The book's complex, cluttered plot focuses on a Northern gentleman and a widowed Creole plantation owner.

In 1894 *Bayou Folk*, a collection of 23 short stories and sketches, was published. Three years later she published *A Night in Acadie,* a collection of stories that included controversial, independent, and strong-willed women. Reaction to these stories was only a prelude to the criticism that she would receive from her novel, *The Awakening.*

She wrote about the search for freedom and self expression. Many of her short stories and novels present the reader with the lesson that the hardships and dangers encountered while searching for freedom are worth the battle. Although her readers accepted the moral thread that ran through her short stories, they were quick to label the main character in her 1899 novel, *The Awakening*, as immoral for abandoning her marriage and children to find her own self-expression. Criticism of *The Awakening* was so strong that Chopin's publisher canceled her contract. She became discouraged, and her later attempts at writing were half-hearted; she never fully recovered her motivation to write.

She died on August 22, 1904, of a brain hemorrhage after spending a strenuous day at the St. Louis World Fair. She is buried in Calvary Cemetery in St. Louis.

Beauregard-Keyes House

1113 Chartres Street
New Orleans, Louisiana 70116

Hours:
Tours on the hour, Monday through Saturday, 10 a.m.-3 p.m.;
Closed on major holidays including Mardi Gras
Admission:
Adults, $4.00; Senior citizens and students, $3.00; Children under 12,
$1.50; Group rate available upon request and with prior reservation
Telephone: (504) 523-7257

Standing on the narrow sidewalk in front of this majestic home, visitors feel the charm of the picturesque New Orleans described in Frances Parkinson Keyes' *Dinner at Antoine's*. Visitors can eavesdrop on the sounds of the French Quarter, and at the same time, look in on the grounds of the eighteenth-century Ursuline Convent from the elevated, four-columned portico.

Built in 1826 by Joseph Le Carpentier, this home has had many owners, including in 1832, John A. Merle, Consul of Switzerland, and after the Civil War, Confederate General Pierre G. T. Beauregard.

In 1925 the home was scheduled to be demolished; however, a group of patriotic women took charge of the home and saved it from destruction. Later, Francis Parkinson Keyes, a widowed U.S. senator's wife, took over the house for a winter home. Over a period of several years, she restored the home to its "original dignity and symmetry."

While restoring the home, nearly 30 coats of paint were stripped from the interior walls. When visitors tour this romantic house, they see rooms painted in the original colors and baseboards that have been restored to their original gray marbleizing which complement the original marble mantels.

The estate includes the original slave quarters and carriage house which were converted into a study as well as two other buildings which were restored to house Keyes' bedroom, a library, and a gift shop.

Her first days at 1113 Chartres Street brought Keyes some unwelcomed attention. Both she and the home had admirers. Although she had the gates closed across the front stairs, tourists would open the gates, gather around, and tap on the windows to get her attention. Writing came first for Keyes. She quickly learned to ignore the interruptions, although she regretted turning away her fans. As soon as the slave quarters were remodeled, she moved her office there.

Keyes wrote 29 of her books while staying here, including *Dinner at Antoine's*, *The Chess Players*, and *Blue Camellia*.

This elegant historical home can be scheduled for special functions.

Frances Parkinson Wheeler Keyes

(1885-1970)

Author of over 50 books

Home—*New Orleans, Louisiana*
Special Collection—*University of Virginia, Charlottesville, Virginia*

Frances Parkinson Wheeler Keyes (pronounced Kize) was born on July 21, 1885, in Charlottesville, Virginia. Spending most of her youth in Boston, she received a worldwide education. She had tutors in Switzerland and Germany and attended the Boston area schools when not traveling with her family. In 1904 she married politician Henry Wilder Keyes, the governor of New Hampshire and later a United States senator. They had three sons.

While her husband worked on Capitol Hill, she wrote articles and short fiction for national magazines. Her works focused on her travels as a youth and on her experiences as the wife of a politician. She was the editor of the *National Historical Magazine* of the Daughters of the American Revolution from 1937 to 1939.

After her husband's death in 1938, she converted to Catholicism and devoted her time to preserving historic shrines such as Arlington, the Lee Mansion on the Potomac, and what is now called the Beauregard-Keyes House. She also devoted a considerable amount of time researching and writing about the lives of the saints. During her lifetime, she wrote more than 50 books—mainly while living at the Beauregard-Keyes house—focusing on biography, travel, and fiction. She was a popular storyteller, capturing her audience with sparkling adventures and romantic characters. *Dinner at Antoine's* (1948) remains a favorite of dedicated romance readers.

She received honorary degrees from George Washington University, Bates College, and the University of New Hampshire, along with receiving the Siena Medal and being named Catholic Woman of the Year in 1946.

She died on July 3, 1970, in New Orleans. She is buried in Newbury, Vermont.

Other Louisiana
Writers
and Sites

Sherwood Anderson
(1876-1941)

Literary Landmark—Pontalba Apartments, New Orleans, Louisiana

(Please see biography in Virginia chapter.)

William Cuthbert Faulkner
(1897-1962)

French Quarter Home—now a bookstore, New Orleans, Louisiana

(Please see biography in Mississippi chapter.)

Lyle Chambers Saxon
(1891-1946)

Biographer and novelist of Louisiana life

Special Collection—Tulane University, New Orleans, Louisiana
Burial Site—Magnolia Cemetery, Baton Rouge, Louisiana

Best known for his nonfiction writing, Lyle Chambers Saxon had only one novel published, *Children of Strangers* (1937). However, the novel was widely read and admired for its realistic treatment of mulatto and African-American people in and about the Cane River region (the Natchitoches area).

Born on September 4, 1891, in Baton Rouge, Louisiana, Saxon graduated from Louisiana State University in 1912. Working first as a reporter in Chicago, he then returned to Louisiana to work for the New Orleans *Item* and later the *Times-Picayune*.

He contributed stories and articles to national magazines and won an O. Henry

Award in 1926. Saxon's first book, *Father Mississippi*, was published in 1927. A
year later *Fabulous New Orleans*, a book full of colorful descriptions and stories with New Orleans settings and characters, was published.

Turning his attention to biography, Saxon wrote an account of the pirate
Jean Lafitte, a character important to the shaping of Louisiana; *Lafitte the Pirate*
was published in 1930. During the 1940s Saxon was appointed director of the
Federal Writers' Projects in Louisiana. He edited *A Collection of Louisiana Folk
Tales: Gumbo Ya-Ya* (1945) which critics say contains some of the best ac-
counts of Louisiana's folk history.

He died on April 9, 1946, in New Orleans, Louisiana.

Tennessee [Thomas Lanier]
Williams
(1911-1983)

Festival—*Tennessee Williams/New Orleans Literary Festival, New
Orleans, Louisiana (annual event in March)*

(Please see biography in Mississippi chapter.)

Lafacadio Hearn
(1850-1904)

Journalist and novelist fascinated with the exotic

Special Collections—*Samford University, Birmingham, Alabama;
W. S. Hoole Special Collections Library, University of Alabama,
Tuscaloosa, Alabama; Claremont Colleges, Claremont, California;
Illinois State University, Normal, Illinois; University of Louisville,
Louisville, Kentucky; Tulane University, New Orleans, Louisiana;
Harvard University Library, Cambridge, Massachusetts; Pierpont
Morgan Library, New York, New York; Ohio University, Athens, Ohio;*

University of Virginia, Charlottesville, Virginia

Lafcadio Hearn continually searched for the novel and exotic in life and in his writing. He began his writing career as a journalism apprentice, reporting on scandalous and outrageous subjects for weekly newspapers. In his spare time, he worked on translating the works of Gautier and Flaubert. He was an editor, educator, fiction writer, and translator. Fascinated by the Louisiana Creoles, he published a collection of Creole recipes, a dictionary of Creole proverbs, and several stories and book-length fiction influenced by the New Orleans lifestyle.

He was born on June 27, 1850, on the Isle of Santa Maura, off the coast of Greece. The island was formerly called "Leucadia," thus his name. At age six, he moved with his mother to Dublin, Ireland. However, an aunt soon took over his legal guardianship and provided a home for him while he attended school. After long disciplinary battles, his aunt sent him in 1869 to the United States to live. Settling in Ohio, he began an apprenticeship in journalism. Here he learned to seek the sensational and the extreme and write about it in a conversational tone.

In 1877 he traveled to the South for a vacation and found a land and people that he could not leave. He accepted a position first as associate editor for the New Orleans *Item* and later as an editor for the *Times-Democrat*. By 1882 his translation of a Gautier short story, "One of Cleopatra's Nights," was published. Two years later he published a collection of Oriental myths which he had rewritten, *Stray Leaves from Strange Literature* (1884). This was followed in 1887 by a second collection of Oriental myths, *Some Chinese Ghosts*.

His fascination with Louisiana and its people is evident in his *La Cuisine Creole* (1885); *"Gombo Zhebes": A Little Dictionary of Creole Proverbs* (1885); and the novelette, *Chita* (1889).

In 1890 he was commissioned by Harper Brothers to work in Japan. For 14 years he wrote books about the country and its people which include *Glimpses of Unfamiliar Japan* (2 vols., 1894); *Japanese Fairy Tales* (5 vols., 1898-1903); and *Japan: An Attempt at Interpretation*. He also lectured at Tokyo Imperial University.

He died on September 26, 1904, in Japan.

John Kennedy Toole
(1937-1969)

Posthumous winner of a Pulitzer Prize

Special Collection—Tulane University, New Orleans, Louisiana
Pulitzer Prize—A Confederacy of Dunces, 1981 (awarded posthumously)

Identified by his friends and co-workers as witty, gracious, and charming, John Kennedy Toole was a talented writer. His most recognized novel, *A Confederacy of Dunces,* was written during the 1960s; however, it was not published until 1980, eleven years after his death. The novel, praised by critics and a large reading audience, resulted in a Pulitzer Prize in 1981.

Born in 1937 in New Orleans, Toole attended Frontier High School where he won a four-year scholarship to Tulane University. He wrote a humor column for his high school newspaper and was a cartoonist for the Tulane *Hullabaloo.*

He went on to earn a master's degree from Columbia University in New York in 1959. After graduation, he accepted a teaching position at Hunter College in Manhattan. He soon moved back to New Orleans to teach at the University of Southwestern Louisiana in Lafayette, Louisiana.

In 1961 he entered the army, serving as an English instructor for Spanish-speaking recruits in Puerto Rico. While there, he began writing his second novel, *A Confederacy of Dunces.* He returned to Louisiana after his tour of duty and submitted the manuscript to a publishing company. An editor requested several revisions but ultimately rejected the manuscript. Toole stored the manuscript in the back of a drawer where his mother found it after his death in 1969.

Critics have praised *A Confederacy of Dunces* for its vivid characterizations and authentic use of various dialects. Toole drew heavily from his own experiences in writing the novel. For example, because his mother taught elocution classes when he was young, he became acutely aware of language and speech patterns. Drawing again from his experiences, he gave the main character jobs as a hot dog vendor and a file clerk in a pants factory. While attending Tulane University, he worked as a stadium hot dog vendor and later in a clothing factory.

Many critics believe the main character of *A Confederacy of Dunces* to be the best comic grotesque in American literature. Toole's comic handling of the harsh themes of cruelty and alienation is evidence of his keen understanding of the American South and of his extensive literary talent.

Toole wrote his only other novel, *The Neon Bible*, for a writing contest when he was 16 years old. The novel, which also focuses on alienation and cruelty, was published in 1987 after a lengthy court battle among Toole's heirs. The main character, a young boy growing up in a small Mississippi town, is a social outcast. Some scholars consider this novel to be more finely constructed than *A Confederacy of Dunces* but recognize that Toole's use of language is not as well developed.

Toole committed suicide in March 1969 in Biloxi, Mississippi, two months after quitting his teaching job at Dominican College in New Orleans.

Maryland

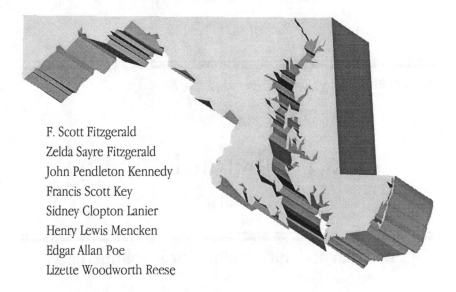

F. Scott Fitzgerald
Zelda Sayre Fitzgerald
John Pendleton Kennedy
Francis Scott Key
Sidney Clopton Lanier
Henry Lewis Mencken
Edgar Allan Poe
Lizette Woodworth Reese

F. Scott Fitzgerald
(1896-1940)

Burial Site—*St. Mary's Catholic Cemetery, Rockville, Maryland*

(Please see biography in Alabama chapter.)

Zelda Sayre Fitzgerald
(1900-1948)

Burial Site—*St. Mary's Catholic Cemetery, Rockville, Maryland*

(Please see biography in Alabama chapter.)

John Pendleton Kennedy
(1795-1870)

Politician and author of political commentary

Special Collections—*Enoch Pratt Free Library, Baltimore, Maryland; Johns Hopkins University, Baltimore, Maryland; University of Virginia, Charlottesville, Virginia; Virginia Historical Society, Richmond, Virginia* **Burial Site**—*Greenmount Cemetery, Baltimore, Maryland*

A well-educated lawyer, John Pendleton Kennedy had a greater interest in writing satire about his community and its people than practicing law. His series of essays, "The Swiss Traveler," appeared in the Baltimore *Portico*. Kennedy wrote several novels and short stories before entering politics. However, after his election to the House of Representatives in 1838, he began writing political commentary. Through essays, fiction, and political commentary, Kennedy's writing, sometimes under the pen name of Mark Littleton, influenced the growth of the South.

Born on October 25, 1795, in Baltimore, Maryland, Kennedy graduated from Baltimore College and joined the Maryland militia. Trained and encouraged by his uncle, he studied law and passed the bar exam in 1816. He was elected to the Maryland House of Delegates in 1820. He married Mary Tenant in 1824, but his marriage lasted only a few months because Mary died in childbirth.

In 1929, he married Elizabeth Gray and returned to writing. His first book, *Swallow Barn* (1832), was both respectful and satirical in its handling of plantation life. In 1835 he published his second novel, *Horse-Shoe Robinson*, which has been labeled his most significant achievement. It received one of the few positive reviews written by Edgar Allan Poe.

In 1838 Kennedy was elected to the House of Representatives, ending his career as a romance novelist. He continued to write, but turned his attention to politics, producing books such as *Quodlibet* (1840), a critique of Jackson's policies, *The Border States* (1860), and *Mr. Ambrose's Letters on the Rebellion* (1865). Kennedy's last literary work focused on the popular statesman William Wirt. The *Memoirs of the Life of William Wirt* (1849) reflected the wit, humor, and common sense of the influential man who served as attorney general under Presidents Monroe and Adams.

He died on August 18, 1870, in Baltimore, Maryland.

Francis Scott Key
(1779-1843)

Author of America's national anthem

Monument—*Baltimore, Maryland*
Special Collection—*Maryland Historical Society, Baltimore, Maryland (includes autographed manuscript of "The Star Spangled Banner")*
Museum—*Francis Scott Key Museum, Frederick, Maryland*
Burial Site—*Mount Olivet Cemetery, Frederick, Maryland*

Best known as the author of the national anthem, "The Star Spangled Banner," Francis Scott Key was also a noted speech writer, penning inspirational speeches that influenced the birth and growth of the United States.

Key was born on August 1, 1779, south of Taneytown, Maryland. He graduated with honors in 1726 from St. John's College in Annapolis, Maryland, and continued his studies, taking private classes in law in Annapolis. In 1801 he began his law practice, and a year later he married Mary Taylor Lloyd. They had 11 children. From 1833 to 1842 Key was the U.S. attorney for the District of Columbia. One of his closest friends was Andrew Jackson.

"Defense of Fort M'Henry" was an anonymous handbill distributed in Baltimore on September 17, 1814. This was the first publication of what we know today as "The Star Spangled Banner." Key received the byline as the song's writer in the September 24, 1814, issue of the Frederick-Town *Herald.* The first recorded public singing of the song was on October 19, 1814, at the Baltimore Holliday Street Theater. However, it was not until 1931 that President Hubert Hoover officially proclaimed "The Star Spangled Banner" as the national anthem.

Key's other works include *Oration . . . in the Rotunda of the Capitol of the U. States, on the 4th of July, 1831* (1831); *The Power of Literature and Its Connexion with Religion: An Oration . . . July 23, 1834 . . .* (1834); and *Speech . . . Before the Colonization Convention, May 9, 1842* (1842).

Key died on January 11, 1843, in Baltimore, Maryland.

Sidney Clopton Lanier
(1842-1881)

Burial Site—*Greenmount Cemetery, Baltimore, Maryland*

(Please see biography in Georgia chapter.)

Henry Lewis Mencken
(1880-1956)

Critic of Southern culture, literature, and authors

Special Collections—*Azusa Pacific College, Azusa, California; San Diego State University, San Diego, California; Yale University, New*

*Haven, Connecticut; Georgetown University Library, Washington, D.C.;
Southern Illinois University, Carbondale, Illinois; University of Kansas,
Lawrence, Kansas; University of Louisville, Louisville, Kentucky; H. L.
Mencken Room, Enoch Pratt Free Library, Baltimore, Maryland; Goucher
College, Towson, Maryland; Dartmouth College, Hanover, New
Hampshire; New York Public Library Research Libraries, New York, New
York; Gettysburg College, Gettysburg, Pennsylvania; University of
Pennsylvania, Philadelphia, Pennsylvania; University of Texas, El Paso,
Texas; University of Virginia, Charlottesville, Virginia*
Burial Site—*Loudon Park Cemetery, Baltimore, Maryland*

As a columnist, reporter, and editor, Henry Lewis Mencken had perhaps the most influence of any one person on Southern literature. His harsh criticism of Southern culture, literature, and authors brought about an awakening for Southern writers. Many of them set out to dispute Mencken's negative appraisal by openly defending Southern lifestyle and literature. In a specific response to his claim that Southern literature was "sterile," some writers gathered to form the South Carolina Poetry Society. On the other hand, some of the South's younger writers—including James Branch Cabell, Paul Green, and Thomas Wolfe—sided with Mencken and turned to a liberal writing style.

Born on September 12, 1880, he attended Baltimore public schools. When he was 18, he became a reporter for the Baltimore *Morning Herald*. In 1906 he moved to the Baltimore *Sunpapers*, an association of newspapers which positioned him as an influential columnist and editor for various publications. His book reviews in the *Smart Set* gave him a platform from which to support controversial writers such as Theodore Dreiser and James Branch Cabell and a forum for his criticism of the mediocrity of American life.

In 1917 Mencken's "The Sahara of the Bozart" was published in the New York *Evening Mail* (reprinted in *Prejudices, Second Series*, 1920). In this essay he claimed the South was almost as artistically, intellectually, and culturally sterile as the Sahara Desert. He claimed preachers and politicians were the cause of the decline of Southern culture. In 1924 Mencken followers were labeled young and sophisticated. As editor of the *American Mercury*, Mencken continued to ridicule the prudish South, specifically its preachers, politicians, and educators.

In 1930, at age 50, he published what he thought was his best work, *Treatise on the Gods*. It went through seven printings before the year's end. However, critics hold his later works to be superior. His autobiographical books—*Happy Days* (1940), *Newspaper Days* (1941), and *Heathen Days* (1943)—became popular with readers. Many critics call *Happy Days* the most perfect picture of an American boyhood since *Huckleberry Finn*.

Although Mencken was a great essayist and social critic, his most lasting work, and perhaps his most all-consuming one, was *The American Language*, first published in 1918 and revised four times before his death. This massive work began as an essay in the Baltimore *Evening Sun* in 1910. Mencken addressed changes in language due to the founding of a new land, to the forming of a new nation, the Civil War, and many other influences. Discussions of pronunciation, spelling, parts of speech, and American slang are based on examples that Mencken collected throughout his years as a newspaperman.

Mencken died on January 29, 1956, in Baltimore, Maryland.

Edgar Allan Poe
(1809-1849)

Statue—Baltimore, Maryland
Burial Site—Westminster Presbyterian Church Cemetery, Baltimore, Maryland

(Please see biography in Virginia chapter.)

Lizette Woodworth Reese
(1856-1935)

Poet and storyteller

Special Collection—Brandeis University, Waltham, Massachusetts
Burial Site—St. John's Episcopal Church, Waverly, Maryland

Poet, essayist, and storyteller, Lizette Woodworth Reese is best known for the sonnet, "Tears." All of her writing, both poetry and prose, had a beauty and honesty that resulted from her life in a small Maryland community.

Born on January 9, 1856, in Waverly, Maryland, she graduated from the local public schools and began teaching which was a lifelong career for her. In her free time she wrote poetry and essays, publishing her first poem, "The Deserted House," in 1874 in *Southern Magazine*. Her first volume of poetry, *A Branch of May*, was published 13 years later in 1887.

In 1899, Reese's famous poem, "Tears," was published in *Scribner's Magazine*. From that time on, she often submitted poetry, essays, and stories to national magazines such as *Atlantic Monthly*, *Scribner's*, and *Smart Set*. She also had five volumes of poetry published during this period.

At age 73, she published a volume of prose anecdotes, *A Victorian Village* (1929). In this book, she told childhood memories and included her recollection of Abraham Lincoln's funeral procession. In 1931, her second book of memories, *The York Road*, was published. It included short stories and fictional character sketches based on her life and acquaintances.

Pastures and Other Poems (1933) was her final volume of poetry. In this collection, she focused on nature, death, and the loss of loved ones. At her death, *The Old House in the Country*, a rhymed narrative poem, and *Worley's*, a fictionalized account of her childhood, were unfinished. Both were published posthumously in 1936.

She died on December 17, 1935, in Baltimore, Maryland.

Mississippi

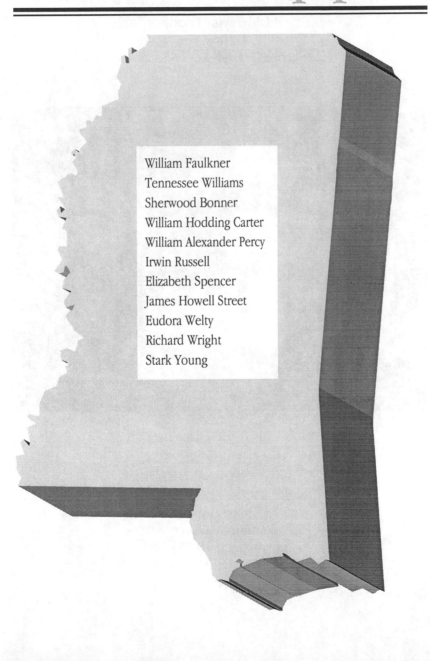

William Faulkner
Tennessee Williams
Sherwood Bonner
William Hodding Carter
William Alexander Percy
Irwin Russell
Elizabeth Spencer
James Howell Street
Eudora Welty
Richard Wright
Stark Young

Rowan Oak

Old Taylor Road
P. O. Box 965
Oxford, Mississippi 38655

Hours:
Tuesday through Saturday, 10 a.m.-12 p.m. and 2-4 p.m.;
Sunday, 2-4 p.m.; Closed on Mondays and major holidays
Admission: Free
Telephone: (601) 234-3284

This two-story white frame home with square columns was built by a pioneer settler in the 1840s. The large rooms and tall ceilings are typical of Southern homes of this era. When William Faulkner bought the home in 1930, he named the home and its 32-acre property in honor of the legendary Rowan tree, which shades the elegant front porch. Folklore says that Scottish peasants placed a cross of Rowan wood over their thresholds to ward off evil spirits and give the occupants a place of refuge, privacy, and peace.

When the Faulkners moved into their new home, it had no lights, no plumbing, and no running water. (They bathed outside in the courtyard.) Faulkner hammered and painted all summer. He and a helper scrubbed the house inside and out, installed plumbing and electricity, and added fresh paint to all the walls. A short time later, Faulkner built the brick wall to shield himself and his wife from the strangers who would often stand in the yard and gawk at the local celebrity.

Included in the furnishings of Rowan Oak are paintings by Faulkner's mother and a bust of Don Quixote, given to Faulkner in 1961 by the president of Venezuela.

The handwritten plot outline of *A Fable* can be seen on the walls of Faulkner's office which he built after being awarded a Nobel Prize in 1949. A portable typewriter sits on the table; a bottle of horse liniment and a carpenter's pencil are nearby, just as they were on the day Faulkner died.

Tourists are welcome to walk around the grounds. Behind the house is a stable and a cook's house and kitchen, used by Faulkner as a smokehouse. Many visitors also enjoy walking from Rowan Oak into town, as Faulkner did almost everyday.

Faulkner lived most of his life in Oxford, his family having moved there when he was four years old. His tales of Yoknapatawpha County were based on his experiences growing up in Oxford. Many of the characters in his writings are composites of people he knew.

William Cuthbert Faulkner
(1897-1962)

Pulitzer and Nobel Prize winner

Homes—*Oxford, Mississippi, and New Orleans, Louisiana (open as a bookstore only)*
Marker—*New Albany, Mississippi*
Park—*New Albany, Mississippi*
Special Collections—*Stanford University, Stanford, California; Yale University, New Haven, Connecticut; Connecticut College Library, New London, Connecticut; Northwestern University Library, Evanston, Illinois; University of Louisville, Louisville, Kentucky; Tulane University, New Orleans, Louisiana; University of New Orleans, New Orleans, Louisiana; Harvard University Library, Cambridge, Massachusetts; Williams College, Williamstown, Massachusetts; University of Michigan, Ann Arbor, Michigan; Mississippi State University, Mississippi State, Mississippi; University of Mississippi, University, Mississippi; Southeast Missouri State University Library, Cape Girardeau, Missouri; University of Nevada, Reno, Nevada; U.S. Military Academy Library, West Point, New York; Wake Forest University, Winston-Salem, North Carolina; Public Library of Cincinnati & Hamilton County, Cincinnati, Ohio; Kent State University Libraries, Kent, Ohio; University of Texas Libraries, Austin, Texas; University of Virginia, Charlottesville, Virginia*
Burial Site—*St. Peter's Cemetery, Oxford, Mississippi*
Nobel Prize for Literature—*1949*
Pulitzer Prizes—A Fable, *1955;* The Reivers, *1963*

Obsessed by an interest in writing, William Faulkner became one of America's best writers producing 20 novels, two collections of poetry, and five short story collections. He incorporated both realism and symbolism in his stream-of-consciousness technique of writing. Awarded a Nobel Prize for Literature in 1949 and Pulitzer Prizes in 1955 and 1963, he achieved international recognition.

Faulkner was born on September 25, 1897, in New Albany, Mississippi. As a child he moved with his family to Ripley, Mississippi, and then to Oxford, which he called home for most of his life. In the spring of 1918, at age 21, he moved to Connecticut to live with his friend Phil Stone, a student at Yale University. That summer he added a "u" to his name (his family name was spelled Falkner) and joined the Canadian Air Force, a career that lasted only a few months.

In 1925, he moved to New Orleans, searching for an atmosphere and motivation for writing. There he met writer Sherwood Anderson, who encouraged him to submit a novel manuscript to a publisher. This resulted in the publication of *Soldiers' Pay* in 1926. Several novels later, he wrote *The Sound and the Fury* (1929), a highly experimental novel immediately acclaimed a masterpiece.

He married Estelle Franklin, a long-time friend, on June 20, 1929. They had two daughters, one who died nine days after birth. Franklin also had two children from a previous marriage. The couple purchased the home now known as Rowan Oak in 1930.

Although *Sanctuary* (1931) shocked his audience with violence, it brought Faulkner fame, sales, and a Hollywood contract. Subsequently, he sought a Hollywood career as a screenwriter while continuing to write short stories for popular magazines. He worked for four studios, including Warner Brothers in 1942. The novel *Intruder in the Dust* (1948) restored his reputation with the nation's readers and again provided him with volume sales.

During his writing career, he received many awards, including election to the American Academy of Arts and Letters on November 23, 1948. Two years later, he received the Nobel Prize for Literature. He received the National Book Award for *Collected Stories* in 1951 and for *A Fable* in 1955. Also in 1955, he received a Pulitzer Prize for *A Fable*.

After receiving the Nobel Prize in 1950, he spent much time traveling and speaking. However, he also found time for writing, producing six novels in 11 years. During this period, he wrote about the changing cultural and political atmosphere in the South, a topic of many of his speeches during this time.

He entered the hospital in Byhalia, Mississippi, on July 6, 1962. A few hours later, he suffered a fatal heart attack.

In 1963, one year after his death, his last novel, *The Reivers* (1961), received a Pulitzer Prize.

Tennessee Williams Birthplace Home and Welcome Center

Corner of Main and Third Street, South
Columbus, Mississippi 39703

Hours: Monday through Sunday, 8:30 a.m.-5:30 p.m.
Closed on major holidays
Admission: Free
Telephone: (601) 328-0222

Built in 1875, this two-story Victorian house was the birthplace home of Thomas Lanier (Tennessee) Williams. Moved in 1995 to its present location, this home now serves as a state welcome center.

Williams lived in this home, then the rectory for St. Paul's Episcopal Church, for three years. Walter Dankin, Williams' grandfather, served as the church's rector.

The home, built of wood native to Mississippi, has been restored to its 1911 condition. Only the first floor is open to visitors, and tourists are welcome to come and go at their leisure. Those interested in the playwright are encouraged to read the newspaper and magazine articles about Williams that are prominently displayed. The home also maintains a collection of Williams' bound works.

Many tourists enjoy walking just one block north to see the stately St. Paul's Episcopal Church where young Williams was baptized.

Tennessee [Thomas Lanier] Williams
(1911-1983)

Award-winning dramatist

Birthplace Home—*Columbus, Mississippi*
Memorial—*Tennessee Williams Fine Arts Building, Florida Key Community College, Key West, Florida*
Special Collections—*University of Arizona, Tucson, Arizona; University of California, Davis, California; University of California, Los Angeles, California; University of Delaware Library, Newark, Delaware; University of Georgia Libraries, Athens, Georgia; Mississippi State University, Mississippi State, Mississippi; St. Louis Public Library, St. Louis, Missouri; Princeton University Libraries, Princeton, New Jersey; Columbia University Libraries, New York, New York; University of Texas Libraries, Austin, Texas*
Festival—*Tennessee Williams/New Orleans Literary Festival, New Orleans, Louisiana (held each March)*
Pulitzer Prizes—A Streetcar Named Desire, *1948;* Cat on a Hot Tin Roof, *1955*

Considered one of the most important Southern playwrights, Tennessee Williams spent much of his youth outside the South. Perhaps best known for the plays—*The Glass Menagerie* (1945), *A Streetcar Named Desire* (1947), and *Cat on a Hot Tin Roof* (1955)—he built a career as a novelist, poet, and a screenwriter for MGM. His writing has an element of sadness that characterized his own life.

Born on March 26, 1911, in Columbus, Mississippi, Williams, along with his mother and older sister Rose, lived with his grandparents while his father traveled across the country selling shoes. In 1919, his father received a promotion and moved the family to St. Louis, a traumatic move that later affected the lives of both children and is reflected in Williams' drama and comedy. Williams attended the University of Missouri, Washington University, and the University of Iowa.

Like many writers of his time, he lived in large cities throughout the country; however, he especially enjoyed vacationing in Florida. He believed that he did his best work in Key West. In fact, he completed the manuscript for *A Streetcar Named Desire* while vacationing there with his grandfather in 1946.

The Glass Menagerie, his first successful play, won a Drama Critics' Circle Award in 1945. *A Streetcar Named Desire* debuted in 1947. Both of these plays, full of Southern nostalgia, are somewhat autobiographical, although Williams exaggerated his emotions to form fictional characters and reflect their changing lifestyles.

Both *A Streetcar Named Desire* and *Cat on a Hot Tin Roof* earned Drama Critics' Awards and Pulitzer Prizes for Williams. Audiences were attracted by his style of writing, which went beyond regional Southern themes and explored universal conflicts. Critics varied widely in their appraisal and interpretation of Williams' plays; however, he maintained a large audience for several years. *Night of the Iguana* debuted in 1961 and also received a Drama Critics' Award; however, it marked the beginning of his decline in popularity.

Williams heavily revised some of his plays before and after production. There are two versions of some of his plays, including *Cat on a Hot Tin Roof*. *Night of the Iguana* had been printed in two versions and even produced differently from the printed scripts.

His screen-writing career spanned more than four decades. He continued to publish until his death on February 25, 1983, in New York. He is buried in Calvary Cemetery in St. Louis, Missouri.

Other Mississippi
Writers
and
Sites

Sherwood Bonner
[Katherine MacDowell]
(1849-1883)

Master of distinctive Southern dialect

Special Collection—*Harvard University Library, Cambridge, Massachusetts*
Burial Site—*Hill Crest Cemetery, Holly Springs, Mississippi*

By the age of 20, Katharine Sherwood Bonner McDowell had contributed stories to newspapers in Boston, Massachusetts, and Mobile, Alabama. A prolific writer, she wrote about life on the mountains, plantations, and country farms with a flavor and truthfulness that has been labeled a remarkable literary form.

Bonner was born February 26, 1849, in Holly Springs, Mississippi. She watched with her family and neighbors as the ravages of the Civil War destroyed their personal property. Confederate soldiers raided Holly Springs more than 60 times. When the area schools were destroyed, 16-year-old Bonner continued to study under her father's guidance.

On February 14, 1871, she married Edward McDowell; they had one daughter. Their troubled marriage ended in divorce in 1881. For many of those ten years, Bonner lived away from her husband in Europe, Boston, Mississippi, and Texas. During her travels, she met Henry Wadsworth Longfellow, and in 1873 she accepted a position with him as his secretary.

In 1878 she published her only novel, *Like Unto Like*. This semi-autobiographical work takes place during the Civil War and Reconstruction. Scholars have acknowledged the historical merits of the novel— sometimes calling the book more fact than fiction.

Bonner is better known for the short stories that she wrote using Southern manners and speech. Giving her characters distinctive regional dialects, she became the first author to publish short stories with such well-defined characteristics. She also led the way in creating short story characters who spoke in African-American dialect. Her "Gran'mammy" stories are thought to be the first such stories published in a monthly journal. Her short stories are compiled in two volumes, *Dialect*

Tales (1883) and _Suwanee River Tales_ (1884).
She died on July 22, 1883, in Holly Springs, Mississippi.

William Hodding Carter
(1907-1972)

Pulitzer Prize-winning newspaper editor

Special Collection—_Mississippi State University, Mississippi State, Mississippi_
Burial Site—_Greenville, Mississippi_
Pulitzer Prize—_Editorial Writing,_ Delta Democrat-Times _(Greenville, Mississippi), 1946_

A novelist, poet, and historian, Hodding Carter is best remembered as a newspaper editor. He used his writing to voice his intolerance of racial bias and bigotry. His editorials in the _Delta Democrat-Times_ received a Pulitzer Prize in 1946.

Born on February 3, 1907, in Hammond, Louisiana, he grew up watching the cruel way whites treated African Americans in his neighborhood. When he was six, he watched a gang of white boys chase an African-American man, and several years later, he stumbled upon the aftermath of a lynching.

After attending Bowdoin College in Maine and Columbia University in New York City, he accepted a position with the New Orleans _Item-Tribune_ in 1929. He went on to serve as night bureau chief for the United Press in New Orleans and bureau chief for the Associated Press in Jackson, Mississippi.

In 1931 he married Betty Brunhilde Werlein. Together they began the _Daily Courier_ in Hammond, Louisiana, where he became known as a relentless foe of U.S. Senator Huey Long. The Carters moved back to Mississippi in 1935 where they began the _Delta Star_ which later became the _Delta Democrat-Times._

During World War II, Carter served in the Army Bureau of Public Relations and in army intelligence activities. He wrote a book on civil defense and served as the editor for _Yank_ and the Cairo edition of _Stars and Stripes._

The Winds of Fear, his best known book, was published in 1944. This somewhat autobiographical novel, featuring a young journalist who tries to bring racial tolerance to a small Southern town, stirred an already boiling racial controversy. He followed this book with *Flood Crest* in 1947.

Where Main Street Meets the River, his autobiography, was published in 1953. The title describes the location of the *Delta Democrat-Times* office during the time he served as publisher. (The newspaper office moved to North Broadway in the 1960s.)

Carter received several awards including the Pulitzer Prize for editorial writing, a Guggenheim Fellowship, and the Southern Literary Award. He was instrumental in the founding of the Levee Press, which published authors such as Eudora Welty, William Faulkner, and William Alexander Percy. From 1962 until 1970, he served as writer-in-residence at Tulane.

He died on April 4, 1972, at his home in Greenville, Mississippi.

William Alexander Percy
(1885-1942)

Lawyer, poet, and political activist

Special Collection—William Alexander Percy Memorial Library,
Greenville, Mississippi
Burial Site—Greenville Cemetery, Greenville, Mississippi

He may be better known in some circles as the cousin and foster-father of the acclaimed novelist, Walker Percy, but William Alexander Percy was also a noted writer. Described once by his adopted son as "the most extraordinary man I have ever known," he wrote several books of poetry as well as his autobiography.

He was born May 14, 1885, in Greenville, Mississippi. He attended local schools and graduated from the University of the South (Sewanee) in 1904. He received a law degree from Harvard Law School in 1908 and returned to Greenville to enter law practice with his father. He never married.

In 1915, *Sappho in Levkas*, his first book, was published. During World War I, he was a member of the Belgian Relief Commission; and, after going on a diet for a month to gain weight, he was able to receive a commission in the United States Army.

After the war, he published his second collection of verse, *In April Once* (1920). His poems reflected his life, his beliefs, and his environment. Critics were never completely kind to his works; however, he received the support of fellow poets such as Carl Sandburg and Hodding Carter.

In addition to his legal practice, Percy involved himself in local politics. He used his political and legal skills to fight against the Ku Klux Klan in 1922, successfully keeping them from attaining power in Greenville. When the Mississippi River flooded in 1927, he led the Red Cross unit that fed and cared for the 120,000 poor field hands who had been left homeless.

He wrote two other volumes of poetry—*Enzio's Kingdom* (1924) and *Selected Poems* (1930). His only prose book, an autobiography, *Lanterns on the Levee* (1941) recounted his life as a planter's son. This book brought acknowledgment of Percy's wisdom, gentleness, and wit but criticism for his social views.

He died in Greenville, Mississippi, on January 21, 1942.

Irwin Russell
(1853-1879)

Creator of non-stereotypical African Americans

Memorial—City Hall, Port Gibson, Mississippi

As a poet and essayist, Irwin Russell is noted for writing about African Americans as memorable individuals, not stereotyped symbols. Published posthumously, only one volume of Russell's poetry, *Poems by Irwin Russell* (1888), exists. However, during his lifetime, Russell's works were published in national publications such as *Scribner's Monthly* and the New Orleans *Times*.

Born on June 3, 1853, in Port Gibson, Mississippi, Russell graduated from what is now St. Louis University in 1869. He passed the bar exam at age 19 and went on to build a successful law practice. Throughout his life, as an avocation, he studied literature and wrote poetry and essays. As a member of the Port Gibson Thespian Society, he wrote at least one play, *Everybody's Business; or, Slightly Mistaken*, which is now lost.

After the yellow fever epidemic of 1878, during which he served as a physician's assistant, he moved to New York. Emotionally and physically exhausted and feeling the effects of alcoholism, he couldn't find the motivation to continue writing. He moved to New Orleans and worked as a fireman on a steamboat. There he tried to renew his writing voice, submitting several poems to the *Times-Picayune*.

Poems by Irwin Russell was published posthumously in 1888 with the assistance of Joel Chandler Harris. In 1917 the book was reprinted as *Christmas-Night in the Quarters*.

Russell contracted yellow fever and died on December 23, 1879, in Port Gibson, Mississippi.

Elizabeth Spencer

(1921-)

Master of original Southern themes

Special Collections—Merrill Building Museum, Carrollton, Mississippi; National Library of Canada, Ottawa, Canada

A prolific fiction writer, Elizabeth Spencer has written more than 50 short stories and nine books. With her first three novels taking place in Mississippi, it has been easy for critics to compare her writing to Faulkner's. However, her approach to Southern themes is fresh and original.

Born on July 10, 1921, in Carrollton, Mississippi, Spencer experienced poor health throughout her childhood. Her parents kept her entertained by telling her stories and encouraging her to read. She learned Bible stories, read mythology and Arthurian romances, and heard accounts of Mississippi's role in the Civil War. In 1938, Spencer graduated as valedictorian of her high school class. She attended Belhaven College in Jackson, Mississippi, and Vanderbilt University in Nashville, Tennessee. In 1956 she married John Rusher.

During her college years, she honed her writing skills, receiving the Chi Delta Poetry Award and placing second in the short story division of the Southern Literary Festival. After graduation, she taught classes in several colleges and for a short time served as a reporter for the Nashville *Tennessean*.

Her first three novels portray the social and political circumstances of the rural South during the first half of the twentieth century. *Fire in the Morning* (1948) enjoyed unusual attention for a first novel. Spencer eloquently handled a complicated plot involving four generations of Mississippians. With *This Crooked Way* (1952) and *The Voice at the Back Door* (1956), she again received critical acclaim. Using a straightforward prose style, Spencer built strong novels resting on characterization and intricate plotting.

For the setting of her next two books—*The Light at the Piazza* (1960) and

Knights and Dragons (1965)—she looked to Europe. In 1960 she received the McGraw-Hill Fiction Award for *The Light at the Piazza*. *Ship Island and Other Stories* (1968) and *The Collected Stories of Elizabeth Spencer* (1981) include short stories which distinguish her talent for relating regional nuances.

With her 1972 novel, *The Snare*, she turned to New Orleans for the setting. She employed skillful use of flashbacks, diary entries, and fragments of memory to explain the actions of the main character. The novel has drawn special notice for its bizarre characters and action.

In the 1980s she published the novel, *The Salt Line* (1984), and a collection of short stories, *Jack of Diamonds and other Stories* (1988). Then in the 1990s *The Night Travelers* (1991) and *Landscapes of the Heart* (1998) were published.

She has received several awards including a grant from the National Institute of Arts and Letters, a Guggenheim Fellowship, and the Rosenthal Award. She continues to write from Chapel Hill, North Carolina.

James Howell Street
(1903-1954)

Reporter, editor, historian, novelist

Special Collection—*W. S. Hoole Special Collection Library, University of Alabama, Tuscaloosa, Alabama*

Beginning his career as a journalist for newspapers such as the Hattiesburg *American*, Pensacola *Journal*, and the New York *World-Telegram*, James Howell Street eventually became a freelance writer. His most popular short story, "The Biscuit Eater," became a popular movie and a musical comedy.

He was born on October 15, 1903, in Lumberton, Mississippi; however, he spent much of his youth in Laurel, Mississippi. He attended the Massey School, Southwestern Theological Seminary, and Howard College (now Samford University). In 1923, he married Lucy Nash O'Briant.

He accepted a position with the Hattiesburg *American* in 1922; however, he quit after only a few months. For the next three years, he served as a Baptist minister in small towns in Missouri, Mississippi, and Alabama.

In 1926 he accepted a position with the Pensacola *Journal* and resumed his journalism career. He wrote and edited for Northern and Southern newspapers for the next ten years. Moving to Connecticut in 1938, and later to Chapel Hill, North Carolina, he devoted himself to full-time freelance writing. He wrote social commentary, historical romances, and based several novels and short stories on his years in the ministry.

Look Away—A Dixie Notebook (1936), his first book, described the anger and turbulence festering in the changing South. From 1940 to 1942, he wrote prolifically, publishing two books in 1941—*In My Father's House* (1941) and *The Biscuit Eater* (1941). He drew on his experiences as a minister for later books such as *The Gauntlet* (1945) and *The High Calling* (1951).

His popular histories include *The Civil War* (1953) and *The Revolutionary War* (1954). *The Velvet Doublet,* published in 1953, is a historical novel based on the life of Juan Rodrigo Bermejo, a man who sailed with Columbus.

He died on September 28, 1954, in Chapel Hill, North Carolina.

Eudora Welty
(1909-)

Master storyteller who captures a sense of place

Special Collections—Millsaps University, Jackson, Mississippi; Eudora Welty Library, Jackson, Mississippi; Mississippi State University, Mississippi State, Mississippi; University of Nevada, Reno, Nevada; Vassar College Library, Poughkeepsie, New York; Bryn Mawr College, Bryn Mawr, Pennsylvania
*Pulitzer Prize—*The Optimist's Daughter, *1972*

Noted for her emphasis on establishing a sense of place, Eudora Welty has an exceptional ability for storytelling. Slow to be accepted, her writing is now heralded for its metaphorical style and complex vision. She is skilled at invoking a reader's senses and emotions as she explores the complexities of family life—its inner struggles and the outside pressures of society. She has received such honors as Guggenheim Fellowships, the William Dean Howells Medal of the American Academy, the American Book Award, and a Pulitzer Prize. She became a member of the American Academy of Arts and Letters in 1971.

Born on April 13, 1909, in Jackson, Mississippi, Welty attended Jackson public schools, Mississippi College for Women, the University of Wisconsin, and the Columbia University Graduate School of Business. During her childhood, fairy tales, legends, and Mississippi history captivated her interest. She has said that her mother, a Southern Democrat, and her father, a Yankee Republican, helped her to understand that "there were two sides to everything." This understanding influenced her life and is reflected in her writing.

After graduate school, where she studied advertising, she accepted a position as junior publicity agent for the Works Progress Administration (WPA) in Jackson. Her duties took her across the state, interviewing Mississippians, taking photographs, and writing feature stories about Southern life. During this time she began describing the Mississippi countryside and painting verbal pictures of Southern towns for her stories.

In 1936 the editors of *Southern Review* stumbled upon Welty's "Death of a Traveling Salesman" which had been published in the small magazine, *Manuscript*. They recognized her talent for placing her characters in conflict with themselves and her metaphorical handling of their personal trials. Two of her early short stories—"A Worn Path" and "The Wide Net"—won O. Henry awards.

In 1942 she published *The Robber Bridegroom*, a novella that blended fantasy and realism in a unique way. This tale of Indians and outlaws received praise by William Faulkner for its blend of history, myth, humor, and cultural critique.

Delta Wedding, her first full-length novel, was published in 1946. The writing style she had honed while working for the WPA spilled over into this novel. The rhythm of Southern speech and detailed place descriptions captured the nuances of the Delta gentry and the personal conflicts that arise in a family built around Southern ceremony and tradition.

She published *The Golden Apples* in 1949. Scholars have acclaimed it as her most distinguished and experimental work. Through a mythological weaving of characters and events, she sent her character—the heroic wanderer, Virgie Rainey—on a journey into the world and brought her back to Mississippi. The creativity of the book makes it hard to define: critics call it a novel, and Welty places it on her list of collected stories.

Losing Battles, published in 1970, is said to be her most ambitious work. In it, she described the struggle between the old and new South, focusing on a 1930s hill-country family confronted by a schoolteacher who attempted to push the family toward cultural improvement.

She received a Pulitzer Prize for her novel, *The Optimist's Daughter*, in 1972. This semi-autobiographical book enjoyed popular attention and brought large sales. In 1978 she published *The Eye of the Story*, a collection of essays and reviews spanning 40 years. *The Collected Stories of Eudora Welty* was published in 1980, and in 1984, *One Writer's Beginnings* (1984), the story of her writing life and career was published.

Throughout her works, she exhibits a love of the South and its people. With a keen insight about human nature combined with an extraordinary sense of creativity, she has built a faithful and admiring audience.

Richard Wright
(1908-1960)

Major literary voice of African Americans

Special Collections—Yale University, New Haven, Connecticut; University of Nevada, Reno, Nevada; Duke University, Durham, North Carolina

A major literary voice of African Americans, Richard Wright unveiled the terrors of racism. He was one of the first writers to explore the social, economic, and moral conditions of the ghetto.

Wright was born on September 4, 1908, near Natchez, Mississippi. His father, a sharecropper, abandoned his family when Richard was five years old. His mother suffered a series of strokes and left him to live with relatives in Mississippi, Tennessee, and Arkansas. He attended several public and private schools, graduating as valedictorian from Smith-Robertson High in Jackson, Mississippi. He married twice—first to Dhima Rose Meadman in 1939 and then to Ellen Poplar in 1941. He had two children.

At age 15, he began working at various jobs after school and during the summer. He worked as a porter, newsboy, and secretary/accountant to an insurance company. During this time he decided he wanted to be a writer. He prepared for a writing career by reading the books mentioned in H. L. Mencken's *Book of Prefaces*.

In 1927, he moved to Chicago, where he worked as a postal clerk, porter, and street-sweeper. He also served as an assistant precinct captain for the Republican party. In 1933 he joined the Communist party, in which he found encouragement to write poetry and short stories. Soon, realizing party officials were trying to influence his writing, he broke away from the party.

He moved to New York in 1937, already having published poetry and short stories in publications such as *New Masses, Left Front, Partisan Review,* and *International Literature*. After months of rejection from New York publishers, he won first prize in a contest sponsored by *Story* magazine.

In 1938 he published *Uncle Tom's Children*. This collection of four short stories dealing with the deplorable conditions brought about by racism in the South won critical acclaim for him. However, he didn't receive a national readership until the publication of *Native Son* in 1940. The novel, chosen as a Book-of-the-Month-Club selection, sold more than 200,000 copies in less than three weeks. A stage version produced by Orson Welles made *Native Son* an even greater success.

His fictionalized autobiography, *Black Boy*, was published in 1945. Covering his years prior to moving to Chicago, it became almost as popular as *Native Son*.

In 1947, he moved his family to Paris and established permanent residence there. He continued to write, but never achieved the popularity he had found in the United States. He wrote two more novels, *The Outsider* (1953) and *The Long Dream* (1958). He also published several travel books including *Black Power* (1954), *The Color Curtain* (1956), and *Pagan Spain* (1957).

He died on November 28, 1960, in Paris, France, and is buried there in Pere Lachaise Cemetery.

Stark Young
(1881-1963)

One of Broadway's most famous critics

Marker—Como, Mississippi
Special Collection—Mississippi State University, Mississippi State, Mississippi
Burial Site—Friendship Cemetery, Como, Mississippi

A leading Broadway theater critic, director, and playwright, Stark Young is perhaps best remembered for his volumes of drama criticism and for having spent more than ten years translating Anton Chekhov's plays for the American theater.

He was born on October 11, 1881, in Como, Mississippi. He grew up in a large family, listening to the stories told by his close relatives. He attended the University of Mississippi and Columbia University in New York, where he received a master's degree in 1902. From 1904 until 1921, he taught English and drama at several universities.

With several published articles to his credit, he resigned from his position at Amherst College in 1921 to devote his time to freelance writing. He moved to New

York and became actively involved in the theater, being appointed to the editorial board of *Theatre Arts Magazine* and drama critic for the *New Republic*. Establishing himself as a leading drama critic, he directed plays on Broadway while also writing his own plays. *The Colonnade* (1924) and *The Saint* (1925) were successful portrayals of his Southern heritage.

After the production of the two plays, he turned his attention to writing novels. He wrote quickly and well, publishing *Heaven Trees* in 1926, *The Torches Flare* in 1928, and *River House* in 1929. Each of his novels focused on the Old South, defending the traditional values of family life and community.

From 1938 to 1941, he spent much of his time on the play *Belle Isle*, later retitled *Artemise* (1942). At the age of 60, he took up painting, an avocation in which he excelled. He soon had exhibits in several well-known galleries and received positive critiques.

In 1947 he retired from his position as drama critic for the *New Republic* where he wrote more than 1,000 essays, sketches, reviews, and articles. Officially retired, he continued to write. In 1948 he published *Immortal Shadows*, a collection of his best theater essays. In 1951 he published his autobiography, *The Pavilion*. In 1953 he helped with the production of the new edition of his best known novel, *So Red the Rose*, first published in 1934.

He continued translating Chekhov's plays, producing in 1957 a one-volume collection titled *Best Plays of Chekhov: The Sea Gull; Uncle Vanya; The Three Sisters;* and *The Cherry Orchard*.

In 1959 he suffered a stroke and couldn't return to writing. He died on January 6, 1963, in Fairfield, Connecticut.

North Carolina

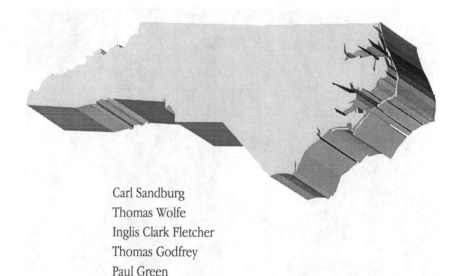

Carl Sandburg
Thomas Wolfe
Inglis Clark Fletcher
Thomas Godfrey
Paul Green
Randall Jarrell
William Sydney Porter
[O. Henry]

Connemara

Carl Sandburg Home National Historic Site
1928 Little River Road
Flat Rock, North Carolina 28731-9766

Hours:
9 a.m.-5 p.m. daily, except Christmas Day
Admission:
Adults, $3; Children under 16, free; No charge to enter
the grounds
Telephone: (704) 693-4178

Connemara was built in 1838 as a summer home for C. G. Memminger, the first Secretary of the Treasury of the Confederacy. This farm with five miles of walking trails is located three miles south of Hendersonville, North Carolina.

In the mid-1940s, Carl Sandburg's wife, Lilian, decided that her prize-winning goats needed more room and a milder climate. She studied temperatures throughout the United States and decided North Carolina was the place for them to live. When Sandburg first saw the view of the Smokey Mountains from the front porch of the farmhouse, he knew his wife had found a perfect home. The farm had everything—a pasture for Lilian's goats, room for Carl's 10,000-volume library, and an agreeable climate for all.

The Sandburgs remodeled the home before moving in. They had the kitchen expanded and updated, ceilings lowered, and bookshelves added. Connemara became home for Sandburg, his wife, three daughters, two grandchildren, Chula the Siamese cat, and Jackson the cocker spaniel.

Sandburg kept a stack of Sears, Roebuck and Company catalogs, a guitar, and a fire extinguisher in each room. He used the catalogs to prop his feet on while playing the guitar. Typically, each morning Sandburg slept late while his wife and daughters took care of household chores and tended the livestock. Upon arising, Sandburg embarked on a strict exercise routine which included calisthenics, a brisk walk, and raising a wooden chair above his head several times. His writing routine included sharing his ideas with his wife and daughters or reciting a new poem or playing a song for them on the guitar. When he was creating new poems, he worked alone and late into the night.

Sandburg wrote his only novel, *Remembrance Rock* (1948), and an autobiography, *Always the Young Strangers* (1953), in the home. He also served as a consultant for the film *The Greatest Story Ever Told* and wrote many poems. In addition, while living here, Sandburg received a Pulitzer Prize for his book *Complete Poems*.

On display in the house are Sandburg's magazines, books, and research materials. Visitors are encouraged to take time to tour the barnyard, gazebo, greenhouse, and spring house. A bookstore is stocked with Sandburg literature and is open during regular hours. The Flat Rock Playhouse, North Carolina's State Theater, is located across the street.

Carl Sandburg
(1878-1967)

"America's Troubador"

Home—*Flat Rock, North Carolina*
Festival—The World of Carl Sandburg *and* Rootabaga Stories, *Asheville, North Carolina (annual performances during summer months)*
Special Collections—*University of Southern California Library, Los Angeles, California; California State University, Northridge, California; University of Delaware, Newark, Delaware; Chicago Public Library, Chicago, Illinois; Newberry Library, Chicago, Illinois; University of Illinois Urbana/Champaign Library, Urbana, Illinois; Indiana University, Bloomington, Indiana; Indiana State University, Terre Haute, Indiana; University of Nevada, Reno, Nevada; University of North Carolina, Charlotte, North Carolina; Dickinson College, Carlisle, Pennsylvania; University of Virginia, Charlottesville, Virginia*
Pulitzer Prizes—Corn Huskers, *1919 (award provided by gifts from the Poetry Society);* Abraham Lincoln: The War Years, *1940;* Complete Poems, *1951*

Carl Sandburg's friendly smile and twinkle in his eyes endeared him to many Americans. Considered the first poet of modern times to write using the language of the people, he wrote about the America he loved. Many people thought of him as America's troubadour. He took any opportunity to sing his folk songs, recite his poetry, and speak on the aspirations of American life.

Sandburg was born January 6, 1878, in Galesburg, Illinois. To supplement his family's income, he dropped out of school after the eighth grade. He never, though, lost his desire to learn.

In 1897, at age 19, he spent a year as a hobo, catching free train rides through Iowa, Missouri, Kansas, Nebraska, and Colorado. He took odd jobs working on farms and steamboats, washing dishes and blacking stoves, but mainly he was learning about people and storing away dialogue and regional expressions that he would later draw upon for his writing.

Volunteering for service in the Spanish-American War in 1898, he became a war correspondent for his hometown newspaper. After a short term in the service, he attended Lombard College in Galesburg, Illinois, where he edited the college journal and yearbook and developed exceptional skills as an orator.

After college, he moved to Wisconsin and took an active role in the Social-Democratic party. He lectured, wrote articles for newspapers, and immersed himself in committee work. While living there, he met Lilian Steichen. They married in 1908 and had three children.

The long hours in the political arena took a toll on their marriage, and in 1909, Sandburg accepted positions as columnist for several Milwaukee newspapers including the *Journal*, the *Daily News*, and the *Sentinel*. In 1910, he was appointed private secretary to Milwaukee's newly elected socialist mayor, Emil Seidel.

In 1912, after Seidel lost re-election, Sandburg moved his wife and daughter Margaret to Chicago. There he found work on newspapers and magazines such as the *World*, *The Day Book*, and *System: The Magazine of Business*. In 1914, he sent some of his poetry to *Poetry* magazine, essentially launching his career as a poet. The nation discovered Carl Sandburg in 1916, when his first book, *Chicago Poems,* was published. He received critical acclaim, being hailed as one of the most energetic and original poets of the time. In 1919 his book *Corn Huskers* earned him an award from the Poetry Society of America (later incorporated as a category in the Pulitzer Prize annual awards).

For 15 years he worked as a reporter for the *Chicago Daily News* while he continued to write poetry. In 1932 he began his career as a full-time writer. He was obsessed with the history of Abraham Lincoln. The storage room of his house overflowed with books, papers, and clippings referring to Lincoln. The collection became so large that at one point that Sandburg annexed a second storage area in a barn. With this information, he wrote a two-volume biography, *Abraham Lincoln: The Prairie Years* (1926) and four volumes of *Abraham Lincoln: The War Years* (1939). He received a Pulitzer Prize in 1940 for the four-volume biography.

The People, Yes (1936) was his last major book of poetry. This epic-prose poem was his response to the economic and social upheaval of the 1930s. During the 1940s, he lectured extensively, worked as a syndicated columnist, and wrote his only novel, *Remembrance Rock* (1948). *Complete Poems* won him another Pulitzer Prize in 1951.

At age 81, he was invited by the U.S. Congress to address a joint session on the

150th anniversary of Lincoln's birth. He spoke for 18 minutes to a standing-room-only crowd.

In 1960, Twentieth Century-Fox offered him a position as creative consultant for the movie *The Greatest Story Ever Told*. Many critics thought this was an honorary position; however, Sandburg worked hard and was disappointed when financial cutbacks caused a delay in the movie's release.

His other works include an anthology of folk songs, *The American Songbag* (1927), and an autobiography of the first 20 years of his life, *Always the Young Strangers* (1953).

He died on July 22, 1967, in Flat Rock, North Carolina. He is buried at his birthplace home in Galesburg, Illinois.

Thomas Wolfe Memorial

48 Spruce Street
Asheville, North Carolina 28801-3006

Hours:
April through October: 9 a.m.-5 p.m., Monday through
Saturday and 1-5 p.m. Sunday; November through March: 10 a.m.-
4 p.m., Tuesday through Saturday and 1-4 p.m., Sunday
Admission: Adults, $1; Students, 50¢
Telephone: (704) 253-8304

This 29-room Queen Anne boarding house, known as The Old Kentucky Home, was Thomas Wolfe's home from 1906 to 1922. Built in 1893, the two-story white frame house has a gabled roof and several porches.

A beautiful home, once adorned with decorative touches, it was stripped to the bare necessities by Wolfe's mother, Julia. When she bought the house and turned it into a boarding house, she created plain, utilitarian rooms that would be easy to furnish and clean. Wolfe accused the house of smelling of "raw wood, cheap varnish, and flimsy, rough plaster."

The city enjoyed a booming tourism business, and Wolfe's mother always had a full house, which meant that Wolfe never slept in one room long enough to call it his own. *Look Homeward Angel,* his first novel, is based on his experiences growing up in this house.

The Old Kentucky Home remains much the same as it was when Wolfe was a child, containing many of the same furnishings. However, one of the upstairs rooms is furnished with items taken from his final New York apartment, including his typewriter, a valise, and several other items.

Thomas Wolfe
(1900-1938)

Author of autobiographical fiction

Childhood Home—*Asheville, North Carolina*
Festival—*Thomas Wolfe Festival, Asheville, North Carolina (last weekend in September)*
Special Collections—*Illinois State University, Normal, Illinois; Harvard University Library, Cambridge, Massachusetts; University of Minnesota, Minneapolis, Minnesota; University of Nevada, Reno, Nevada; Hampden-Booth Theatre Library at the Players, New York, New York; New York University, New York, New York; Pack Memorial Library, Asheville, North Carolina; University of North Carolina, Chapel Hill; University of Virginia, Charlottesville, Virginia*
Burial Site—*Riverside Cemetery, Asheville, North Carolina*

At six-foot-six, Thomas Wolfe was a big man in stature as well as emotions and desires. As a novelist, he earned a large audience of admirers even though critics accused him of not knowing when to stop writing and of destroying any suspense that would draw a reader into a story.

Wolfe was born on October 3, 1900, in Asheville, North Carolina, where he grew up in a boarding house surrounded by a diverse group of strangers. Neighbors did not realize how deeply the strain of his family life affected young Wolfe. His mother was busy with the boarders and had little time to spend with him. His father had refused to move into the boarding house and often burdened his son with complaints and self-pity stemming from the separation from his family. Thomas learned to cope with his feelings with ambivalence.

He attended North State Fitting School, where he was accepted because of his writing skills. His father encouraged him to attend the University of North Carolina, with the hopes that he would make good contacts for a career in North Carolina politics. However, Wolfe focused on literature and began his writing career by becoming a member of the Carolina Playmakers.

While in graduate school at Harvard, he began to write about his hometown, its people, and the tourists with whom he had lived. In 1924, he accepted a position teaching English at New York University. He often occupied his evenings with writing, creating a pile of paper. Editor Maxwell Perkins helped him turn a massive manuscript into his first novel, *Look Homeward, Angel* (1929). The autobiographical novel was a great success, earning him nationwide acclaim. People in his hometown, however, rejected the work, feeling offended and let down.

His next challenge was to write about restless, modern America. Writing as prolifically as before, his ideas multiplied into a plan for a series of novels spanning the history of the nation. The project became so complex that Perkins once again helped him organize the manuscript. *Of Time and the River* (1935) was the outcome. Critics accused the book of being an anthology-like uneven piece of work, crediting it for some magnificent parts that conveyed the quality of the nation and other parts that were overwritten and wearisome.

After publishing his third book, *From Death to Morning* (1935), a collection of stories, Wolfe set aside his historical series to concentrate on a saga about a character named George Webber. However, he died before completing the manuscript. Edward Aswell, an editor at *Harper's*, developed three books—*The Web and the Rock* (1939), *You Can't Go Home Again* (1940), and *The Hills Beyond* (1941)—from the massive narrative that Wolfe had created.

Wolfe died on September 15, 1938, in New York.

Other North Carolina Writers and Sites

Inglis Clark Fletcher
(1879-1969)

Most widely read historical novelist of her day

Burial Site—*National Cemetery, Wilmington, North Carolina*

Born October 20, 1879, in Alton, Illinois, Inglis Clark spent hours listening to stories told by her great-grandfather. She attended Washington University in St. Louis, Missouri, but dropped out to marry John G. Fletcher, a mining engineer. In the early 1930s she published two novels based on traveling she had done in Africa.

Her interests then turned to her Southern heritage. She began writing what turned out to be a series of 12 novels about North Carolina. The first book was *Raleigh's Eden*, published in 1940. It began for Fletcher a popularity that lasted more than 20 years. Hers were the most widely read historical novels of their day. The novels covered a period of 200 years, from the founding of Roanoke Island colony to the ratification of the Constitution.

In 1944 she and her husband moved to a North Carolina plantation home near Edenton, where she lived until it burned in 1963.

She died on May 30, 1969, in Edenton, North Carolina.

Thomas Godfrey
(1736-1763)

First American-born playwright

Burial Site—*St. James Church, Wilmington, North Carolina*

The author of over 20 poems for children, Thomas Godfrey's most important literary contribution to American literature was the drama, *The Prince of Parthia*. This five-act tragedy is the first one written and published by a native-born

American and the first play written in America performed on a professional stage.

Thomas Godfrey was born on December 4, 1736, in Philadelphia, Pennsylvania. Although his formal education is undocumented, it is known that the Provost of the Academy and College of Philadelphia encouraged Godfrey to study literature and the arts. After serving in the Pennsylvania militia during the French and Indian War, he accepted a position as a businessman in Wilmington, North Carolina, where he spent the rest of his life.

He found particular interest in the theater while living in Pennsylvania. He had some connections with the theatrical troupe headed by David Douglass. *The Prince of Parthia*, intended to be performed by that company for the 1759 season, contained 40 scenes, a complicated task that Godfrey could not complete in time. The play was performed in 1767, four years after his death.

His poetry found in *Juvenile Poems on Various Subjects* (1765) addresses conventional themes in conventional forms. The elegies, pastorals, and songs imitate heavily the works of Chaucer and Pope. Scholars agree that Godfrey was a better dramatist than poet.

He died in 1763, in Wilmington, North Carolina.

Paul Green
(1894-1981)

Creator of the "symphonic drama"

Paul Green Theater—*University of North Carolina, Chapel Hill, North Carolina*
Festivals—The Lost Colony, *Waterside Theatre, Roanoke Island, Roanoke, North Carolina, (annual performance held in June-August);* Cross and Sword, *St. Augustine, Florida (annual performance held in June-September)*
Burial Site—*Old Chapel Hill Cemetery, Chapel Hill, North Carolina*
Pulitzer Prize—In Abraham's Bosom, *1927*

The American playwright Paul Green had a creative technique that caused his audiences to compare his works with the dramas of Eugene O'Neill. His "heritage dramas" incorporated themes of democratic humanity that still captivate audiences today.

Born on March 17, 1894, in Lillington, North Carolina, Green always called North Carolina home. He attended the University of North Carolina, Chapel Hill, and upon graduation he accepted a position teaching philosophy there. He married Elizabeth Lay in 1922; they had four children.

In 1924, Green's writing ability was recognized with the publication of the play *The No'Count Boy* in *Theatre Arts Magazine* and by his winning the Belasco Cup competition in New York City. Due to this success, two volumes of his plays were published.

From 1926 to 1928 he captured the attention of New York audiences with three plays—*In Abraham's Bosom; The Field God;* and *The House of Connelly*. He received a Pulitzer Prize in 1927 for *In Abraham's Bosom*. His next four plays received poor reviews, causing him to turn his attention away from New York productions. In 1937 he published *The Lost Colony*, writing specifically for the outdoor summer productions that were becoming popular in the South. Working with Richard Wright, Green adapted Wright's *Native Son* for the stage in 1941.

He developed a writing technique he called "symphonic drama." His new plays, which were written to be performed outdoors, combined music, dance, and dialogue in a new way. His new theater performances captivated his audiences once again. His first "symphonic drama," *The Lost Colony* (1937), is still performed annually in North Carolina.

Green died on May 4, 1981, in Chapel Hill, North Carolina.

Randall Jarrell
(1914-1965)

National Book Award winner for poetry

Special Collections—University of Nevada, Reno, Nevada; New York Public Research Libraries, New York, New York; University of North Carolina, Greensboro, North Carolina
Burial Site—New Garden Friends Cemetery, Greensboro, North Carolina

Best known for his poem "Death of the Ball Turret Gunner," Randall Jarrell was a poet, critic, novelist, and teacher. His choice of words and skill for varying tense and voice combined to form powerful, emotion-filled writing. His wit and keen appraisals made him a distinguished critic.

Jarrell was born on May 6, 1914, in Nashville, Tennessee; however, his family moved to Long Beach, California, when he was an infant. When his parents divorced, 11-year-old Jarrell went to live with his grandparents in Hollywood. In 1931, at the age of 17, he returned to Nashville to live with his mother. He attended Hume Fogg High School and Vanderbilt University, where he received bachelor's and master's degrees. He married twice—first to Mackie Langham in 1940 and then to Mary Eloise von Schrader in 1952.

While attending Vanderbilt, he took several classes taught by the noted literature professor John Crowe Ransom. Through him, Jarrell met some of the popular writers of the day including Robert Penn Warren and Allen Tate. After graduating from Vanderbilt, Jarrell accepted a position as an English instructor at Kenyon College in Gambier, Ohio. Two years later, in 1937, he moved to Austin to teach at the University of Texas.

In 1940 he published his first collection of poems in the anthology *Five American Poets*. Two years later he published *Blood for a Stranger* (1942), his second collection of poetry. Some critics have said that his best poems have a woman or child as the central character; they cite such poems as "A Girl in a Library," "Next Day," and "Woman." In 1960 Jarrell received a National Book Award for his collection of poems, *The Woman in the Washington Zoo* (1960).

He enlisted in the Army Air Corps in 1942. He wrote about the war years and his experiences in the service in two books, *Little Friend, Little Friend* (1945) and *Losses* (1948). Both books are highly respected for their contribution to World War II literature. After his discharge from the Army in 1946, he received a Guggenheim Post-Service Fellowship and began teaching at Sarah Lawrence College in Bronxville, New York. During this time he also served as poetry editor of the *Nation*. He later became a regular contributor to the *Partisan Review* and then to the *Yale Review*.

In 1947 he joined the teaching staff at the University of North Carolina, Greensboro. He also taught classes at Princeton University and the University of Illinois. His experience teaching led him to write two books of criticism, *Poetry and the Age* (1953) and *A Sad Heart at the Supermarket* (1962).

In 1954 he published a satirical novel, *Pictures from an Institution*. He also wrote three children's books: *The Gingerbread Rabbit* (1963), *The Bat Poet* (1964), and *The Animal Family* (1965).

He died on October 14, 1965, in Chapel Hill, North Carolina, after being struck by a car.

William Sydney Porter
[O. Henry]
(1862-1910)

Museum—*Greensboro Historical Museum, Greensboro, North Carolina*
Special Collection—*Greensboro Public Library, Greensboro, North Carolina*
Burial Site—*Riverside Cemetery, Asheville, North Carolina*

(Please see biography in Texas chapter.)

South Carolina

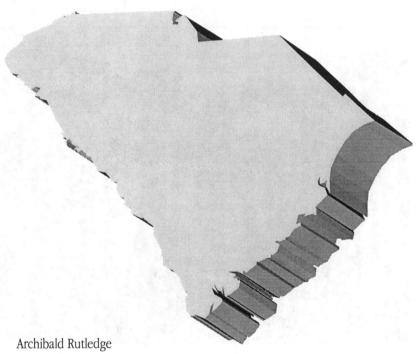

Archibald Rutledge
Mary Boykin Miller Chestnut
DuBose Heyward
Julia Mood Peterkin
Josephine Lyons Scott Pinckney
William Gilmore Simms
Henry Timrod

Hampton Plantation
State Park

Archibald Rutledge Home
1950 Rutledge Road
McClellanville, South Carolina 29458

Hours:
Year-round: Saturday and Sunday, 1-4 p.m.;
April 1-Labor Day: Thursday-Monday, 1-4 p.m.
Park is open year round, Thursday-Monday, 9 a.m.-6 p.m.
Closed on Tuesdays and Wednesdays.
Admission: Adults, $2; Children, $1; Under 6, free
Telephone: (803) 546-9361

Begun in the mid-1700s, this Greek Revival house was constructed of yellow pine and cypress. It began as a simple six-room farmhouse, and by the 1780s consisted of 12 large rooms, including the elegant ballroom. Shortly before a visit by President George Washington in 1791, the Rutledges added the Adam-style portico.

Through the years, the Rutledges managed what has been called one of the grandest homes and most prosperous agricultural enterprises in America. However, the Civil War caused Hampton Plantation to decline. The house went unpainted; cotton was stored in the ballroom; and by 1923, the home was abandoned.

In 1937 Archibald Hamilton Rutledge, the first poet laureate of South Carolina, returned to his boyhood home and restored it to its original charm. The unfinished interior of the home highlights the architectural detail. The cutaway sections of walls and ceilings allow visitors to follow the building's stages of construction.

While there, many tourists take time to explore the grounds surrounding the mansion. Cypress swamps, abandoned rice fields, and the magnificent forest of hardwoods and pines are a reminder of the earliest days of plantation life.

Archibald Hamilton Rutledge

(1883-1973)

First poet laureate of South Carolina

Home—*McClellanville, South Carolina*
Festival—*Hampton Plantation Spring Festival (last Saturday in March), McClellanville, South Carolina*
Burial Site—*Hampton Plantation, McClellanville, South Carolina*

Recipient of 17 honorary degrees and more than 30 awards, Archibald Hamilton Rutledge became the first poet laureate of South Carolina. He wrote more than 1,000 poems, essays, short stories, and articles, most of which appeared in popular magazines and literary journals. His works have also been published in various collections.

He was born on October 23, 1883, in McClellanville, South Carolina. He attended Porter Military Academy in Charleston and Union College in New York. In 1904 he accepted a teaching position at Mercersburg Academy in Pennsylvania, where he remained until his retirement in 1937. He married Florence Louise Hart in 1907; they had three sons. After the death of his first wife in 1934, he married his childhood sweetheart, Alice Lucus, in 1936.

The landscape and social activities of Hampton Plantation, his family home, became the focus for much of Rutledge's writing throughout the years. Stories of hunting and nature walks in the woods of Hampton were well received by the readers of popular magazines.

After his retirement, he and Alice returned to Hampton Plantation, where he continued to write while restoring his family home, creating a writing retreat out of the original log house that his father had built. The log house was destroyed by Hurricane Hugo in 1989; it has since been rebuilt with materials from the original.

His works include the following: *The Heart's Quest* (1904), *Under the Pines, and Other Poems* (1906), *The Banners of the Coast* (1908), *Tom and I on the Old Plantation* (1918), *Old Plantation Days* (1921), *The Beauty of the Night* (1947), *Brimming Tide and Other Poems* (1956), *The World Around Hampton* (1960), and *The Woods and Wild Things I Remember* (1970).

Rutledge died on September 15, 1973, in McClellanville, South Carolina.

Other South Carolina
Writers
and Sites

Mary Boykin Miller Chesnut (1823-1886)

The Confederacy's diarist

Special Collection—*University of South Carolina, Columbia, South Carolina*
Memorabilia Collection—*Hampton-Preston Mansion, Columbia, South Carolina*
Marker—*Chesnut Cottage, Columbia, South Carolina*
Burial Site—*Knight's Hill, Camden, South Carolina*

Author of what became the primary source of information about Confederate leaders and Southern society during the Civil War, Mary Chesnut had only one published book, and it was published posthumously. However, *A Diary from Dixie* (1905, 1949)—and the revision, *Mary Chesnut's Civil War* (1981)—is said to be the finest literary work of the Confederacy. It is praised for Chesnut's irreverent wit and use of irony and metaphor.

Mary Miller was born on March 31, 1823, in Stateboro, South Carolina. Her father was a U.S. congressman and senator. She attended private schools in Camden and Charleston, South Carolina; however, her education ended abruptly when her mother's death in 1838 required Mary to return to her family home in Camden. In 1840, she married James Chesnut, Jr.

Elected to the U.S. Senate in 1858, her husband resigned his appointment shortly after Abraham Lincoln was elected President. He was one of the leaders of the secessionist movement in South Carolina, and Mary traveled with him as he served under Jefferson Davis and as Commander of South Carolina's reserve forces. Her job was to entertain the Confederate elite.

From 1861 to 1865 she wrote about her experiences in a series of diaries. After the Civil War the Chesnuts moved back to Camden, where they found themselves seriously in debt. Mary tried her hand at fiction, producing three novels; however, none were ever published. In the early 1880s she worked on revising her Civil War diaries into what was to become *A Diary from Dixie*. Since she had no ties to the literary establishment, she felt no compulsion to incorporate the defensiveness and sentimentality that is evident in much of the writing of the period.

She set scenes and rounded out characters using skills that she had developed from writing fiction. The original manuscript, which was published posthumously, has been edited twice and released once in 1949 and again in 1981. Historians and literary critics still view this extensive account of the Civil War era as a valued resource.

Chesnut died on November 22, 1886.

DuBose Heyward
(1885-1940)

Creator of *Porgy and Bess*

Marker—Charleston, South Carolina
Special Collections—Charleston Library Society, Charleston, South Carolina; College of Charleston Library, Charleston, South Carolina
Burial Site—St. Philip's Protestant Episcopal Church, Charleston, South Carolina

DuBose Heyward's characters are more famous than he is. His first novel, *Porgy* (1925), was an immediate success. The characters Porgy and Bess made an indelible impression on the nation through first the play (1927) and later George Gershwin's opera *Porgy and Bess* (1935).

Heyward's characters met difficult challenges with "the secret rhythm of life"—faith, community, and a common history of suffering. This same philosophy also applied to Heyward's life. He was born on August 31, 1885, in Charleston, South Carolina. His father died when Dubose was two years old. At age 14, he dropped out of school and went to work in a hardware store to support his family. When he was 18, he contracted polio, typhoid, and pleurisy.

After holding several jobs and writing short stories in his leisure time, he moved in 1917 to Hendersonville, North Carolina, and took up painting. He developed friendships with John Bennett and Hervey Allen, who encouraged him to write poetry. Together, in response to H. L. Mencken's criticism of Southern culture, the three established the South Carolina Poetry Society.

In 1923 Heyward married Dorothy Hartzell Kuhns; they had one child. Heyward gave up his business and turned to full-time literary activities, speaking on Southern literature and devoting much time to his novel *Porgy*. As an established playwright, Dorothy collaborated with her husband to write the play version of this novel. Later, Heyward wrote the libretto and most of the lyrics for the opera *Porgy and Bess*.

He wrote 11 more books—fiction, poetry and drama—and worked on the screenplays for two movies, *The Emperor Jones* and *The Good Earth*.

He had planned to create an opera version of *Star Spangled Virgin* (1939), but before completing the project, he died on June 16, 1940, in Tryon, North Carolina.

Julia Mood Peterkin
(1880-1961)

Author of popular Creole stories

Burial Site—*Peterkin Cemetery, Fort Motte, South Carolina*
Pulitzer Prize—Scarlet Sister Mary, *1929*

Julia Mood Peterkin, mistress of Lang Syne Plantation in South Carolina, wrote about plantation characters in "a patient struggle for fate." Her novels gained attention from African-American intellectuals such as W. E. B. DuBois who said, "She is a Southern white woman, but she has the eye and the ear to see beauty and know truth."

She was born on October 31, 1880, in Laurens County, South Carolina. She received a bachelor of arts degree from Converse College at the age of 16. After getting a master's degree, she taught two years in a one-room schoolhouse. She married William George Peterkin in 1903; they had one son.

She first published short stories and sketches in the *Smart Set* and the *Reviewer*. Here she found an enthusiastic following for her Gullah (Creole) narratives. She attributed her ease of storytelling to the influence of the Creole nurse who raised her.

In 1924 her first book, *Green Thursday*, a collection of 12 mythic stories, was published. Over the next eight years she wrote three novels: *Black April* (1927), *Scarlet Sister Mary* (1928), and *Bright Skin* (1932).

In 1929 she received a Pulitzer Prize for *Scarlet Sister Mary*. The novel explored the life of Mary Pinesett, a character dealing with sexual indiscretions and social conflicts. It sold more than one million copies. Four years later, Peterkin's next novel, *Bright Skin* (1932), received poor reviews by critics and fans alike. It was such a disappointment to Peterkin that she never wrote fiction again.

Her next book, *Roll, Jordan, Roll*, a nonfiction account of life on a plantation, was published in 1933. Her last book, *A Plantation Christmas* (1934), was a sentimental book that received little attention. Lack of readership and poor sales led Peterkin to end her writing career.

She died on August 10, 1961, in Orangeburg, South Carolina.

Josephine Lyons Scott Pinckney (1895-1957)

Bestselling author of Charleston novels

Burial Site—*Magnolia Cemetery, Charleston, South Carolina*

A poet, nonfiction writer, and novelist, Josephine Pinckney is best remembered for her skillfully written novels focusing on Charleston manners—*Three O'clock Dinner* (1945) and *Splendid in Ashes* (1958).

Born on January 25, 1895, in Charleston, South Carolina, she studied at the College of Charleston, Columbia University, and Radcliffe. Her interests focused on preserving Charleston architecture and African-American spirituals. She was a member of the South Carolina Poetry Society.

She wrote poems and articles for a variety of magazines, as well as several successful novels. In 1927 her first book, *Sea-Drinking Cities*, was published. This collection of poetry was about Pinckney's native Charleston set in verse. Each selection focused on familiar Charleston people, scenes, or atmosphere.

Hilton Head (1941) was her first published novel. She built a successful historical romance around the life of an English surgeon, Henry Woodward, as he played a major role in building a colony. Her second novel, *Three O'clock Dinner* (1945), was her most popular book. It became a feature for the Literary Guild, and screen rights were sold to a Hollywood producer. Set in twentieth-century Charleston, this novel of Southern manners follows the attempts of a young German immigrant as she tries to fit into Charleston society.

Pinckney focused her next two novels on fantasy. *Great Mischief* (1948) pursued the main character's fascination with evil spirits and witchcraft; *My Son and Foe* (1952) took place on an enchanted Caribbean Island.

Splendid in Ashes (1958) was her last novel. Returning to her familiar Charleston for the setting, she successfully blended memories and flashbacks to tie past

events with 1950s Charleston.
She died on October 4, 1957, in New York.

William Gilmore Simms
(1806-1870)

Poet, historian, biographer, and editor

Bust—*White Point Park at the Battery in Charleston*
Special Collections—*Charleston Library Society, Charleston, South Carolina; University of Virginia, Charlottesville, Virginia; Duke University, Durham, North Carolina*
Burial Site—*Magnolia Cemetery, Charleston, South Carolina*

A prolific writer with a keen sense of humor, William Gilmore Simms wrote about what he knew best—the South, its people and their lifestyles. He was a spokesman for social and political concerns and used his writing to illustrate his views. The author of more than 80 books of history and geography, biography, essays and literary criticism, poetry, and fiction, he had a love for the South and a respect for the Southern way of life.

Born on April 17, 1806, in Charleston, South Carolina, he lived most of his childhood with his maternal grandmother, his mother having died when Simms was two years old. He had little formal education, and at age 12 he was apprenticed to an apothecary. Rejecting the career that was chosen for him, he studied law largely on his own and passed the bar in 1827.

His first marriage was to a childhood sweetheart who died in 1832, six years after their marriage. In 1836 he married Chevilette Roach, the daughter of a South Carolina plantation owner.

His earliest recognition was as a poet. His most notable poem, "Atlantis," was published in 1832; previously, though, he had published several volumes of poetry.

From 1828 to 1829 Simms was the editor of the *Southern Literary Gazette*. In 1830 he bought the Charleston *City Gazette,* which he had to sell two years later because of its decline in subscriptions after it came out in support of the Union in the Nullification Controversy.

Simms moved to New York and established himself as a fiction writer, publishing *Martin Faber* (1833) and *Guy Rivers* (1834). A diverse audience of readers embraced these two novels. In 1835 Simms published *The Yemassee*, which was heralded as the most widely read novel that year. It described the Carolina Indian conflicts of the eighteenth century.

In 1836 Simms returned to South Carolina to live at Woodlands, the plantation owned by his father-in-law. Here he wrote most of his 80 volumes of work, experimenting with various forms, including humor. *Paddy McGann* (1863) was his first attempt at humor. In this short novel, Southern gentlemen farmers listened as a whiskey-loving Irish backwoodsman, Paddy McGann, told a tall tale about an enchanted gun.

Simms often spent his winters on the plantation and his summers in the North near publishing centers. He was editor of several magazines, including the *Southern and Western Monthly Magazine* and the *Southern Quarterly Review*.

Taking an active role in politics, he served in the South Carolina legislature from 1844 to 1846. A staunch defender of slavery, he served as an advisor for several influential politicians on Civil War issues. In 1865 Union troops burned Woodlands.

Suffering from the death of his spouse, the loss of several children, and the destruction of his home, which included an 11,000-volume library, Simms began a newspaper to occupy his time and mind. He edited the *Phoenix* from March to October 1865. His rigorous schedule damaged his health and caused him to retire.

He died on June 11, 1870, in Charleston, South Carolina.

Henry Timrod
(1828-1867)

Poet called the "Harp of the South"

Monument—Washington Park, Charleston
Park—Florence, South Carolina
Special Collections—Charleston Library Society, Charleston, South Carolina; Duke University, Durham, North Carolina
Burial Site—Trinity Episcopal Churchyard, Columbia, South Carolina

Considered the best Southern poet of his time, equaled only by Edgar Allan Poe, Henry Timrod is almost unknown today. He has been called the

"Laureate of the Confederacy" and the "Harp of the South."

Born on December 8, 1828, in Charleston, South Carolina, he followed in his father's footsteps as a poet. His father, William, was the author of *Poems on Various Subjects* (1814). After attending the University of Georgia for two years, Henry took a position as a private tutor for a plantation family.

He and his childhood friends, Paul Hamilton Hayne and William Gilmore Simms, began publishing *Russell's Magazine* in 1857. The literary magazine ceased publication in 1860. During this period, Timrod's poetry appeared in *Russell's* and the *Southern Literary Messenger*. His poems usually yielded no pay, but they yielded much criticism. Some critics have accused Timrod of having little imagination and unoriginal ideas.

However, Timrod's war poems were different. Although he opposed regionalism in poetry, believing that poetry belonged to the world, he turned to poetry to express his frustrations with the Civil War. He focused on the losses and sorrows of the war. Critics have judged his war poetry to be his best with "At Magnolia Cemetery" being the most notable and perhaps the most quoted.

During his lifetime, only one volume of his poetry was published, and it was financed by his friends. Since his death, six books containing his collected works have been published. One, *The Essays of Henry Timrod* (1942), contains his critical commentary in which he describes the South as a literary backwater, uninterested in intellectual and poetic knowledge.

He was a correspondent for the Charleston *Mercury* from 1851 to 1864. In 1864 he became a part owner and editor of the *South Carolinian*, which was destroyed by Union troops a year later.

He died on October 7, 1867, in Columbia, South Carolina.

Tennessee

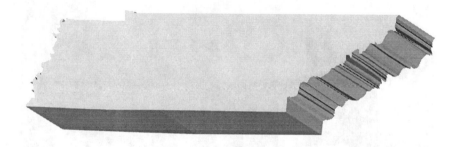

Alexander Palmer Haley
James Rufus Agee
Randall Jarrell
John Crowe Ransom
T.S. Stribling
Peter Hillsman Taylor

Alex Haley State House Museum

200 South Church Street
Henning, Tennessee 38041

Hours:
Tuesday-Saturday, 10 a.m.-5 p.m.; Sunday, 1-5 p.m.
Admission: Adults, $2.50; Children 6 to 16, $1.00
Gift Shop: Open during tours
Telephone: (901) 738-2240

"The front porch of this home is, in fact, the birthplace of *Roots*," said Alex Haley. This ten-room bungalow, constructed from 1918 to 1921 by his grandfather, Will E. Palmer, has been restored to model the home as it looked when Haley was born. Some of the 1919 furniture which decorates the home belonged to his family.

When he was six weeks old, Haley and his parents showed up, quite unexpectedly, on the front porch of this Southern home. His maternal grandparents had received no correspondence from their daughter since she and her husband had gone away to college in Ithaca, New York.

Here, just 35 miles north of Memphis, Haley grew up under the supervision of the Palmers. His doting grandparents reared him in a loving, family-centered home. On this front porch he listened to stories of his ancestors, including Kunte Kinte and Queenie. Here in Henning, Tennessee, his roots as a master storyteller also began.

Haley's childhood home is the first state-owned historic site devoted to an African American in Tennessee. Displayed throughout the house are photographs and memorabilia from the Haley family. A gift shop is also open during tour hours.

Alexander Palmer Haley
(1921-1992)

Famed author of *Roots* and other novels

Childhood Home—*Henning, Tennessee*
Statue—*Morningside Park, Knoxville, Tennessee*
Festival—*Alex Haley Memorial Picnic, Knoxville, Tennessee*
Special Collection—*University of Tennessee, Knoxville, Tennessee*
Burial Site—*Childhood Home, Henning, Tennessee*
Pulitzer Prize—Roots: The Saga of an American Family, *1977*

In 1959, at the end of his military career, Alex Haley chose to support his family as a freelance writer. His success came when he accepted a position with *Playboy* as a staff writer. In that position, he interviewed Malcom X and went on to write his first book, *The Autobiography of Malcom X* (1965).

Haley was born on August 11, 1921, in Ithaca, New York, where his parents were attending college, both in their first year of graduate study. Six weeks after his birth, his parents took him to live with his grandparents in Henning, Tennessee. He graduated from high school at age 15 and completed two years of college before enlisting in the United States Coast Guard in 1939. He married twice—first to Nannie Branch and then to Juliette Collins; he had three children.

He served in the Coast Guard for 20 years. In his leisure time he read prolifically and wrote letters and adventure stories. In 1949 his writing practice paid off—he was appointed as the first chief journalist for the Coast Guard.

Roots: The Saga of an American Family (1976) was his second book. The family stories he had heard as a child came to life as he spent 12 years researching his maternal ancestry. His stories of Kunte Kinte became instantly famous. The book was made into a television drama only weeks after it went on sale in bookstores. He received a Pulitzer Prize, a National Book Award, and several other honors for this literary saga. It was the basis for a television sequel and for the television series *Palmerstown USA*, both productions supervised by Haley.

The 1980s found Haley deep in work on two projects. The first, a short Christmas tale—*A Different Kind of Christmas*—was published in 1988. However, most of his time was spent on researching his father's family history. The story of Queenie, the daughter of white slave owner and Civil War colonel James Jackson, was to span from eighteenth-century Ireland to colonial America. When Haley suffered a heart attack in 1992, the manuscript was left incomplete. However, NBC had already begun production of the saga, and the novel had been scheduled for publication in 1993.

For several years after his retirement from the Coast Guard, Haley worked on *Henning*, a fictionalized account of his childhood in Tennessee, often putting it aside for more important projects. The manuscript remains unpublished although many of the stories have been printed in various magazines.

He died on February 10, 1992, in Seattle, Washington.

Other Tennessee
Writers
and Sites

James Rufus Agee

(1909-1955)

Prize-winning author of autobiographical fiction

Special Collections—University of Nevada, Reno, Nevada; University of Texas Libraries, Austin, Texas
*Pulitzer Prize—*A Death in the Family, *1958*

Best known for his autobiographical fiction, James Agee was posthumously awarded a Pulitzer Prize for his novel, *A Death in the Family*. Called a dedicated Southerner, he has been accused of playing the part of a hillbilly trapped in the world of academia.

He was born on November 27, 1909, in Knoxville, Tennessee, where he spent his childhood. At age 10, he entered St. Andrew's School in Sewanee, Tennessee. He returned to Knoxville and attended Knoxville High School one year before entering Phillips Exeter Academy (Massachusetts) in 1925. While attending Exeter, he began writing regularly, contributing to the school's monthly publication. As a student at Harvard College, he wrote poetry and fiction for the *Harvard Advocate*, a publication which he edited from 1931 to 1932.

Upon graduation from Harvard College, he accepted a position as a staff writer for *Fortune* magazine. He later accepted a position with *Time* as a book reviewer and later a film critic. He also wrote a biweekly column for the *Nation* during this time. From his experience as a critic, he went to Hollywood and became a screenwriter, working on movies such as *The African Queen* and *The Night of the Hunter*.

He experimented with various forms of writing as indicated in his first book, a collection of poetry titled *Permit Me Voyage* (1934). While researching an article about sharecroppers for *Fortune*, he dug down to his Southern roots. His compassion for the Southern tenant farmer is depicted in his second book, *Let Us Now Praise Famous Men* (1941). His third book, *The Morning Watch*, was patterned on his experiences at St. Andrew's. Published in 1951, it focuses on the conflict of community and solitude of a parochial school.

Agee suffered a fatal heart attack on May 15, 1955, and died in New York. He is buried a few miles from his farm in Hillsdale, New York. Since his death, several volumes of his letters, collected poems, short stories, and film scripts have been published.

John Crowe Ransom

(1888-1974)

Poet, critic, and editor

Special Collections—*University of Nevada, Reno, Nevada; University of North Carolina, Greensboro, North Carolina; Vanderbilt University Library, Nashville, Tennessee*

Poet, critic, and editor, John Crowe Ransom has been called one of the most influential American men of letters of the first half of the twentieth century. His distinctive writing style invokes deep feeling and emotion; however, as a writer, he maintains a detachment from that emotion.

Born on April 30, 1888, in Pulaski, Tennessee, he was the son of a Methodist minister and missionary. Because his family moved often, going from one church to another, he received his early education from his parents' tutoring. At the age of 12, he entered Bowen Academy in Nashville; three years later he enrolled at Vanderbilt University. He attended Oxford University as a Rhodes Scholar, receiving a degree in 1913. Upon returning to the United States in 1914, Ransom accepted a teaching position at Vanderbilt University.

Poems About God (1919) was his first book. Through these poems, Ransom, often revealing skepticism, explored the way God manifests Himself in the world. His later poems took on a different tone; a cool, detached manner and subtle irony are evident in much of his poetry.

From 1922 until 1925, he teamed with several literary associates, including Robert Penn Warren and Allen Tate, to produce a literary magazine, the *Fugitive*. This magazine, considered by some critics to be the best of its kind to be published in America, contained poetry and literary critiques. *Chills and Fever* (1925) and *Two Gentlemen in Bonds* (1927) are collections of Ransom's poems that were first published in the *Fugitive*.

His best known poem, "Bells for John Whiteside's Daughter," was published in 1924. The narrator takes the voice of a bystander contemplating the unexpected death of a child. Some critics have labeled "The Equilibrists" (1925) as his best poem. Through a careful choice of words, Ransom emulates the emotions of lovers kept apart by honor.

In 1937 he moved to Gambier, Ohio, where he accepted a position at Kenyon

College. There he founded and edited the *Kenyon Review*, a publication that concentrated on critical essays in the spirit of New Criticism.

In 1930 he participated with several other Southern literary scholars and writers in writing the book, *I'll Take My Stand*. Through this book the writers commented on social, economic, and political circumstances resulting from the Southern (agrarian) way of life as opposed to the dehumanizing consequences of the Industrial Revolution. He continued his social critique with three more books focusing on some of the major vices in America—*God Without Thunder* (1930), *The World's Body* (1938), and *The New Criticism* (1941). In *The New Criticism*, a book that received a great deal of attention, he outlined a system of critical thought that dominated the scene for nearly three decades. This method of literary critique was based on a study of the structure and texture of poetry instead of content.

He died on July 30, 1974, in Gambier, Ohio. He is buried in Kenyon College Cemetery in Gambier.

T.S. Stribling
(1881-1965)

Pioneer of realism in Southern literature

Burial Site—Clifton City Cemetery, Clifton, Tennessee
*Pulitzer Prize—*The Store, *1933*

Short-story writer and novelist, T. S. (Thomas Sigismund) Stribling constructed the foundation for the Southern Literary Renascence of the mid-1920s. Although some critics have sought to discredit him, and others have labeled him merely a literary footnote, Stribling paved the way for Southern realism. He was one of the first to write openly about bigotry and ignorance in the South.

He was born on March 4, 1881, in Clifton, Tennessee. He attended Clifton Masonic Academy and Southern Normal College in Huntingdon, Tennessee. In 1902, he enrolled in what is now the University of North Alabama in Florence, Alabama, where he completed the requirements for teacher-training in one year. After teaching math and gymnastics at Tuscaloosa High School in Tuscaloosa, Alabama, for a year, he entered law school at the University of Alabama. Again, he completed the required course work in one year, obtaining a law degree in 1905.

He practiced law in Florence, Alabama, for a few years. However, he maintained an interest in writing that he had developed while in high school. In 1900 he served for a brief time as editor of the *Clifton News*, and in 1907, having been offered a position at the *Taylor-Trotwood Magazine* in Nashville, he promptly resigned from the law firm. While working at *Taylor-Trotwood*, he developed a skill for writing Sunday School stories and gained confidence in his writing ability. Writing these stories came so easily for him that he often produced seven in one day.

In 1921, *Century Magazine* contracted with him to serialize his novel *Birthright* in seven of its issues and then to publish it in book form in 1922. A serious commentary on prejudice, the novel brought Stribling's name to the attention of major book publishers and magazine editors.

For his next two novels—*Fombombo* (1923) and *Red Sand* (1924)—he drew upon experiences from his earlier travels to South America. These light, melodramatic adventures were much like his first novel, *The Cruise of the Dry Dock* (1917). Readers found them entertaining, but whatever serious message Stribling tried to communicate became lost in melodrama.

Teeftallow (1926) explored bigotry and ignorance in a small Tennessee town. The novel became a popular and critical success, perhaps due to the 1925 Scopes Trial, a trial that took place in Dayton, Tennessee, and debated the principles of evolution. The book became a Book-of-the-Month Club selection and sold over 40,000 copies within a few months. A sequel novel, *Bright Metal* (1928), didn't receive as much attention.

Stribling then turned to lighter subjects. *Strange Moon* (1929), set in Venezuela, focused on romance and aristocracy, and in the same year, a collection of five previously published short stories, *Clues of the Caribbees*, was published.

In 1933, he received a Pulitzer Prize for his novel *The Store*, the second volume of a trilogy about the changing South from the Civil War to the 1920s. *The Forge* (1931) and *Unfinished Cathedral* (1934) combine with *The Store* to make what critics have called his most significant contribution to literature. Set in Florence, Alabama, the trilogy examines the actions and effects of bigotry and materialism.

Stribling chose the North for the setting of his last two novels. *The Sound Wagon* (1935) took place in New York and Washington, D.C., and focused on corruption within the American political system. *These Bars of Flesh* (1938), set at a New York City university, poked fun at the poor ethical judgment of professors and students within a metropolitan university.

From 1943 until the mid-1950s, Stribling wrote mystery short stories for magazines such as *Ellery Queen, Famous Detective, Smashing Detective Stories*, and *Saint Detective*.

He died on July 8, 1965, in Florence, Alabama.

Peter Hillsman Taylor

(1917-1994)

Acclaimed novelist and short-story writer

Special Collection—Vanderbilt University, Nashville, Tennessee
Pulitzer Prize—A Summons to Memphis, *1987*

Placing affluent characters in the Southern settings where he grew up, Peter Taylor wrote short stories and plays for nearly 60 years. He studied under such noted Southern writers as Allen Tate, John Crowe Ransom, and Robert Penn Warren.

Taylor was born on January 8, 1917, in Trenton, Tennessee. He attended Southwestern University in Memphis, Vanderbilt University, Kenyon College, and Louisiana State University. After receiving his undergraduate degree from Kenyon College in 1940, he studied briefly at Louisiana State University before joining the U.S. Army. From 1941 to 1945 he served at bases in this country and in England. He married Eleanor Lilly Ross in 1943; they had two children.

He was a teacher, lecturer, and writer. He said that he maintained a teaching job so that he wouldn't become dependent on writing for a livelihood. Throughout his career, he enjoyed writing short stories more than any other literary form. He began by submitting stories to *The New Yorker*, establishing a publishing relationship that lasted a lifetime. Because of their depth and detail, his short stories have been called miniature novels.

His first collection of short stories, *A Long Fourth and Other Stories,* was published in 1948. Two years later he published the novella, *A Woman of Means.* Each of his stories received critical acclaim and steadily increased his readership. Although critics endorsed his writing from the beginning, his short stories slowly achieved nationwide acclaim simply because the short story form had taken a back seat to the novel for popular reading. Many of these short stories are collected in volumes such as *Happy Families Are All Alike* (1959), *Miss Leonora When Last Seen, and Fifteen Other Stories* (1963), and *The Collected Stories of Peter Taylor* (1969).

His short stories and novels are set in urban Nashville, Memphis, or St. Louis. He often created characters from small Southern towns and moved them to the big city. There the characters were confronted and had to come to grips with a different set of values and demands. Through his acute attention to detail, Taylor presented social commentary based on Southern manners and morals that reached out to a universal audience.

Elected to the National Institute of Arts and Letters in 1969, he earned many honors including a Guggenheim Fellowship in 1950, a Fulbright Fellowship in 1955, and a Pulitzer Prize in 1987. The *New York Times Book Review* proclaimed him to be "one of the best writers America has ever produced."

In the mid-1980s, readers took a new interest in his writings. *The Old Forest, and Other Stories* (1985), a collection of his works from 1930 to the 1980s, won for him the PEN/Faulkner award for fiction. Then, in 1987, he received a Pulitzer Prize for *A Summons to Memphis*, a novel built around the emotional upheaval resulting from a father moving his family from Nashville to Memphis.

He died on November 2, 1994, in Charlottesville, Virginia.

Texas

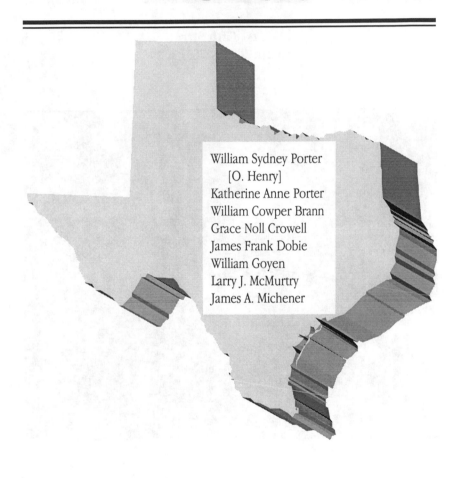

William Sydney Porter
[O. Henry]
Katherine Anne Porter
William Cowper Brann
Grace Noll Crowell
James Frank Dobie
William Goyen
Larry J. McMurtry
James A. Michener

O. Henry Museum

409 East Fifth Street
Austin, Texas 78701

Hours:
Wednesday through Sunday, 12-5 p.m.
Admission: Donation
Telephone: (512) 472-1903
Visitors are requested to wear flat, soft-soled shoes to
prevent damage to the floors.

Tourists who visit this Victorian cottage see the original Bastrop pine floors and many items that belonged to William Sydney Porter, best known by his pseudonym, O. Henry. The home also has other period pieces on display.

In 1893, Porter, his wife, and daughter moved into this cottage, which was then located at 308 East Fourth Street. (The home was moved in 1930 because of the rezoning of the neighborhood.) The family lived here until 1896 when Porter moved to Houston to work for the *Houston Post*.

While living at the house, Porter worked as a teller at the First National Bank and published *The Rolling Stone*, a weekly humor publication.

William Sydney Porter
[O. Henry]
(1862-1910)

A popular short story writer

Museums—Greensboro Historical Museum, Greensboro, North Carolina; O. Henry Museum, Austin, Texas
Marker—Austin, Texas
O. Henry Bridge—San Antonio, Texas
Annual Festival—O. Henry Pun-Off World Championship, Austin, Texas
Special Collections—Greensboro Public Library, Greensboro, North Carolina; Austin History Center, Austin, Texas; University of Virginia, Charlottesville, Virginia; University of Wisconsin, Madison, Wisconsin
Burial Site—Riverside Cemetery, Asheville, North Carolina.

While serving time in a federal prison, William Sydney Porter became one of America's most popular short story writers. He wrote almost 400 short stories, many of them published in major New York-based magazines, under the carefully guarded pseudonym, O. Henry.

Born on September 11, 1862, near Greensboro, North Carolina, Porter moved to Texas when he was 20 years old. What began as rest and recuperation from a bad cough resulted in his calling Austin, Texas, home. He took a job in a cigar store and joined the Hill City Quartet, where he played the guitar and mandolin. In 1887, he married Athol Estes Roach; they had one daughter, Margaret.

After his marriage, he worked as a draftsman for the General Land Office of Texas, a politically appointed position. When a new governor was elected in 1891,

Porter lost his job. He then accepted a position as a teller at the First National Bank. He found the banking job to be a burden and failed to keep his records properly. He spent more and more time reading, dreaming, and writing short stories.

In 1894, he launched a comic weekly publication, *The Rolling Stone* (first called the *Iconoclast*), as an outlet for the tensions of his banking job. However, in 1895, he was fired from the bank and had to give up his weekly paper. He accepted a job at the *Houston Post* as a columnist, a position he held for only eight months.

In the summer of 1896 facing charges of embezzlement from the bank where he had worked, he fled to South America. He intended to make a new home in Honduras for his family; however, when Athol was stricken with tuberculosis, he returned to Austin to be with his ailing wife and was subsequently arrested.

Seven months after Athol's death, Porter was convicted of a federal crime. He was sentenced in 1898 to the Ohio Federal Penitentiary, where he served a little over two years. While in prison, he continued to write short stories and chose for himself the pseudonym, O. Henry. He mailed the stories to national magazines such as *Harpers Monthly* and the *New Yorker*. The publication of these stories established for him an admiring audience.

After his release from prison in 1902, he moved to New York, maintaining a successful career writing under his pen name. His experiences in Honduras and the activity of New York life provided him with unlimited inspiration. He soon signed a contract with *The New York World Sunday Magazine*, agreeing to provide it with one story per week.

During the last eight years of his life, he published 381 stories (collected in nine volumes) and became America's favorite short story writer. Despite his success, he could never manage his money.

He died on June 3, 1910, in New York. It took almost 17 years for his daughter to pay off his debts using the royalties from his publications.

Katherine Anne Porter Museum

508 West Center Street
Kyle, Texas 78640

Hours:
Saturday, 10 a.m.-4 p.m.; On the first Sunday of each month—
April to August—2-5 p.m.
Admission: Free
Telephone: (512) 268-2220

Built in 1880, this historic home is a beautiful tribute to one of the nation's most admired writers. Furnished with period pieces and collections of works by Southwestern writers, artists, and poets, this home also displays a unique collection of Katherine Anne Porter's photographs, recordings, and videos. A collection of her letters and manuscripts is also maintained at this site.

From the age of two, she lived with her paternal grandmother at this home in Kyle, Texas. Here she received the inspiration for some of her best short stories.

Visitors can begin their tour with the front yard, the scene of many of Porter's impromptu plays. Also in the front yard is the "upping block" used by her grandmother to mount and dismount horses.

Porter left Texas after a life-threatening battle with tuberculosis. She lived for a while in Mexico, Paris, and Berlin. The experiences she had while living abroad provided inspiration for several of her short stories. She returned to the United States in 1936.

The Katherine Anne Porter Museum is regularly scheduled for community and monthly events and is open for public meetings, classes, and weddings when scheduled in advance.

Katherine Anne Porter
[Callie Russell]
(1890-1980)

Pulitzer Prize-winning short story author

Childhood Home—*The Katherine Anne Porter Museum, Kyle, Texas*
Markers—*Indian Creek, Texas; Kyle, Texas*
Statue—*San Antonio, Texas*
Special Collections—*University of Maryland Library, College Park, Maryland; University of Nevada, Reno, Nevada*
Burial Site—*Cremated ashes buried in Indian Creek Cemetery, Indian Creek, Texas*
Pulitzer Prize—Collected Stories, *1966*

Katherine Anne Porter's writing reflected a life full of disappointments that included her mother's death, growing up in a poor family, and several unsuccessful marriages. Throughout her works readers can find a recurring theme of human failure and resulting evil.

She was born on March 15, 1890, in Indian Creek, Texas. When her mother died, Katherine Anne was two years old. She and her siblings moved in with their grandmother in Kyle, Texas. She attended Thomas School in San Antonio and later taught music and dramatic reading in Victoria, Texas. She married John Henry Koontz in 1906.

Eleven years later, after a tumultuous marriage and an unsuccessful attempt at acting, she accepted a position as staff writer for the Fort Worth *Critic* and then the *Rocky Mountain News*. From 1919 to 1930 she wrote poetry, short stories, and book reviews while making regular visits to Mexico. She drew inspiration for her best creative works from her life experiences and surroundings.

Mexico was a strong influence in her early writing. Her first published story, "Maria Concepcion," appeared in *Century* magazine in 1922. "Flowering Judas," another story with Mexico as a setting, soon followed. It became the title story for her first collection of short stories, *Flowering Judas and Other Stories* (1930).

She had three more unsuccessful marriages. She traveled extensively—living for a time in Mexico, Madrid, Paris, and Berlin. After her return from Europe in 1936, she wrote *Noon Wine* (1937) and *Pale Horse, Pale Rider: Three Short Novels* (1939). Her only full-length novel, *Ship of Fools*, was published in 1962.

She won a Pulitzer Prize and the National Book Award for *The Collected Stories of Katherine Anne Porter* (1965). She also received several honorary degrees, a Guggenheim Fellowship, the O. Henry Memorial Award, the first Annual Gold Medal for Literature, and the Emerson-Thoreau Gold Medal for Fiction. She published her last book in 1977. *The Never-Ending Wrong* was a memoir of the Saco-Vanzetti case. Shortly after its publication, she suffered several strokes.

She died on September 18, 1980, in Silver Springs, Maryland.

Other Texas
Writers
and Sites

William Cowper Brann
(1855-1898)

Iconoclastic literary critic

Burial Site—*Oakwood Cemetery, Waco, Texas*

Perhaps one of the most vicious critics in the history of American literature, William Cowper (pronounced Cooper) Brann had negative comments for almost everyone. His stinging barbs reached from Baylor University in Waco, Texas, to Thomas Carlyle and Victor Hugo in Europe. His sharp tongue and disagreeable manner never served him well.

He was born on January 4, 1855, in Humboldt, Illinois. His mother died when he was two years old, leaving him to live most of his childhood on the farm of William Hawkins. There he learned to hate farming and at age 13 ran away from home. He worked at several jobs—bell boy, painter, drummer, and printer—while reading extensively and teaching himself foreign languages. He married Carrie Martin in 1877.

Also in 1877, he accepted a position as editorial writer for the St. Louis *Globe-Democrat*. Several years later, he moved his family to Texas, where he became the chief editorialist for the Houston *Post*.

Having received criticism from his employers that his editorials were too radical, he bought his own printing office in Austin, Texas, and established the *Iconoclast*. The first issue, dated July 1891, was full of biting commentary and criticism. The negative tone, which some described as a roasting mill, was not profitable. The magazine lasted less than a year.

In 1894 Brann sold the printing business to William Sydney Porter (O. Henry), who salvaged the name but turned the publication into a humor magazine. Under Porter's supervision, the *Iconoclast* steadily gained readership. Brann was so insulted that he made Porter remove the name from the humor magazine. He then moved his family to Waco and began publishing *Brann's Iconoclast*. (Porter continued to publish the humor magazine, simply changing the name to *The Rolling Stone*.) Within four years Brann built *Brann's Iconoclast* to a readership of more than 90,000. However, people still recognized it as a "blatant journal of opinion."

His books include *Brann's Speeches and Lectures* (1895?), *Potiphar's Wife* (1897), and *Brann's Scrapbook* (1898).

Over the years, many people learned to hate Brann. After having criticized the wrong person, he found himself in a duel. He died on April 2, 1898, in Waco, Texas, from a gunshot wound. Many people attended his funeral, not so much to pay their respects but to see that he was actually dead.

Grace Noll Crowell
(1877-1969)

State poet laureate and children's poet

Burial Site—*Sparkman-Hillcrest Memorial Park, Dallas, Texas*

Grace Noll Crowell's first attempt at poetry haunted her throughout her lifetime with a feeling of failure. Growing up on a farm, she loved her family and home. She believed the beauty of her father's field could only be described through the elegant rhythm of poetry. As she attempted to describe the field in a November dusk, words failed her. However, she overcame this disappointment and became heralded as one of America's best loved children's poets.

Born on October 31, 1877, in Inland, Iowa, she attended German-English College in Iowa, where she received an A.B. degree in 1898. She married Norman H. Crowell in 1904; they had three children. In the early 1920s she and her family moved to Texas, settling in Dallas.

Her first poem, "The Marshland," was printed in *Outing Magazine* in September 1906, and *Scribner's Magazine* published her second poem. In 1925 her first volume of poetry, *White Fire*, was published. It was also published in England and later reissued in Braille. This book was followed quickly by *Silver in the Sun* (1928), *Miss Humpety Comes to Tea and Other Poems* (1929), and *Flames in the Wind* (1930).

Crowell became poet laureate of Texas in 1935. Three years later she was chosen by the Golden Rule Foundation as American Mother of the Year and by American Publishers as one of the ten outstanding women of 1938.

Later in her career, she focused on devotional books such as *A Child Kneels to Pray* (1950) and *My Book of Prayer and Praise* (1955). Still read today, her books are often praised for the inspiration they give to people who are sick and suffering.

She died on March 31, 1969, in Dallas, Texas.

James Frank Dobie

(1888-1964)

Chronicler of the Southwest

Special Collections—University of California, Berkeley, California; Wake Forest University, Winston-Salem, North Carolina; University of Texas Libraries, Austin, Texas; Texas A&M University, College Station, Texas (book collection); University of Texas, El Paso, Texas; Baylor University, Waco, Texas
Burial Site—Texas State Cemetery, Austin, Texas

A loyal citizen of the Southwest, J. Frank Dobie took on a life-long task to preserve his Southwestern heritage. He wrote books as well as pamphlets and articles for magazines and newspapers publicizing his beloved land and people.

He was born on September 26, 1888, in Live Oak County, Texas. His mother encouraged him to read, and his father read nightly to the family from the Bible. A graduate of Southwestern University in Georgetown, Texas, and Columbia University in New York, he spent much of his life as an educator.

In 1910 he began teaching at a high school in Alpine, Texas. During the summers, he worked as a newspaper reporter. After receiving a master's degree from Columbia, he returned to teach at the University of Texas at Austin. In 1922 he became editor of the Texas Folklore Society. He married his college sweetheart, Bertha McKee, in 1916.

A Vaquero of the Brush Country (1929), Dobie's first book, prompted a regional literary revival. With the Southwest cattle country for a setting, Dobie examined cowboy life. His second book, *Coronado's Children* (1930), brought him national attention and won for him an admiring Texas audience. He began publishing articles in magazines and continued writing book manuscripts. In 1939, he started a syndicated newspaper column, "My Texas."

He wrote about universal human values using the symbols of the Southwest. His most popular book, *The Longhorns,* was published in 1941. Interweaving Southwest history and folklore, he compared the strength, vitality, freedom, and endurance of the longhorn steer with that of the hard-working pioneers of the region. He wrote four more books about the Southwest, including *Tales of Old-Time Texas* (1955) and *Cow People* (1964).

In 1943, he began a two-year assignment as a visiting professor at Cambridge

University in England. *A Texan in England*, published in 1945, is an account of his experiences.

He died on September 18, 1964, at his home in Austin, Texas.

William Goyen
(1915-1983)

Novelist, short story author, and screenwriter

Special Collections—University of Texas Libraries, Austin, Texas; Rice University, Houston, Texas

Beginning his writing career with short fiction, William Goyen was first published in the *Southwest Review*, a small magazine that awarded him a Literary Fellowship in 1948. He earned several awards, including two Guggenheim fellowships.

Born on April 24, 1915, in Trinity, Texas, Goyen attended Rice University, where he won every prize offered for fiction and drama. He received a bachelor's and a master's degree from Rice. After college, he served several years in the U.S. Navy, using his spare time for writing. However, his work wasn't published until 1945 when he submitted a short story to *Southwest Review*. He married Doris Roberts in 1963.

House of Breath, his first novel, was published in 1950, earning him two awards, one for the best first work by a Texan. Accepting a position with McGraw-Hill as an editor, he moved to New York, where he became involved in the theater. A dramatic adaptation of *House of Breath* was performed in 1953. While in New York, Goyen taught drama and worked at the Lincoln Center Repertory Theatre.

In 1955 he published *In a Farther Country*, a romance novel with a Spanish-American woman as the central character. His 1963 novel, *The Fair Sister*, expanded on a previous short story. The central character, a black woman evangelist, faces a world full of store-front churches.

Goyen's one nonfiction book, *A Book of Jesus*, was published in 1973. His screenplays include *The House of Breath* (1956), *The Diamond Rattler* (1960), *Christy* (1964), and *The House of Breath Black/White* (1971).

In 1983, two months after his death, his novel *Arcadio* was published. The narrative has been heralded as his finest achievement.

Goyen died on August 30, 1983, in Los Angeles, California.

Larry J. McMurtry
(1936-)

Storyteller of the vanishing West

Special Collections—*University of Arizona, Tucson, Arizona; University of North Texas, Denton, Texas; University of Houston, Houston, Texas*
Pulitzer Prize—Lonesome Dove, *1986*

As the son and grandson of cattle ranchers, Larry McMurtry grew up hearing stories of the often lonesome, frequently dangerous, and always romantic life on the range. His novels of Texas small towns and the vanishing cowboy captured the attention of a large readership across the United States. In all 21 novels, two collections of essays, and over 30 screenplays, McMurtry's themes remain universal. His realistic characters confront complicated battles and often fail when confronting the battle within themselves.

He was born on June 3, 1936, in Wichita Falls, Texas, and grew up in nearby Archer County. He attended Rice University, North Texas State College (now the University of North Texas), and Stanford University. He has taught at Texas Christian University and Rice University. He married Josephine Ballard in 1959; they have one child.

Horseman, Pass By, his first novel, was published in 1961. Readers were first introduced to the fictional Texas town of Thalia, a romantic western town resembling Archer City, a town near McMurtry's childhood home. His second novel, *Leaving Cheyenne*, was published in 1963 and continued the story of Thalia. In 1968 *The Last Picture Show* was published and later made into a movie. McMurtry's vivid descriptions of the west Texas landscape framed a novel of dissatisfaction, frustration, and loneliness.

In a Narrow Grave, also published in 1968, is a collection of his essays, focusing on Texas and its literary heritage.

Writing about Texas of the present and the West of the past, McMurtry has developed a vast following of fans across the nation. Although some critics have had biting comments, most agree that he writes stories that are emotionally gripping and entertaining.

In 1969 he moved to Washington, D.C., where he taught creative writing at George Mason University and American University. While living in Washington, he completed *Moving On* (1970) and two other novels—*All My Friends Are Going to*

Be Strangers (1972) and *Terms of Endearment* (1977). Each novel featured Texas characters and focused on marriage and the urban experience.

He published the novel *Somebody's Darling* in 1978. This comedy of manners and vulgarity featured movie people and movie making. McMurtry was perhaps his harshest critic, calling the novel "an interesting failure." In the 1980s he published four novels. *Cadillac Jack* (1982) followed the adventures and misadventures of a former rodeo cowboy who visited Washington, D.C. Next, he embarked on a more complex project—an epic tale of the post-Civil War West—called *Lonesome Dove*. In 1983, he realized the need for a break from his massive work on *Lonesome Dove* and allowed himself a three-week "writer's holiday." He used this time to write *The Desert Rose* (1983), a story of a mother and daughter who both work as show girls.

Lonesome Dove was published in 1986 and was an immediate hit. It won favor with critics and fans alike, and McMurtry was soon identified as "masterful." Critics praised his ability to weave comic scenes into dramatic intrigue. He received a Pulitzer Prize for this novel in 1986. Three years later the novel became one of television's most popular miniseries.

He revisited western legend with *Anything for Billy* (1988) and *Buffalo Girls* (1990). He brought historical figures such as Billy the Kid and Calamity Jane into present-day Texas. He blended comic scenes with drama to draw a sad picture of the changing West.

A "compelling storyteller," McMurtry maintains homes in Texas and Arizona and continues to write. In 1997 he co-authored *Zeke and Ned* with Diana Ossana and also published *Comanche Moon*. His Archer City, Texas, bookstore, Booked Up, specializes in finding and selling rare books.

James A. Michener
(1907-1997)

Author of epic novels

Museum—*James A. Michener Arts Center, Bucks County, Pennsylvania*
Special Collection—*University of Northern Colorado, Greeley, Colorado*
Burial Site—*Austin Memorial Park, Austin, Texas*
Pulitzer Prize—Tales of the South Pacific, *1948*

James A. Michener was noted for his entertaining and monumental sagas of places such as *Hawaii* (1959), *Texas* (1985), and *Alaska* (1988). His first novel, *Tales of the South Pacific*, brought him a Pulitzer Prize in 1948. He wrote more than 40 books that have sold approximately 75 million copies worldwide.

An orphan adopted by Mabel Michener, he said that he was born on February 3, 1907, in New York City. He grew up in Doylestown, Pennsylvania, and attended the public schools there. In 1925 he received a scholarship to Swarthmore College, where he graduated with honors. From 1931-33, he traveled in Europe, studying at St. Andrew's University in Scotland for a brief period. He married three times: first to Patti Koon in 1935, second to Vange Nord in 1948, and third to Mari Yoriko Sabusawa in 1955.

In 1937, after he received a master's degree from the University of Northern Colorado, he accepted a position there as associate professor. He spent three years teaching and writing social studies articles and textbooks. In 1941, he became associate editor at Macmillan Publishing Company in New York.

He enlisted in the U.S. Navy during World War II and served as chief naval historian for the area from Australia to French Oceania. His job required him to move from island to island, studying the people and their culture. The hours that he spent listening to stories from the residents and servicemen eventually became *Tales of the South Pacific*. The book achieved only a moderate success at first; however, in 1948 it received a Pulitzer Prize and was then adapted as a musical and performed on Broadway.

In 1949, Michener published his second novel, *The Fires of Spring*, based on his childhood in Bucks County, Pennsylvania. His next three books focused on World War II. *Return to Paradise* (1951), was set in the South Pacific; *The Bridges at Toko-Ri* (1953) featured a fictional group of Korean fighter pilots; and *Sayonara: The Floating World* (1954) chronicled the romance of an American officer and a Japanese woman.

In the late 1950s, he began writing the massive epics for which he became so well known. *Hawaii*, published in 1959, was chosen as a Book-of-the-Month Club selection, reprinted by *Reader's Digest* Condensed Books, and adapted for a movie. *The Source*, set in Israel, followed in 1965; *Centennial*, set in Colorado, in 1974; *Chesapeake* in 1978; *The Covenant*, set in South Africa, in 1980; *Poland* in 1983; *Texas* in 1985; and *Caribbean* in 1989.

Michener approached his writing as a professional. When he began a project, he did indepth research and worked hard at capturing accurate details. To prepare to write most of his epic novels, he often lived for a time at the location. He would meet people, listen to their stories, and collect detailed information about the area and its history.

In addition to his novels, he wrote nonfiction accounts and commentary. *Kent*

State, focusing on the fatal shooting of students at Kent State University, was published in 1971. His other works include *Sports in America* (1976), *The Quality of Life* (1980), *This Nobel Land: My Vision for America* (1996), and *A Century of Sonnets* (1997).

He was also noted for his philanthropy and service to the country. He served on the U.S. Food for Peace program, the U.S. Advisory Commission on Information, the Bi-centennial Advisory Committee, and the NASA Advisory Council, among others. President Gerald Ford awarded him the Medal of Freedom in 1977. Throughout his lifetime he donated millions of dollars to selected colleges and universities.

He died October 16, 1997, at his home in Austin, Texas.

Virginia

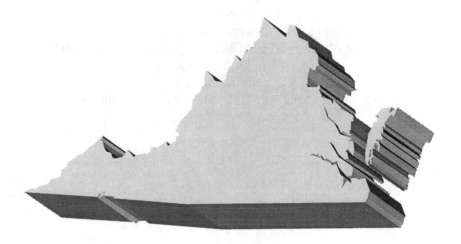

John Fox, Jr.

Edgar Allan Poe

Booker T. Washington

Mason Locke Weems

Sherwood Anderson

William Hervey Allen, Jr.

James Branch Cabell

John Esten Cooke

Clifford Dowdey

Ellen Glasgow

Mary Johnston

Thomas Nelson Page

William Styron

St. George Tucker

Nathaniel Beverley Tucker

John Reuben Thompson

John Fox, Jr., Museum

Shawnee Avenue East
Big Stone Gap, Virginia 24219

Hours:
Open June through Labor Day on weekends only
Tuesday and Wednesday, 2-5 p.m.; Thursday through Saturday, 2-6 p.m.;
Sunday, 2-5 p.m.
Admission:
Adults, $3; Students, $1; Children under ten free with adults
Telephone: (540) 523-2747

John Fox, Jr., and his family moved to this 20-room house in the 1890s. Here he worked clearing timber for mining operations, becoming friends with the Virginia mountaineers, and establishing his writing career.

This nineteenth-century house has natural cedar shingles and large screened porches off both stories. In 1908, Fox had an addition built to the house and married actress Fritzi Scheff. Although the marriage lasted only five years, this portion of the house is referred to as the Fritzi Scheff addition.

The house contains many items of furniture and memorabilia that belonged to Fox and his family. Tourists can see his large oak desk where he wrote his first short story, "A Mountain Europa," as well as the novels *The Trail of the Lonesome Pine* and *The Little Shepherd of Kingdom Come* and his many other works.

Fox's *The Trail of the Lonesome Pine* is performed mid-June through Labor Day weekend at the June Tolliver Playhouse located on Jerome Street and Clinton Avenue. The playhouse adjoins an arts and crafts center which displays nineteenth-century furnishings and arts and crafts made by Virginia artists. For reservations and information call 1-800-362-0149 or (540) 523-1235.

John William Fox, Jr.
(1863?-1919)

Friend of Virginia's mountaineers

Home—*Big Stone Gap, Virginia*
Drama—The Trail of the Lonesome Pine, *Big Stone Gap, Virginia (annual performance)*
Special Collection—*Alderman Library, University of Virginia, Charlottesville*
Burial Site—*Paris, Kentucky*

A friendly, colorful Southern gentleman, John Fox, Jr., began his writing career as a reporter for the New York *Sun* in 1884. He wrote many stories of the Cumberland Mountain region and its people.

Probably born in 1863, he attended the boys' school taught by his father and moved on to be the youngest of his class (1883) to graduate from Harvard University. He contracted tuberculosis while in college, causing him to resign his job at the New York *Sun* and withdraw from Columbia University Law School. Doctors in New York offered little hope for his recovery.

He returned home and worked with his father and brothers clearing land for mining and timber operations. He became friends with many of the Virginia mountaineers, learning their ways and receiving their affection. In 1890, he moved with his family to Big Stone Gap, Virginia. Continuing to clear land during the day, he spent his evenings writing.

He had friends in many places, among them fiction writer and historian Thomas Nelson Page, journalist Richard Harding Davis, and President Theodore Roosevelt. He earned his popularity with stories focusing on mountain characters and their lifestyle. He painstakingly distinguished mountaineers from "poor white trash." However, today he is most remembered for his historical fiction, notably *The Little Shepherd of Kingdom Come* (1903) and *The Trail of the Lonesome Pine* (1908).

He died on July 8, 1919.

Edgar Allan Poe Museum

1914-16 East Main Street
Richmond, Virginia 23223

Hours:
Tuesday through Saturday, 10 a.m.- 4:00 p.m. with guided
tours on the hour; Sunday and holidays, 1-4 p.m.
Admission: Adults, $5; Senior citizens, $4; Students, $3;
Call for group rates.
Telephone: (804) 648-5523

Although Poe never lived in this location, visitors see a staircase, mantel, and bed from his childhood home on 14th Street. A number of Poe's personal effects are on also on display here.

The museum occupies five buildings, the center of which is Richmond's oldest structure, the Old Stone House, built around 1737. Guided tours allow visitors to trace Poe's time in Richmond by viewing a large-scale model of Richmond as Poe knew it. A brief film also helps place his years in Richmond in the larger context of his life.

Behind the house is the Enchanted Garden, inspired by Poe's poems, "To One in Paradise" and "To Helen." The garden also contains a pergola built of the bricks from the building that housed the *Southern Literary Messenger*, the influential magazine where Poe worked as editor. Inside the museum visitors can see the desk and chair which he is said to have used while working at the *Messenger*.

The museum also contains an extensive research library that is open to the public by appointment.

Edgar Allan Poe
(1809-1849)

Inventor of the detective story

Museum—*Richmond, Virginia*
Dorm Room—*University of Virginia, Charlottesville*
Statue—*Baltimore, Maryland*
Library Room—*Enoch Pratt Library, Baltimore, Maryland*
Special Collections—*University of California, San Diego, La Jolla, California;
University of Chicago Library, Chicago, Illinois; Indiana University,
Bloomington, Indiana; University of Iowa Libraries, Iowa City, Iowa; Harvard
University Library, Cambridge, Massachusetts; Johns Hopkins University,
Baltimore, Maryland; Bronx County Historical Society, Bronx, New York; Free
Library of Philadelphia, Philadelphia, Pennsylvania; Brown University,
Providence, Rhode Island; University of Texas Libraries, Austin, Texas; University
of Virginia, Charlottesville, Virginia*
Burial Site—*Westminster Presbyterian Churchyard, Baltimore, Maryland*

Edgar Allan Poe was proficient in a wide range of literary and journalistic endeavors. He worked as an editor, literary critic, essayist, and fiction writer. Although he is best remembered for his eerie, yet musical poetry, some scholars believe his most significant contribution to literature was his invention of the detective story.

His writing had a universal theme; he didn't focus on Southern lifestyle or characters. Wanting readers to concentrate on the themes or atmospheres within his stories, not on stereotypical concepts, he employed new, unfamiliar settings. Unlike many Southern writers of his time, he believed literature should affect the emotions and that moral judgment and intellectual rhetoric should be left to sermons and speeches.

He was born on January 19, 1809, in Boston, Massachusetts. By the time he was two years old, both of his parents had died. He moved into the Richmond home of John Allan, a distant relative, who became his guardian. A tobacco merchant, Allan provided a good education and a stable home life for young Poe but never formally adopted him. After Poe entered the University of Virginia, he was, for the most part, on his own. He married Virginia Clemm, his cousin, in 1835; they had no children.

Dropping out of college after an argument with Allan, Poe published his first volume of poetry, *Tamerlane and Other Poems,* in 1827. In May of the same year, at the age of 18, he enlisted in the U.S. Army under the name of Edgar A. Perry. He spent nearly two years at Fort Moultrie in Charleston, South Carolina. After his discharge, he self-published another volume of poems, *Al Aaraaf, Tamerlane, and Minor Poems* (1829). He entered West Point in 1830 and spent almost a year writing a third manuscript. When it was ready for publication, he solicited a court-martial by "neglecting his duties." The new volume included some of his most remembered poems: "To Helen," "Israfel," and "The City in the Sea."

After his marriage, he supported his wife and her mother (Poe's aunt), by submitting literary criticism to the *Southern Literary Messenger*, a Richmond-based magazine for which he would later became an editor for two years. His reputation for being an industrious and skillful editor and a leading literary critic grew as did his reputation for emotional instability and drunkenness. In 1837, he left the magazine to establish one of his own; however, he was never financially secure enough to do so. He did buy a weekly newspaper, the *Broadway Journal*, in 1845. It ceased publication less than a year later.

Poe worked as an editor for brief periods with various magazines, including *Burton's Gentleman's Magazine*, *Graham's Magazine*, and the New York *Evening Mirror.* During this period he focused more on his poetry and fiction writing than on his editing positions. "The Raven" appeared in the *Evening Mirror* in January 1845; by the end of the year it was published in a collection of poetry titled *The Raven and Other Poems*. His collection of short fiction, *Tales,* was also published that year.

It was also during this period that he invented the detective story, what he called the "Tale of Ratiocination." He created a form of literature that offered the reader an opportunity to accompany the main character in solving a crime. M. Auguste Dupin was the forerunner of sleuths such as Sherlock Holmes and Nero Wolfe. "The Murders in the Rue Morgue," "The Purloined Letter," and "The Gold Bug" are Poe's best treatment of the new literary form.

When his wife died in 1847, Poe became deeply depressed. His inability to concentrate worsened, but he continued to write and to produce poetry and stories that are enjoyed by readers today.

In October 1849, while on his way to New York from Richmond, Poe stopped in Baltimore and collapsed in a street. He died a few days later, on October 7, 1849, and is buried in Westminster Presbyterian Churchyard in Baltimore.

Booker T. Washington National Monument

12130 Booker T. Washington Highway
Hardy, Virginia 24101

Hours:
9 a.m.-5 p.m. daily, except Thanksgiving, Christmas, and
New Year's Day; Guided tours on the hour
Admission: Free
Telephone: (540) 721-2094

Booker T. Washington was born here on April 5, 1856. Today the national park includes most of the original 207-acre tobacco plantation that he knew. Tourists can see slave cabins and farm buildings similar to those in Washington's time. Guided tours begin with a documentary film about him. The one-quarter mile Plantation Trail effectively transports visitors back to the 19th century.

A self-guided, walking tour is also an option for visitors. Tourists are invited to bring their lunch and enjoy the wooded picnic area before or after a tour.

Washington was freed from slavery and left the plantation at age nine. When he returned to visit in 1908, he was a college president and a noted statesman; however, his boyhood experiences continued to influence his life and shape his philosophy.

(Please see biography in Alabama chapter.)

Weems-Botts Museum

The Corner of Duke and Cameron Streets
P. O. Box 26
Dumfries, Virginia 22026

Hours:
April-October, Monday-Saturday, 10 a.m.-5 p.m., Sunday, 1-5
p.m.; November-March, Monday-Saturday, 10 a.m.-4 p.m., Sunday,
1-4 p.m. Closed on Mondays except when it falls on a holiday.
Admission: Adults, $3.00; Senior citizens, $2.00; Children, $1.50.
Group rates available.
Telephone: (703) 221-3346

Mason Locke Weems bought this home in 1798 to use as a bookstore and for lodging while he traveled the East Coast. He was a traveling bookseller and did much of his business in Dumfries.

This split-level home was built at different times. The smaller section, which now houses the Weems bookstore and attic, was purchased by Weems. However, it isn't clear when the second portion of the house was built.

In 1802, he moved his family to a brick home off Route 640 in Dumfries. (This home is now privately owned and not open to the public.) He sold the home at 300 Duke Street to Benjamin Botts, one of Aaron Burr's attorneys.

This building is thought to be the oldest structure in Dumfries. It is furnished with items representing the period of Weems' ownership.

Weems wrote biographies of Francis Marion, William Penn, and Benjamin Franklin. He also wrote numerous almanacs and sermon tracts.

A number of his works are on display, and the museum maintains sources for the Weems family genealogy.

Mason Locke Weems
(1759-1825)

Storyteller and publishing pioneer

Home—*Dumfries, Virginia*
Burial Site—*Dumfries, Virginia*

Bookseller, promoter, and author—Mason Locke Weems was the first biographer of George Washington. He was, in fact, the creator of the story about young George and the cherry tree. A former minister, Weems first wrote moralistic pamphlets and later biographies and almanacs.

Born in Marshes Seat, Maryland, on October 11, 1759, he was the youngest of 19 children. Evidence indicates that young Weems traveled to England, perhaps aboard a ship owned by his older brothers. There he is said to have studied medicine, serving as a surgeon for the Royal Navy during the Revolutionary War. After a brief trip to America when his father died, he returned to England to continue his studies, this time focusing on religion.

Ordained as a priest by the Archbishop of Canterbury on September 12, 1784, he became rector of All Hallows Church in Davidsonville, Maryland, and later served at St. Margaret's in Westminister, Maryland. However, after 1793, Sunday mornings found short, balding Weems more often in the congregation than behind the pulpit. He soon found more joy in wandering the countryside selling books than in his clerical post.

Sermons and pamphlets warning of the evils of bad habits were the first to bear his name. Most of these were simply reprints of pamphlets already in circulation with some moralizing by Weems added. In 1793 he became an agent for the publisher, Mathew Carey, selling books on commission and living the life of a traveling salesman.

He published his first biography in 1800. *The Life of George Washington,* after much editing and expansion, became one of the most popular biographies ever printed. It includes the story of Washington "barking" a cherry tree (cutting deeply into the tree's trunk, causing it to die). He wrote three more biographies—*The Life of Francis Marion, The Life of Benjamin Franklin,* and *The Life of William Penn.* None of these ever reached the popularity of the Washington biography, which went through 70 editions.

Weems wrote 26 books, pamphlets, and almanacs. These include *The Grand Republican Almanac, God's Revenge Against Murder, The Devil Done Over,* and *The Bad Wife's Looking Glass.*

As a salesman, he is regarded as an innovator. He developed what would be known today as a total marketing system, including the principles of price cutting and special sales. Scholars credit him with inventing the term "best seller" and being the first to use a brief commentary on the cover of books. He was also a pioneer in obtaining celebrity endorsements from people such as Thomas Jefferson and Dolly Madison.

While traveling through the Southeast on a promotional tour, he died on May 23, 1825, in Beaufort, South Carolina.

Other Virginia
Writers
and Sites

Sherwood Anderson
(1876-1941)

Popular novelist and short story writer

Markers—*Marion, Virginia; New Orleans, Louisiana*
Special Collections—*Clyde Public Library, Clyde, Ohio*
Burial Site—*Round Hill Cemetery, Marion, Virginia*

One of the best examples of man caught between the pull of a business lifestyle and the call of creativity, Sherwood Anderson left a successful business career in Elyria, Ohio, to pursue writing. His influence on American literature came not only from his own pen but also from his support of beginning writers such as William Faulkner and Ernest Hemingway.

Born on September 13, 1876, in Camden, Ohio, Anderson grew up in Clyde, Ohio. He attended the local school, but never graduated, leaving school to work to support his family. Called "Jobby," because he had held so many jobs, he never lost his dream of a glorious future for himself. In 1895, after the death of his mother, he moved to Chicago, where he worked as a laborer before enlisting in the armed forces in 1898. Upon his release from the army at the end of the Spanish-American War, he enrolled in Whittenberg Academy in Springfield, Ohio. From there he went to Chicago and accepted a position as an advertising writer. He experimented with creative writing in his spare time and contributed essays and sketches to the employee newspaper.

He married four times—to Cornelia Lane in 1904 (they had three children), to Tennessee Mitchell in 1916, to Elizabeth Prall in 1924, and to Eleanor Copenhaver in 1933.

After he suffered a nervous breakdown in 1911, he left his business and family, returning to Chicago and to copywriting in 1912. There he met several writers, including Carl Sandburg, and joined a group known as the Chicago Renaissance. In 1916, his first novel, *Windy McPherson's Son*—which he had begun writing while living in Elyria—was published. Focusing on a young man and his desire for material success, the book contains many autobiographical elements. His second book, *Marching Men*, was published the following year. *Winesburg, Ohio* (1919) was his most successful book. Through this collection of short stories, he effectively influenced a change in the way American short stories were written. He constructed realistic characters and put them in engaging and thorough plots.

Although he was almost 40 years old before he published his first story, he became a prolific writer. He published 27 major books in 26 years. Much of his writing focuses on the frustrations and desires of common people trapped by the demands of material success.

In 1923 he and his third wife, Elizabeth, lived in New Orleans. There he enjoyed the creative influence of the area and of his fellow writers such as F. Scott Fitzgerald, William Faulkner, and Gertrude Stein. He published stories in the local *Double Dealer Magazine* alongside Hemingway, Faulkner, and Thornton Wilder. Also, while living in New Orleans, he worked on the novel *Dark Laughter* (1925).

In 1924, he moved to Marion, Virginia, where he became the editor of *Smyth County News* and the Marion *Democrat*. While he and his wife vacationed in Troutdale during the summer of 1925, they bought property that he named Ripshin Farm. He published more than 15 books while living here. In 1932 *Beyond Desire* was published. *Death in the Woods and Other Stories* followed quickly in 1933. He wrote about his travels throughout the United States in *Puzzled America* (1935), and his novel, *Kit Brandon*, was published in 1936.

Anderson died on March 8, 1941, while traveling to South America.

William Hervey Allen, Jr.
(1889-1949)

Poet, biographer, and novelist

Special Collections—Harvard University, Cambridge, Massachusetts; University of Pittsburgh, Pittsburgh, Pennsylvania
Burial Site—Arlington National Cemetery, Arlington, Virginia

Searching for a release from the stress of his war experiences, William Hervey Allen, Jr., turned to writing. He had written some poetry and prose while in college and had published a collection of poems, *Ballads of the Border* (1916). It was after World War I, though, that he began writing regularly. *Anthony Adverse*, his 1933 historical novel, sold a record-breaking 395,000 copies the first year.

Born on December 8, 1889, in Pittsburgh, Pennsylvania, Allen was the youngest of five children. After attending public schools and the U.S. Naval Academy, he graduated from the University of Pittsburgh in 1915. As a first lieutenant in the National

Guard, he served overseas during World War I, taking part in many battles and eventually being assigned to teach English to French soldiers.

After the war, he settled in Charleston, South Carolina. In 1921 he accepted a position there teaching high school English. He became friends with Charleston native DuBose Heyward. They, along with John Bennett, founded the Poetry Society of South Carolina, chiefly as a retort to H. L. Mencken's attack on Southern culture and literature.

In 1922 Allen published a second collection of poetry, *Wampum and Old Gold*. This collection included "Blind Man" and other war-inspired poems. However, by 1926 his attention had turned to the life of Edgar Allan Poe. In that year, he published the two-volume *Israfel: The Life and Times of Edgar Allan Poe*. Scholars still consider it one of the best accounts of Poe's life.

He married Annette Hyde Andrews in 1927. That year they moved to Bermuda. He spent the next five years writing *Anthony Adverse*, a novel that traces the adventures of the main character from his birth in 1775 to his death in 1825. This huge, best-selling novel has been compared to *Don Quixote* and *Tom Jones*.

Due to the success of the novel, he and his wife returned to the United States and bought an estate in Maryland. *Action at Aquila*, his second novel, was published in 1938. This Civil War narrative received poor reviews by critics and readers. Some people viewed it as simply a formula romance. In his next book, *It Was Like This* (1940), composed of two short stories, he voiced his opinion of war and the exploitation of people touched by war.

Returning to his most successful type of writing, he formulated the outline for a five-part series on colonial America. *The Forest and the Fort* (1943), *Bedford Village* (1944), and *Toward the Morning* (1948) are filled with adventure and realistic details of the mid-1700s.

He died on December 28, 1949, in Miami, Florida. He was working on the fourth book in his planned series.

James Branch Cabell
(1879-1958)

A controversial novelist

Special Collections—University of California, Los Angeles, California; University of California, Santa Barbara, California; Yale University, New

Haven, Connecticut; University of Louisville, Louisville, Kentucky; University of Michigan Library, Ann Arbor, Michigan; Detroit Public Library, Detroit, Michigan; University of North Carolina, Chapel Hill, North Carolina; Wake Forest University, Winston-Salem, North Carolina; Free Library of Philadelphia, Philadelphia, Pennsylvania; University of Texas Libraries, Austin, Texas; University of Virginia, Charlottesville, Virginia; Richmond Public Library, (bust) Richmond, Virginia ; Virginia Commonwealth University, Richmond, Virginia; College of William and Mary, Williamsburg, Virginia
Burial Site—*Hollywood Cemetery, Richmond, Virginia*

A brilliant man born into the Virginia aristocracy, James Branch Cabell poked fun at the vanities of the lifestyle that surrounded him. He found inconsistencies in the stories of the Confederacy told by his elders and built comic myths for his time.

Born on April 14, 1879, in Richmond, Virginia, Cabell graduated with honors from the College of William and Mary. During his college years, he wrote poetry for the campus literary magazine. Toward the end of his schooling, rumors of homosexuality haunted him, linking him with a college librarian; however, the rumors diminished before his graduation.

After graduating from William and Mary, he worked for the Richmond *Times* and the New York *Herald*. Angered by rumors that he had murdered one of his mother's cousins, he left the newspaper industry and acquired work as a genealogist. He also began writing short stories for national magazines and published his first novel, *The Eagle's Shadow*, in 1904.

From 1911 to 1913 he worked in the West Virginia coal mines, gathering material and firsthand experience for his writing. During this time, he met Priscilla Bradley Shepherd, a widow with five children. They married in 1913 and had one son.

The year 1919 proved to be the most eventful year of Cabell's life. He had already published 11 books and numerous short stories. However, this was the year that he returned to full-time literary work. He accepted a position as editor of the Virginia War History Commission and a second position as genealogist of the Virginia chapter of the Sons of the American Revolution. Most importantly, 1919 was the year that his book *Jurgen* was published.

The story of a middle-class pawnbroker, *Jurgen* made him an international figure in 1920. Havng already twice been the center of personal controversy, he now became the most controversial writer in America. Public outcry labeled *Jurgen* a lewd and lascivious book, and soon Cabell faced a lawsuit for violating New York's pornography law. The court exonerated the book, but Cabell retained his reputation as an indecent writer. Because of this controversy, he became a symbol of ultrasophistication, aligned with the "smart set," and changed his publishing name to Branch Cabell. His strongest defender was H. L. Mencken.

The Biography of the Life of Manuel was his most ambitious work. It appeared in 18 volumes from 1927 to 1930 as the Storisende Edition of *The Works of James Branch Cabell*. From this point, his writing became autobiographical and philosophical, and his audience steadily declined. He served as an editor of *The American Spectator* from 1932 to 1935 when his health began to weaken. He spent his remaining years living in St. Augustine, Florida, and Richmond, Virginia.

He died on May 5, 1958, in Richmond, Virginia.

John Esten Cooke
(1830-1886)

Master of charm, grace, and romance

Special Collection—University of Virginia, Charlottesville, Virginia

John Esten Cooke wrote poetry, historical novels, and biographies as well as accounts of the Civil War battlefield for Southern newspapers. Some scholars call him the most talented novelist of his time. His writing depicts easy charm, superficial grace, and romantic pictures of Virginia.

Born on November 3, 1830, in Winchester, Virginia, Cooke was a cousin to John Pendleton Kennedy, a noted writer and statesman from Baltimore, Maryland. Cooke moved with his family to Richmond, Virginia, when he was 10 years old. He attended Richmond Academy. While studying law with his father, he wrote numerous poems and prose for the *Southern Literary Messenger*. In 1851, he passed the law exams for the state of Virginia. However, he continued to write, and by 1854 he had published four books and turned his career focus from law to writing.

Some critics consider *The Virginia Comedians* (1854) and *Henry St. John, Gentleman* (1859) his best works. Those novels describe Virginia society through a blend of history and romance using a technique, often employed by Washington Irving, that allows the writer to mingle his own comments with those of the fictional characters.

During the Civil War, Cooke served with General J.E.B. Stuart and wrote numerous accounts of war life for Southern newspapers. He used these accounts later for the basis of *Wearing of the Gray* (1867). (This collection of articles was published in 1861 as *Outlines from the Outpost*.) He also wrote seven books about the war, including biographies of Stonewall Jackson and Robert E. Lee.

From 1870 to 1879, he wrote nearly 100 articles and short stories but published only half of them. He also published numerous books during this period. With the war over, he worked during the day on his farm and used his spare time to write. *Surry of Eagle's Nest* (1866) and its sequel, *Mohun* (1868), use military developments and Confederate leaders to tell of the Civil War. *Hilt to Hilt* (1869) was again based on his war experiences and romanticized battles and military leaders.

His later books such as *Pretty Mrs. Gaston* (1874) and *My Lady Pokahontas* (1885) were charming and graceful glimpses of Southern society. His writing bridged the antebellum and postwar plantation romance. His literary career incorporated the Old South, the Civil War and Reconstruction, and the beginnings of the New South. At the end of his writing career, he kept up with the modern trends by blending romance and realism into his novels.

He died on September 27, 1886, at his home, The Briars, in Boyce, Virginia.

Clifford Dowdey
(1904-)

Civil War historian

Special Collection—University of Virginia, Charlottesville, Virginia

Best known for his series of Civil War histories, Clifford Dowdey began his career as an editor and freelance writer for pulp fiction magazines. He contributed numerous westerns and confession romances to these magazines during the Depression years. With the publication of his first nonfiction book, *Experiment in Rebellion* (1946), he was accepted as a talented historian by both his critics and readers.

He was born on January 23, 1904, in Richmond, Virginia. He attended the local public schools and Columbia University. After college, he accepted a position with the Richmond *News Leader* but stayed only a few months. He moved to New York to edit pulp magazines in 1926. For ten years, he worked as editor and freelance fiction writer during the day and researched Civil War history at night.

In 1937 he published his first book, *Bugles Blow No More*. This account of Richmond under siege earned him a Guggenheim Fellowship. For the next eight years, he wrote and traveled, settling for short periods in Vermont, California, and Texas. During this time he wrote four more historical novels, each well received by his growing audience.

Settling back into his boyhood home in Richmond, he turned to writing nonfiction. His serious research for *Experiment in Rebellion* (1946) resulted in its being a featured selection for the History Book Club.

His series of Civil War histories include *Death of a Nation: The Story of Lee and His Men at Gettysburg* (1958) and *Lee's Last Campaign: The Story of Lee and His Men Against Grant 1864* (1960). These nonfiction works established him as an authority on the background and the events of the war. Scholars have praised his extensive knowledge of the Army of Northern Virginia and of the men who influenced the Virginia campaigns—Robert E. Lee and Stonewall Jackson.

Dowdey also has written about the history and people of colonial Virginia.

Ellen Glasgow
(1873-1945)

Novelist who challenged social customs of her day

Special Collections—*University of Nevada, Reno, Nevada; University of Virginia, Charlottesville, Virginia*
Burial Site—*Hollywood Cemetery, Richmond, Virginia*
Pulitzer Prize—In This Our Life, *1942*

Receiving almost no formal education, Ellen Glasgow published her first novel, *The Descendant* (1897), at age 24. Her rebellion toward the social ideas of the day were evident in this examination of the class conflicts growing out of the Civil War.

She was born in Richmond, Virginia, on April 22, 1873, the eighth of ten children. Throughout her life, she suffered great bitterness due to the death of her mother, the suicide of her sister's fiancé, the death of her brother, and several devastating love affairs. Her rejection of the rules for feminine conduct placed her as a target for gossip and rumor.

At age 25, she set a goal of writing "a series of sketches dealing with life in Virginia." This goal resulted in a series of novels now referred to as a social history of Virginia. She used realism and irony to illustrate the themes of tradition vs. change, matter vs. spirit, and the individual vs. society.

She was a popular writer, with her works appearing on the best-seller list five times. *The Sheltered Life*, a comedy published in 1932, is considered her finest work. In this novel, her female characters respond to the stereotyped ideals of the day. She received a Pulitzer Prize in 1942 for her last novel, *In This Our Life*.

She died on November 21, 1945, in Richmond, Virginia.

Mary Johnston
(1870-1936)

Author of *To Have and To Hold*

Special Collection—*Alderman Library, University of Virginia, Charlottesville*
Burial Site—*Hollywood Cemetery, Richmond, Virginia*

A prominent member of the women's suffrage movement, Mary Johnston is best remembered for her historical romance, *To Have and to Hold* (1900). Set in colonial Virginia, the book sold more than 500,000 copies and has been made into a movie twice. She published 23 novels and more than 35 short stories.

She was born on November 21, 1870, in Buchanan, Virginia. Her father was a former Confederate officer who held positions requiring the family to travel to Europe and to live in several cities including New York City; Birmingham, Alabama; and Richmond, Virginia. When Mary was 19, her mother died, and she accepted the responsibility for running the household and rearing her five siblings.

Inspired by the need to help financially support the family, she published several books during this period. Within six years she had published *Prisoners of Hope* (1898), *To Have and To Hold* (1900), *Audrey* (1902), and *Sir Mortimer* (1904).

When the family moved back to Richmond, her writing interest turned to the history and people of Virginia. Two of her most notable Civil War epics are *The Long Roll* (1911) and *Cease Firing* (1912). After the publication of these books, she and two of her sisters built a house in Warm Springs, Virginia, where she lived for the rest of her life.

In 1909, she, Ellen Glasgow, and Lila Meade Valentine founded the Equal Suffrage League of Virginia. Johnston often shared her feminist views through speaking engagements, addresses to state legislatures, and other political conferences. Many of her later novels address feminist issues; *Hagar* (1913) is a good example.

She died on May 9, 1936, in Warm Springs, Virginia.

Thomas Nelson Page

(1853-1922)

Essayist, novelist, biographer, historian

Special Collections—Duke University, Durham, North Carolina; University of Virginia, Charlottesville, Virginia; College of William and Mary, Williamsburg, Virginia

A popular fiction writer and historian, Thomas Nelson Page established the first public library in Richmond, Virginia, as a memorial for his first wife, Anne Bruce. (She died two years after their marriage.) Throughout his life, he was a generous supporter of struggling writers. He wrote essays, stories, sketches, and long fiction on a variety of topics ranging from local color stories of the Old South to Christmas recollections to histories of Robert E. Lee to Mount Vernon preservation.

He was born on April 23, 1853, north of Richmond, Virginia. He attended Washington College and the University of Virginia. Practicing law, he specialized in business, inventions, and mining. He married Anne Bruce in 1886. When Anne died, the heartbroken Page left for Colorado and then Europe, working long hours practicing law. He returned to the United States in 1891.

In 1893, he married Florence Field and devoted his career to full-time writing. His first volume of stories, *In Ole Virginia* (1887), focused on the romantic beauty of the region before and during the Civil War. He became a leader in the local-color movement. (Local color emphasized a particular setting, including its customs, clothing, dialect, and landscape.)

Elsket and Other Stories (1891), *The Burial of the Guns* (1894), and *Bred in the Bone* (1904) used African-American dialect and focused on the Old South and its aristocracy. In two of his novels, *Gordon Keith* (1903) and *John Marvel, Assistant* (1909), he allowed the South to meet the North. In both, he contrasted the well-born Southerners with the big-city Yankees.

He also wrote semi-historical work and biographies such as *Robert E. Lee, Man and Soldier* (1911) and a volume of dialect verse, *Befo' de War* (1888).

In 1913 he was appointed as ambassador to Italy. He and his wife involved themselves with official duties and campaigning for the poor. After returning to the United States, he wrote about Italy, politics, and a commentary on Dante.

He died on October 31, 1922, at his family plantation, Oakland, in Montpelier, Virginia.

William Styron

(1925-)

Pulitzer Prize-winning author

Special Collections—University of Nevada, Reno, Nevada; Duke University, Durham, North Carolina
*Pulitzer Prize—*The Confessions of Nat Turner, *1968*

Although his writing doesn't focus on Southern history and culture, Southern heritage has influenced William Styron's writing and still finds its way into his novels. Critics claim that the literary technique he used in writing the novel *Lie Down in Darkness* was influenced by the writings of William Faulkner and Robert Penn Warren.

Born on June 11, 1925, in Newport News, Virginia, Styron attended Davidson College in North Carolina and later Duke University, where he studied creative writing. After graduation, he moved to New York and accepted a position as editor for McGraw-Hill, a job that he held for only six months. He married Rose Burgunder in 1953; they have four children. He served as an officer in the U.S. Marine Corps during World War II and the Korean War.

His first novel, *Lie Down in Darkness* (1951), was published while he was on active military reserve duty. It received enthusiastic reviews and has been praised for its insightful treatment of the complex paradox of a dutiful child who tries to please one parent at the displeasure of the other.

In 1952, he went to Paris, where he, along with such writers as George Plimpton, was influential in the founding of the *Paris Review*. Also during his stay in Paris, he wrote (in only six weeks) a novella based on his military experience; *The Long March* was published in 1953 and is now regarded as a modern classic. Some critics have compared it with Melville's *Billy Budd*.

His most controversial novel, *The Confessions of Nat Turner*, published in 1967, won great critical acclaim and a Pulitzer Prize. However, protests from the general public overwhelmed Styron. Many people, especially African Americans, criticized his treatment of the historical leader and his followers during the 1831 slave rebellion in Virginia.

In 1979 Styron wrote a comic play, *In the Clap Shack*, set in an American Navy hospital during World War II. *Sophie's Choice* (1979) is perhaps his most widely read novel. The forces of death and chaos are revealed to the main character as he becomes acquainted with a couple who experienced the horrors of a Nazi concentration camp. In 1982 he published *This Quiet Dust*, a collection of essays, reviews, and reminiscences.

He has stated that his fiction focuses on "humanly contrived situations which cause people to live in wretched unhappiness." In each of his novels, there is an individual whose will to endure triumphs over any human institution.

St. George Tucker
(1752-1827)

Poet, legal scholar, and satirist

Special Collections—University of Virginia, Charlottesville, Virginia; College of William and Mary, Williamsburg, Virginia

An attorney, judge, and professor of law, St. George Tucker is credited with having written the most important law book of his time. *Blackstone's Commentaries* (1803) is a five-volume, annotated reference on the body of English legal principles laid down by William Blackstone in the 1700s. Tucker's work contributed to the shaping of American court decisions during the 1800s.

Born on June 29, 1752, in Bermuda, Tucker came to the United States to attend the College of William and Mary, where he graduated in 1772 and taught law from 1790 to 1803. After a brief stay in Bermuda, he served in the Virginia militia as a lieutenant colonel during the Revolution. He married Frances Randolph in 1778; they had two children. In 1791, after her death, he married Lelia Shipwith Carter.

He practiced law for a time; then in 1788 he was elected a judge of the General Court of Virginia. From 1804 to 1811 he served as a judge in the Virginia Superior Court of Appeals. Then he served 12 years as a Federal District Court judge for eastern Virginia.

The Knight and the Friars: An Historical Tale (1786) was his first book. He wrote hundreds of poems, most of which he stored with his law papers. However, he did circulate a few pieces among friends. He published only patriotic verse such as "Liberty, A Poem on the Independence of America" (1788).

His 1796 publication, *A Dissertation on Slavery*, offered a plan for the gradual emancipation of slaves. Also in 1796, his collection of political satire, *Probationary Odes of Jonathan Pindar*, was published.

Another volume of political satire, *Up and Ride, or the Borough of Brooklyn,* and a musical comedy, *The Times, or the Patriots Roused,* are among several manuscripts that remain unpublished and are stored in the collection of his papers at the College of William and Mary. *The Poems of St. George Tucker of Williamsburg, Va., 1752-1827* was published in 1977.

He died on November 10, 1827, in Nelson County, Virginia.

Nathaniel Beverley Tucker

(1784-1851)

Author with special insight into Southern politics

Special Collection—College of William and Mary, Williamsburg, Virginia

His writings won the admiration of William Gilmore Simms and Edgar Allan Poe. Nathaniel Beverley Tucker's works remain a topic of study by scholars of Southern politics and economics. Although he wrote only three novels, his depiction of the Southern plantation and his insight into the conflict between the North and South were important contributions to the writers who came after him.

Born on September 6, 1784, in Chesterfield County, Virginia, Tucker was the son of St. George Tucker, a prominent attorney and judge in Virginia. He attended the College of William and Mary, where he studied law. After serving in the War of 1812, he moved to Missouri, where he practiced law and later was elected a judge. In 1834 he accepted a position as professor of law at the College of William and Mary. He married three times.

His letters and political essays reflect his support of secession and his belief in a slave-based economy. *George Balcombe*, published in 1836, was his first and most notable novel. Edgar Allan Poe labeled it the best American novel ever written. Set in Virginia and Missouri, the novel painted an idealized portrait of plantation life.

His second novel, *The Partisan Leader: A Tale of the Future* (1836), which carried the printing date of 1856, was published under an assumed name. Through reflective study of political trends, he predicted many of the events that were to happen over the 20-year period. The novel has caused scholars to reflect on Tucker's keen understanding of politics that allowed him to predict the war between the North and South.

He died on August 26, 1851.

John Reuben Thompson
(1823-1873)

Mentor to great writers

Burial Site—*Hollywood Cemetery, Richmond, Virginia*

Perhaps most remembered for his position as editor of the *Southern Literary Messenger*, John Reuben Thompson wrote poetry and many non-fiction magazine articles. However, his greatest contribution to literature is the influence he had on America's writers.

Born on October 23, 1823, in Richmond, Virginia, Thompson graduated from the University of Virginia with a degree in law. In 1845 he began practicing law but soon abandoned that career to work on magazines. He accepted a position at the *Southern Literary Messenger* as editor in 1847. He worked closely with Edgar Allan Poe and eventually wrote *The Genius and Character of Edgar Allan Poe*, which was published in 1929, more than five decades after Thompson's death.

Poe, however, wasn't the only writer Thompson knew. He visited such notables as Alfred Lord Tennyson, Charles Dickens, and Robert and Elizabeth Barrett Browning. He worked with popular writers such as William Gilmore Simms, Henry Timrod, John Greenleaf Whittier, and William Cullen Bryant.

In 1860, he left the *Southern Literary Messenger* because of poor health, which was later diagnosed as tuberculosis. During the war years, he lived in England but continued to support the Confederacy with his writing for the Louisville *Journal* and the New Orleans *Picayune*. In 1866, when the war was over, he returned to Richmond. The South had few periodicals left in which its writers could publish. In 1868, when Thompson published an article in the North-based magazine *Harper's*

Monthly, he was labeled a traitor to the South. Undaunted, he moved to New York and became editor of the New York *Evening Post*, a position he held until his death. He died on April 30, 1873, in New York.

West Virginia

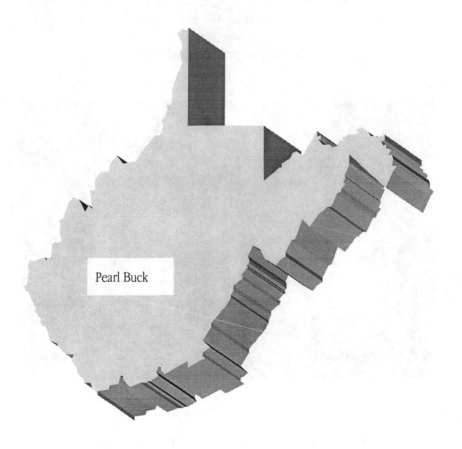

Pearl Buck

Pearl S. Buck Birthplace Museum

Stulting House
Route 219
Hillsboro, West Virginia 24946

Hours: May-October: 9 a.m.-5 p.m., Monday-Saturday;
1-5 p.m. Sunday; Closed Thanksgiving,
Christmas, and New Year's Day
Admission: Adults, $4; Students, $1
Telephone: 304-653-4430
Luncheon available with advance notice.

Built by Pearl Buck's grandparents in 1875, this 12-room farmhouse is constructed of three layers of brick covered with wood siding. Much of the original woodwork is still intact.

On display in the house are some of the furniture owned by Buck's grandparents, a Chinese Bible used by her missionary father, and a settee dating back to 1850. Tour guides dressed in period costumes also show a unique collection of Buck's personal items.

Buck was born here in 1892. Three months later she and her missionary parents left for China. At age nine, she returned to the United States to spend the summer with her grandparents at this home. In 1909, at age seventeen, she returned to Hillsboro for further education. She had an unmistakable love for this home as evidenced by her statement, "From that house there has come so much life that it ought never to die or fall into ruin.... For me that house was a gateway to America."

While visiting, many tourists enjoy seeing the log house where Pearl Buck's father grew up. This old home was moved from Greenbrier County, some 40 miles away, to its present location.

Pearl Comfort Sydenstricker Buck (1892-1973)

Winner of Nobel Prize

Homes—*Hillsboro, West Virginia; Perkasie, Pennsylvania*
Special Collections—*Princeton University Library, Princeton, New Jersey; Randolph-Macon Women's College, Lynchburg, Virginia; West Virginia Wesleyan College, Buckhannon, West Virginia*
Pearl Buck Writer's Festival—*held in August, Hillsboro, West Virginia*
Nobel Prize for Literature—*1938*
Pulitzer Prize—The Good Earth, *1942*

The first American woman to receive a Nobel Prize for literature, Pearl Buck is remembered for creating portraits of life in China. Her narrative style attracted a large audience who had little knowledge or understanding of Chinese customs. A born storyteller, Buck also wrote about the United States and dealt realistically with topics such as injustice, racial discrimination, and generational conflicts.

Born on June 26, 1892, in Hillsboro, West Virginia, Pearl Sydenstricker moved with her father, mother, and older brother to Tsingkiangpu, China. There she spent her childhood in a missionary house surrounded by a gray brick wall. Much of what she saw of the outside world—a continuous parade of knee-length robes and brown feet, some in tiny velvet slippers—was through the crack that separated the gate from the ground.

Her mother encouraged her at an early age to begin writing stories. At age eight, Buck's first short story was published in a Chinese newspaper. From that time on she continued to write, drawing from personal experiences and using familiar characters and settings.

In 1909, sharing an attic room with two other girls, she attended a boarding school in Shanghai. There she first learned of prejudice; her roommates, also children of missionaries, felt whites were better than Chinese and were astonished to see Pearl writing letters in Chinese to her friends. They were horrified that Pearl wanted to study Chinese history and spoke of the similarities between Buddhism and Christianity. Her roommates reported her as a heretic and had her moved into a room of her own so that she wouldn't contaminate the other students. Pearl hardly found this a punishment. She was then able to stay awake long after the other students were asleep. She used these extra hours to write poems, short stories, and even a novel.

During her stay at the boarding school, Pearl learned about "good works." The principal of the school sent her to work at a rescue home for Chinese slave girls and later at a shelter for prostitutes. During spring break, when Pearl told her parents of the good works she had done, her father declared it time for her to enter an American college. At age 18, she enrolled at Randolph-Macon Women's College in Lynchburg, Virginia, where she received a bachelor's degree in psychology in 1913. She was different from the other students and knew she always would be, but she put away her Chinese clothes, adopted a Southern drawl, and learned the new language of "slang."

In 1917, she went back to China and met a young missionary, John Buck. Against her parents' advice, they married and moved to the northern part of China. They had one child, Carol, who was diagnosed as retarded a few years after birth. Pearl wasn't happy in her marriage, but she didn't complain. She occupied her time caring for her daughter and by quietly writing a biography about her mother, who had died a short time after Carol's birth. When she completed the book, she hid it gently in the top of her closet.

In 1925 the couple came to the United States seeking medical attention for Carol. While here, Pearl studied at Cornell University in Ithica, New York, won first honors in a school essay competition for "China and the West," and tried her hand at magazine writing. "In China, Too," a story that contrasted the radical youth trends in America with the trends that were appearing among the young people of China, received immediate publication in *Atlantic Monthly*. When the publisher of *Forum* read the article, he wrote to Buck requesting the same type of article for his magazine. Now, she was not only a published writer, but one whose work was in demand.

Her first book, *East Wind: West Wind* (1930), a compilation of two short stories, became an immediate success. It was followed by *The Good Earth* in 1931, a novel of Chinese peasant life. This parable-like telling of old Chinese narrative sagas, captured the attention of American audiences and critics; in 1932 Buck received a Pulitzer Prize for the book.

In 1934, she moved to the United States. She divorced John Buck and married Richard Walsh, her publisher. Two years later she published the biography of her mother, *The Exile*, and another of her father, *Fighting Angel*. In 1938 these works, and her novels of Chinese peasant life, were labeled masterpieces by the Nobel Prize Committee.

With *This Proud Heart* (1938), Buck's first serious novel with an American setting, she attempted to become an "American" writer. She used clichés and colloquialisms awkwardly; however, the book received good reviews from critics and the general public.

She was a prolific writer, producing two or three books each year. This caused her publisher a great deal of difficulty with marketing. He suggested she assume a pseudonym. So, from 1945 to 1953, "John Sedges" published five novels, and Buck continued to produce an unceasing stream of novels, short stories, essays, and children's books. She wrote almost to the moment of her death.

She died March 6, 1973, in Perkasie, Pennsylvania. She is buried there on the Green Hills Farm.

Appendix

Homes, Markers, and Other Sites

The following list includes homes, museums, or other sites, most of which are open to the public. However, some sites may be open on a limited basis. If you are interested in visiting a site, please call the owner or curator to schedule a visit and to inquire about current admission charges. Many sites require a one-month prior notice for group tours.

Alabama

Samuel Ullman Museum
2150 15th Avenue, South
Birmingham, AL 35205
(205) 934-5634
For tour information write to: UAB
Center for International Programs, 318
Hill University Center, 1400 University
Boulevard, Birmingham, AL 35294-1150.

Ullman Building
University of Alabama at
Birmingham
1212 University Boulevard
Birmingham, AL 35294-3350
Used for classes only

Weeden House Museum
300 Gates Avenue, SE
Huntsville, AL 35801
(205) 536-7718
Home of poet Howard Weeden

Alabama Women's Hall of Fame
A. Howard Bean Hall
Judson College
Marion, AL
Bronze plaque and photograph

Bishop's House
307 Conti Street
Mobile, AL
Marker honoring Father Abram Joseph
Ryan

Ryan Park
Springhill Avenue, Saint Francis, and Scott
Streets
Mobile, AL
Bronze statue of Father Abram Joseph
Ryan

The Cottage
2564 Springhill Avenue
Mobile, AL
Marker honoring Augusta Jane Evans
Wilson

Monroe County Heritage Museum
Old Courthouse
On the Old Courthouse Square
P. O. Box 214
Monroeville, AL 36461
(334) 575-7433
Special collections and memorabilia
Truman Capote and Harper Lee

On Old Courthouse Square
Monroeville, AL
Monument to fictional lawyer, Atticus
Finch (*To Kill a Mockingbird*)

Site of Truman Capote Home
Two blocks south of Old Courthouse
Square
Monroeville, AL
Monument

F. Scott and Zelda Fitzgerald
Home/Museum
919 Felder Avenue
Montgomery, AL 36106
(334) 264-4222

Montgomery Museum of Fine Arts
Montgomery, AL 36101
Memorial to Zelda Sayer Fitzgerald

Ivy Green
300 West North Commons
Tuscumbia, AL 35674
(205) 383-4066
Helen Keller birthplace

The Oaks
Tuskegee Institute
1212 Old Montgomery Road
Tuskegee, AL 36083
(334) 727-3200
Booker T. Washington home

Tuskegee National Forest
Route 29
Tuskegee, AL
Replica of Booker T. Washington birth-
place

Florida

Zora Neale Hurston National Museum of
Fine Arts
227 East Kennedy Boulevard
Eatonville, FL 32751

Marjorie Kinnan Rawlings State Historic
Site
Route 3, Box 92
Hawthorne, FL 32640
(904) 466-3672

Ernest Hemingway Home
907 Whitehead Street
Key West, FL 33040
(305) 294-1136

Florida Key Community College
Key West, Florida
Tennessee Williams Fine Arts Building

Bok Tower Gardens
1151 Tower Boulevard
Lake Wales, FL 33853
Edward Bok memorial

Girl Scout Log House
442 South Eucalyptus Street
Sebring, FL
Marker honoring Rex Beach

Georgia

Wren's Nest
1050 Ralph David Abernathy Blvd., SW
Atlanta, GA 30310
(404) 753-7735
Joel Chandler Harris home

Margaret Mitchell House
990 Peachtree Street
Atlanta, GA 30309-3964
(404) 249-7012

Atlanta Historical Society
3099 Andrews Drive, NW
Atlanta, GA
Memorabilia of Margaret Mitchell, Erskine
Caldwell, Joel Chandler Harris, Sidney
Lanier, Flannery O'Connor, and others

1401 Peachtree St.
Atlanta, GA
Marker near Margaret Mitchell's childhood
home

Margaret Mitchell Park
Peachtree Street and John Wesley Dobbs
Avenue
Atlanta, GA

Road to Tara Museum
Stone Mountain, Georgia
Gone with the Wind memorabilia; clips of
the making of *Gone with the Wind*; cos-
tume gallery

State Archives
330 Capitol Avenue, SE
Atlanta, GA
Items relating to Southern authors

Poet's Monument
Green Street (between 7th and 8th)
Augusta, GA
Commemorates Paul Hamilton Hayne,
James Ryder Randall, Father Abram Joseph
Ryan, and Sidney Lanier

Wildwood Avenue and Garrard Street
Columbus, GA
Marker indicates birthplace of Augusta
Jane Evans Wilson

1519 Starke Avenue
Columbus, GA
Marker indicates childhood home of
Carson McCullers

West Marion and West Lafayette Streets
Eatonton, GA
Marker indicating Joel Chandler Harris
birthplace

Eatonton Courthouse
Eatonton, GA
Statue of Brer Rabbit, character created by
Joel Chandler Harris

Jefferson Street
Eatonton, GA
Marker honoring Joel Chandler Harris

Uncle Remus Museum
Turner Park
Route 441
Eatonton, GA

Gwinnett Courthouse Square
Lawrenceville, GA
Marker honoring Charles Henry Smith
[Bill Arp]

Sidney Lanier Cottage
935 High Street
P. O. Box 13358
Macon, GA 31208-3358
(912) 743-3851

Oglethorpe University
Milledgeville, GA
Sidney Lanier's dorm room

Flannery O'Connor Childhood Home
207 East Charlton Street
Savannah, GA 31401
(912) 233-6014
Oglethorpe Avenue (across from Colonial

Park Cemetery)
Savannah, GA
Marker indicating Conrad Aiken's homes

Washington, GA
Marker indicating Holley Chivers birthplace

Kentucky

Robert Penn Warren Birthplace
Third and Cherry Street
P. O. Box 296
Guthrie, KY 42234
(502) 483-2683

St. Boniface Friary
Louisville, KY
Marker honoring Father Joseph Abram
Ryan

Louisiana

Bayou Folk Museum
P. O. Box 411
Cloutierville, LA 71416
(318) 379-2233
Kate Chopin home

Beauregard-Keyes House
1113 Chartres Street
New Orleans, LA 70116
(504) 523-7257
Frances Parkinson Keyes home

Faulkner House Books
624 Pirate's Alley
New Orleans, LA 70116
(504) 524-2940
William Faulkner's residence (now a bookstore)

540B St. Peter Street
New Orleans, LA
Marker honoring Sherwood Anderson

Maryland

29th Street
Baltimore, MD
Bronze statue of Edgar Allan Poe

Eutaw Place and Lanvale Street
Baltimore, MD
Monument to Francis Scott Key

Francis Scott Key Museum
123 South Bentz Street
Frederick, MD

Mississippi

Merrill Building Museum
Carrollton, MS
Elizabeth Spencer collection

Tennessee Williams Birthplace Home and
Welcome Center
Corner of Main and Third Street, South
Columbus, MS 39703
(601) 328-0222

Oak Street
Como, MS
Marker indicating Stark Young birthplace

Mississippi Department of Archives and
History
Jackson, MS
Eudora Welty collection

New Albany Presbyterian Church
204 Cleveland Street
New Albany, MS
Marker indicating William Faulkner birthplace

William Faulkner Park
Union County Fair Grounds
New Albany, MS

Rowan Oak
Old Taylor Road
P. O. Box 965
Oxford, MS 38655
(601) 234-3284
William Faulkner home

Irwin Russell Memorial (City Hall)
Southeast College and Coffee Streets
Port Gibson, MS
Russell collection

North Carolina

Thomas Wolfe Memorial
48 Spruce Street
P. O. Box 7143
Asheville, NC 28801 3006
(704) 253-8304

College Street
Asheville, NC
Marker indicating birthplace of Thomas
Wolfe

Paul Green Theater
University of North Carolina
Chapel Hill, North Carolina

Connemara
1928 Little River Road
Flat Rock, NC 28731-9766
(704) 693-4178
Carl Sandburg home

Greensboro Historical Museum
130 Summit Avenue
Greensboro, NC 27401
(919) 373-2043
Tuesdays-Saturdays, 10 a.m. - 5 p.m.
Sundays, 2-5 p.m.
Closed on city holidays
Family memorabilia of William Sydney
Porter [O. Henry]

South Carolina

South Carolina Historical Society
100 Meeting Street
Charleston, SC
Collection of papers belonging to DuBose
Heyward, William Gilmore Simms, Henry
Timrod

White Point Park at the Battery
Charleston, SC
Bust of William Gilmore Simms

Washington Park
Charleston, SC
Monument to Henry Timrod

76 Church Street
Charleston, SC
Marker indicates DuBose Heyward's home

Chesnut Cottage
1718 Hampton Street
Columbia, South Carolina
Marker honoring Mary Boykin Chesnut

Hampton-Preston Mansion
1615 Blanding St.
Columbia, SC
Mary Chesnut lived here during the Civil
War

South Carolina State House
Columbia, SC
Portrait of Henry Timrod

Park and shrine
Timrod Drive and South Coit Street
Florence, SC
Honors Henry Timrod

Hampton Plantation State Park
1950 Rutledge Road
McClellanville, SC 29458
(803) 546-9361
Archibald Hamilton Rutledge birthplace

Tennessee

Alex Haley State House Museum
200 Church Street
Henning, TN 38041
(901) 738-2240

Morningside Park
Knoxville, Tennessee
Bronze statue of Alex Haley

Texas

Austin History Center
Austin, TX
Collection of William Sydney Porter [O. Henry] memorabilia

Booked Up
216 S. Center
Archer, City, TX 76351
(940) 574-2511
Fax: 940-574-4245
Open 10 a.m.-5 p.m., 6 days
Larry McMurtry's book shop

O. Henry Museum
409 East 5th Street
Austin, TX 78701
(512) 472-1903

Trailway Bus Station
10th and Congress Street
Austin, TX
Marker recognizing William Sydney Porter [O. Henry] as publisher of the *Rolling Stone*

Indian Creek, Texas
Marker recognizing Katherine Anne Porter

O. Henry Bridge
San Antonio, TX

San Antonio, TX
Statue honoring Katherine Anne Porter

Katherine Anne Porter Museum
508 West Center Street
Kyle, TX 78640
(512) 286-2220

Kyle, TX
Marker recognizing Katherine Anne Porter

Virginia

John Fox, Jr. Museum
Shawnee Ave., East
Big Stone Gap, VA 24219
(540) 523-2747
Home of John Fox, Jr.

University of Virginia
Charlottesville, VA
#13, West Range
Edgar Allan Poe's dorm room

Weems-Botts Museum
The Corner of Duke and Cameron Streets
P. O. Box 26
Dumfries, VA 22026
(703) 221-3346
Home of Mason Locke Weems

Edgar Allan Poe Museum
1914-16 East Main Street
Richmond, VA 23233
(804) 648-5523

Booker T. Washington National
Monument
12130 Booker T. Washington Highway
Hardy, VA 24101
(504) 721-2094

Route 11
Marion, Virginia
Marker honoring Sherwood Anderson

West Virginia

Pearl S. Buck Birthplace Museum
Route 219
Hillsboro, WV 24946
(304) 653-4430

State Capitol
Charleston, WV
Monument to Booker T. Washington

Libraries

The following libraries have special collections relevant to the authors in this book. Many special collections are available for use on a restricted basis. If you are doing research or have a special interest in these materials, please contact the library to schedule an appointment to review the collection.

Alabama

Birmingham Public Library
2100 Park Place
Birmingham, AL 35203
Samuel Ullman

Samford University
Special Collection Library
800 Lakeshore Drive
Birmingham, AL 35229
Lafcadio Hearn

Alabama Department of Archives and History
624 Washington Avenue
Montgomery, AL 36130
Sidney Lanier

University of Alabama
W. S. Hoole Special Collections Library
P. O. Box 870266
Tuscaloosa, AL 35487-0266
Rare first editions by William March, Lafcadio Hearn, and James Howell Street
Manuscripts and papers of Samuel Mintern Peck, Augusta Jane Evans Wilson, and Hudson Strode

Arizona

University of Arizona
University Library
Special Collections
Tucson, AZ 85721
Larry McMurtry
Tennessee Williams

California

Azusa Pacific College
Marshburn Memorial Library
Citrus and Alosta
Azusa, CA 91702
Ernest Hemingway
H. L. Mencken

University of California, Berkeley
Bancroft Library
Manuscript Division
Berkeley, CA 94720
James Frank Dobie

Francis Bacon Library
655 North Dartmouth Avenue
Claremont, CA 91711
Helen Keller

Claremont Colleges
Honnold Library
Ninth and Dartmouth
Claremont, CA 91711
Ernest Hemingway

Claremont Colleges
Ella Strong Dennison Library
Scripps College
Claremont, CA 91711
(714) 621-8000
Lafcadio Hearn

University of California, Davis
Shields Library
Department of Special Collections
Davis, CA 95616
Tennessee Williams

University of California, San Diego
Central University Library
Mandeville Department of Special
Collections
La Jolla, CA 92093
Ernest Hemingway
Edgar Allan Poe

University of California, Los Angeles
Research Library
Department of Special Collections
405 Highland Avenue
Los Angeles, CA 90024-1575
James Branch Cabell
Tennessee Williams

University of Southern California Library
American Literature Collection
Los Angeles, CA 90089-0182
(213) 740-5946
Carl Sandburg

California State University, Northridge
Delmar T. Oviatt Library
Special Collections
1811 Nordhoff Street
P. O. Box 1289
Northridge, CA 91328-1289
(818) 885-2832
Carl Sandburg

San Diego State University
Malcolm A. Love Library
5300 Campanile Drive
San Diego, CA 92182
H. L. Mencken

Huntington Library
Art Gallery and Botanical Gardens
1151 Oxford Road
San Marino, CA 91108
Conrad Aiken

University of California, Santa Barbara
University Library
Department of Special Collections
Santa Barbara, CA 93106
James Branch Cabell

Stanford University Libraries
Cecil H. Green Library
Stanford, CA 94305
William Faulkner
Ernest Hemingway

Connecticut

Yale University
Beinecke Rare Books and Manuscripts
Library
Wall and High Streets
New Haven, CT 06520
James Weldon Johnson
Richard Wright

Yale University
Sterling Memorial Library
Box 1630A
Yale Station
New Haven, CT 06520
James Branch Cabell
William Faulkner
James Weldon Johnson
H. L. Mencken
Robert Penn Warren

Connecticut College Library
Mohegan Avenue
New London, CT 06320
William Faulkner

Washington, D.C.

Georgetown University Library
Special Collection Division
37 and O Streets, NW
Washington, DC 20057
(202) 687-7444
H. L. Mencken
James Ryder Randall

Library of Congress
Manuscript Division
Washington, DC 20540
Booker T. Washington

Delaware

University of Delaware Library
Newark, DE 19717
(302) 831-2229
Erskine Caldwell
Ernest Hemingway
Carl Sandburg
Tennessee Williams

Florida

University of Florida
Gainesville, FL
Marjorie Kinnan Rawlings

University of Miami
Louise Calder Memorial Library
P. O. Box 016950
Miami, FL 33101
547-6441
Carson McCullers

Rollins College
Olin Library Archives
1000 Holt Avenue
Winter Park, FL 32789
(407) 646-2421
Rex Beach

Georgia

University of Georgia Libraries
Special Collections Division
Athens, GA 30602
Tennessee Williams

Atlanta-Fulton Public Library
10 Pryor Street, SW
Atlanta, GA 30303
Margaret Mitchell memorial

Emory University
Robert W. Woodruff Library
Atlanta, GA 30322
(404) 727-6887
Joel Chandler Harris

Oglethorpe University Library
4484 Peachtree Road, NE
Atlanta, GA 30319
Sidney Lanier

Agnes Scott College
McCain Library
East College Avenue
Decatur, GA 30030
Margaret Mitchell
Robert Frost

Georgia College
Ina Dillard Russell Library
Special Collection Department
Milledgeville, GA 31061
Flannery O'Connor

Georgia Southern Library
Statesboro, GA 30458
Conrad Aiken

Idaho

Boise State University Library
Special Collection Department
1910 University Drive
Bosie, ID 83725
(208) 385-3958
Ernest Hemingway

Illinois

Southern Illinois University, Carbondale
Delyte W. Morris Library
Special Collection Department
Carbondale, IL 62901
H. L. Mencken

Chicago Public Library
Special Collection Department
400 State Street
Chicago, IL 60605
(312) 747-4876
Carl Sandburg

University of Chicago Library
Department of Special Collections
1100 East 57th Street
Chicago, IL 60637
(312) 702-8705
Edgar Allan Poe

Newberry Library
60 West Walton Street
Chicago, IL 60610
Ernest Hemingway
Carl Sandburg

Northwestern University Library
Special Collection Department
1937 Sheridan Road
Evanston, IL 60201
William Faulkner
Ernest Hemingway

Knox College
Henry M. Seymour Library
Galesburg, IL 61401
Ernest Hemingway

Illinois State University
Milner Library
Department of Special Collections
Normal, IL 61761-6901
(309) 438-2871
Lafcadio Hearn
Thomas Wolfe

Oak Park Public Library
834 Lake Street
Oak Park, IL 60301
Ernest Hemingway

University of Illinois Urbana/Champaign
Library
Rare Books Room
346 Library
Urbana, IL 61801
Carl Sandburg

Indiana

Indiana University
Lilly Library
Seventh Street
Bloomington, IN 47405
(812) 855-2452
Scott Fitzgerald
Ernest Hemingway
Edgar Allan Poe
Carl Sandburg

Indiana State University
Cunningham Memorial Library
Department of Rare Books and Special
Collections
Terre Haute, IN 47809
Carl Sandburg
Jesse Stuart

Iowa

University of Iowa Libraries
Department of Special Collections
Iowa City, IA 52242
(319) 335-5921
Edgar Allan Poe

Kansas

University of Kansas
Kenneth Spencer Research Library
Special Collections Department
Lawrence, KS 66045
H. L. Mencken

Kentucky

Boyd County Public Library
1740 Central Avenue
Ashland, KY 41101
Jesse Stuart

Berea College Library
Berea, KY 40404
James Still collection

University of Kentucky
Margaret I. King Library
Department of Special Collections
Lexington, KY 40506-0039
James Lane Allen
James Still (use by author permission only)
Jesse Stuart
Robert Penn Warren

University of Louisville
Ekstrom Library
Rare Books and Special Collections
Belknap Campus
Louisville, KY 40292
(502) 588-6762
William Faulkner
Lafcadio Hearn
James Branch Cabell
H. L. Mencken

Morehead State University
Camden-Carroll Library
Morehead, KY 40351
(606) 783-2829
James Still
Jesse Stuart

Pogue Special Collection Library
Murray State University
Murray, KY 42071
Jesse Stuart Suite
Irwin Shrewsbury Cobb

Louisiana

Tulane University
Howard-Tilton Memorial Library
Special Collection Division
7001 Freret Street
New Orleans, LA 70118
William Faulkner
Lafcadio Hearn
Lyle Chambers Saxon
John Kennedy Toole

University of New Orleans
Earl K. Long Library
Lakefront
New Orleans, LA 70148
(504) 286-6354
William Faulkner

Maryland

Enoch Pratt Free Library
Humanities Department
400 Cathedral Street
Baltimore, MD 21201
John Pendleton Kennedy
H. L. Mencken Room
Edgar Allan Poe Room
Lizette Woodworth Reese

Johns Hopkins University
Milton S. Eisenhower Library
3400 N. Charles Street
Baltimore, MD 21218
(401) 516-8348
John Pendleton Kennedy
Sidney Lanier
Edgar Allan Poe
Lizette Woodworth Reese

Maryland Historical Society Library
201 West Monument Street
Baltimore, MD 21201
(410) 685-3758
Francis Scott Key

University of Maryland Library
College Park, MD 20742
Flannery O'Connor
Katherine Anne Porter

Goucher College
Julia Rogers Library
Dulaney Valley Road
Towson, MD 21204
H. L. Mencken
Lizette Woodworth Reese

Massachusetts

Boston University
Mugar Memorial Library
Special Collection Department
771 Commonwealth Avenue
Boston, MA 02215
(617) 353-3696
Margaret Mitchell
John Patrick [Gogan]

John F. Kennedy Library
Columbia Point
Boston, MA 02125
(617) 929-4500
Ernest Hemingway

Harvard University Library
Houghton Library
Cambridge, MA 02138
William Hervey Allen
Conrad Aiken
Sherwood Bonner [Katherine MacDowell]
Margaret Mitchell
William Faulkner
Lafcadio Hearn
Edgar Allan Poe
Booker T. Washington
Thomas Wolfe

Howard University Library
Houghton Library
Cambridge, MA 02138
Booker T. Washington

Brandeis University
Goldfarb Library Special Collections
415 South Street
Waltham, MA 02154
(617) 736-4685
Lizette Woodworth Reese

Wellesley College
Department of Special Collections
Wellesley, MA 02181
James Weldon Johnson

Williams College
Chapin Library of Rare Books
P. O. Box 426
Williamstown, MA 01267
William Faulkner

Michigan

University of Michigan
Special Collections Library
Ann Arbor, MI 48109
(313) 764-9377
James Branch Cabell
William Faulkner

Detroit Public Library
Rare Books Department
5201 Woodward Avenue
Detroit, MI 48202
(313) 833-1476
James Branch Cabell

Minnesota

University of Minnesota
Meredith Wilson Library
309 19th Avenue South
Minneapolis, MN 55455
Thomas Wolfe

Minnesota Historical Library
690 Cedar Street
St. Paul, MN 55101
F. Scott Fitzgerald

Mississippi

Eudora Welty Library
300 North State Street
Jackson, MS 39201
Mississippi writers room with exhibits for
Eudora Welty, William Faulkner,
Tennessee Williams, and others

Millsaps University
Millsaps-Wilson Library
Jackson, MS 39210-0001
(601) 974-1070
Eudora Welty

Mississippi State University
Mitchell Memorial Library
Box 5408
Mississippi State, MS 39762
Hodding Carter
William Faulkner
Eudora Welty
Tennessee Williams
Stark Young

University of Mississippi
John Davis Williams Library
Archives and Special Collections
University, MS 38677
(601) 234-6091
William Faulkner
Stark Young

Missouri

Southeast Missouri State
University Library
Cape Girardeau, MO 63701-4799
William Faulkner

St Louis Public Library
Rare Books and Special Collections
1301 Olive Street
St. Louis, MO 63103
(314) 241-2288
Tennessee Williams

Washington University
John M. Olin Library
Campus Box 1061
St. Louis, MO 63130
Conrad Aiken
Ernest Hemingway
Flannery O'Connor

Nevada

University of Nevada, Reno
University Library
Special Collection Department
Reno, NV 89557
James Agee
Conrad Aiken
Erskine Caldwell
William Faulkner
F. Scott Fitzgerald
Ellen Glasgow
Ernest Hemingway
Randall Jarrell
Carson McCullers
Flannery O'Connor
Katherine Anne Porter
John Crowe Ransom
Carl Sandburg
William Styron
Robert Penn Warren
Eudora Welty
Thomas Wolfe
Richard Wright

New Hampshire

Dartmouth College
Baker Memorial Library
Hanover, NH 03755
Erskine Caldwell
H. L. Mencken

New Jersey

Princeton University Library
Rare Books and Special Collections
Princeton, NJ 08544
(609) 258-3174
Pearl Buck
F. Scott Fitzgerald
Zelda Sayer Fitzgerald
Ernest Hemingway
Tennessee Williams

New York

American Foundation for the Blind
McMigel Memorial Library and
Information Center
15 West 16th Street
New York, NY 10011
Helen Keller

Bronx County Historical Society
Bronx County Research Library
3309 Bainbridge Avenue
Bronx, NY 10467
Edgar Allan Poe

Columbia University Libraries
Rare Books and Manuscripts Library
Butler Library, 6th Floor
535 West 114 Street
New York, NY 10027
(212) 854-2231
Tennessee Williams

New York Public Library
Research Libraries
Berg Collection of English and American
Literature
Fifth Avenue and 42nd Street
New York, NY 10018
(212) 930-0802
Randall Jarrell
H. L. Mencken

New York Public Library
Schomburg Center for Research in Black
Culture
515 Malcom X Boulevard
New York, NY 10037
(212) 491-2218
Richard Wright

New York University
Elmer Holmes Bobst Library
Division of Special Collections
Washington Square, South
New York, NY 10012
Thomas Wolfe

Pierpont Morgan Library
29 East 36 Street
New York, NY 10016
Lafcadio Hearn

State University of New York, Stoney
Brook
Melville Library Department of Special
Collections
Stoney Brook, NY 11794
Conrad Aiken

Syracuse University Library
Syracuse, NY 13244
Erskine Caldwell

U. S. Military Academy Library
West Point, NY 10996
William Faulkner

Vassar College Library
Rare Books and Manuscripts Collection
Box 20
Pougkeepsie, NY 12601
Eudora Welty (correspondence only)

North Carolina

Pack Memorial Public Library
North Carolina Collection
67 Haywood Street
Asheville, NC 28801
Thomas Wolfe

University of North Carolina, Chapel Hill
Wilson Library
Rare Book Collections
Chapel Hill, NC 27514
(919) 962-1143
James Branch Cabell
Thomas Wolfe

University of North Carolina, Charlotte
J. Murrey Atkins Library
UNCC Station
Charlotte, NC 28223
Carl Sandburg

Duke University
William R. Perkins Library
Special Collections Department
Durham, NC 27706
(919) 684-3372
Thomas Holley Chivers
Paul Hamilton Hayne
Sidney Lanier
Carson McCullers
Thomas Nelson Page
William Gilmore Simms
William Styron
Henry Timrod
Richard Wright

Greensboro Public Library
201 North Greene Street
P. O. Box 3178
Greensboro, NC 27402-3178
(919) 373-2471
O. Henry

University of North Carolina, Greensboro
Walter Clinton Jackson Library
Special Collections Department
1000 Spring Garden Street
Greensboro, NC 27412
Randall Jarrell
John Crowe Ransom

Wake Forest University
Smith Reynolds Library
Box 7777
Reynolds Station
Winston-Salem, NC 27109
(919) 759-5755
James Frank Dobie
William Faulkner
James Branch Cabell

Ohio

Ohio University
Vernon R. Alden Library
Department of Archives and Special
Collections
Athens, OH 45701-2978
(614) 593-2710
Lafcadio Hearn

Public Library of Cincinnati and Hamilton
County
Department of Rare Books and Special
Collections
800 Vine Street
Library Square
Cincinnati, OH 45202
William Faulkner

Kent State University Libraries
Department of Special Collections and
Archives
Kent, OH 44242
William Faulkner

Pennsylvania

Dickinson College
Boyd Lee Spahr Library
West High Street
Carlisle, PA 17013
Carl Sandburg

Bryn Mawr College
Canady Library
Bryn Mawr, PA 19010
Eudora Welty

Gettysburg College
Musselman Library
Gettysburg, PA 17325
(717) 337-7011
H. L. Mencken

Free Library of Philadelphia
Rare Books Department
1901 Vine Street
Philadelphia, PA 19013-1189
(215) 686-5416
James Branch Cabell
Edgar Allan Poe

University of Pennsylvania
Van Pelt Library
Rare Books Collection
34 and Walnut
Philadelphia, PA 19104
H. L. Mencken

University of Pittsburgh
Hillman Library
Special Collections Department
Pittsburgh, PA 15260
William Hervey Allen

Rhode Island

Brown University
John Hay Library
20 Prospect Street
Providence, RI 02912
Edgar Allan Poe

South Carolina

Charleston Library Society
164 King Street
Charleston, SC 29401
DuBose Heyward
William Gilmore Simms
Henry Timrod

College of Charleston Library
Special Collections Department
Charleston, SC 29401
Paul Hamilton Hayne
DuBose Heyward

University of South Carolina
1021 Wheat Street
Columbia, SC 29201
Mary Boykin Chesnut

Tennessee

University of Tennessee, Knoxville
University Library
Knoxville, TN 37996
James Agee
Alex Haley

Vanderbilt University
Jean and Alexander Heard Library
Nashville, TN 37212
John Crowe Ransom
Peter Hillsman Taylor
Robert Penn Warren

Texas

University of Texas Libraries
Hoblitzelle Theatre Arts Library
Austin, TX 78712
William Faulkner

University of Texas Libraries
Humanities Research Center
P. O. Box 7219
Austin, TX 78713-7219
(512) 471-9119
James Agee
James Branch Cabell
James Frank Dobie
William Faulkner
William Goyen
Ernest Hemingway
Carson McCullers
Edgar Allan Poe
Tennessee Williams

Cushing Memorial Library
Texas A&M University
College Station, TX 77803
J. Frank Dobie (book collection)

University of North Texas
Denton, Texas 76203-5188
Larry McMurtry

University of Texas, El Paso
University Library
Special Collections Department
El Paso, TX 79968
James Frank Dobie
H. L. Mencken

Rice University
Fondren Library
Woodson Research Center
61005 Main Street
P. O. Box 1892
Houston, TX 77001
William Goyen

University of Houston
Anderson Memorial Library
University Park
Houston, TX 77004
Larry McMurtry

Baylor University
Moody Memorial Library
Texas History Collection
Waco, TX 76706
James Frank Dobie

Virginia

University of Virginia
Alderman Library
Clifton Waller Barrett Collection
Charlottesville, VA 22901
James Branch Cabell
Erskine Caldwell
John Esten Cook
Clifford Dowdey
William Faulkner
John William Fox, Jr.
Ellen Glasgow
Joel Chandler Harris
Lafcadio Hearn
Ernest Hemingway
Mary Johnston
John Pendleton Kennedy
Francis Scott Key
Frances Parkinson Keyes
Sidney Lanier
H. L. Mencken
Thomas Nelson Page

Edgar Allan Poe
William Sydney Porter [O. Henry]
Carl Sandburg
William Gilmore Simms
John Reuben Thompson
St. George Tucker
Thomas Wolfe

Randolph-Macon Women's College
Lipscomb Library
Lynchburg, VA 24503
(804) 846-7392
Pearl Buck

The Edgar Allan Poe Library
1914-16 East Main Street
Richmond, VA 23223
(804) 648-5523
Edgar Allan Poe

Richmond Public Library
101 East Franklin Street
Richmond, VA 23219
James Branch Cabell (bust)

Virginia Commonwealth University
James Branch Cabell Library
Richmond, VA 23284
James Branch Cabell

Virginia Historical Society
P. O. Box 7311
Richmond, VA 23221
John Pendleton Kennedy

College of William and Mary
Earl Gregg Swem Library
Williamsburg, VA 23185
James Branch Cabell
Thomas Nelson Page
St. George Tucker
Nathaniel Beverly Tucker

West Virginia

West Virginia Wesleyan College
Annie Merner Pfeiffer Library
Buckhannon, WV 26201
Pearl Buck

Wisconsin

University of Wisconsin, Madison
Memorial Library
British and American Language and
Literature Collection
728 State Street
Madison, WI 53706
Kate Chopin
William Sydney Porter [O. Henry]

CANADA

National Library of Canada
395 Wellington Street
Ottawa K1A ON4 Canada
(613)995-9481
Elizabeth Spencer

University of Saskatchewan Library
Saskatoon, 57N OWO, Canada
Conrad Aiken

Festivals

A number of festivals across the country are dedicated to a piece of literature, a particular Southern author, or a collection of authors.

Alabama

To Kill a Mockingbird
Monroe County Heritage Museums
P. O. Box 214
Monroeville, AL 36641
(334)575-7433
Annual performance—May

Fitzfest
Huntingdon College
1500 East Fairview Avenue
Montgomery, AL 36106-2148
(334) 833-4414
Annual event—June

The Miracle Worker
Ivy Green
300 West North Commons
Tuscumbia, AL 35674
(205) 383-4066
Annual performance—June and July

Florida

Zora Neale Hurston Festival of the Arts and Humanities
Eatonville, Florida
Annual event—last weekend in January

Hemingway Days Festival
P. O. Box 4045
Key West, FL 33041
(305) 294-4440
Annual event—July

Cross and Sword (1964 play by Paul Green)
St. Augustine, FL
Annual performance—June to September

Georgia

Joel Chandler Harris Birthday Celebration
December 9
Wren's Nest
1050 Ralph David Abernathy Blvd., SW
Atlanta, GA 30310
(404) 753-7735

Flannery O'Connor Childhood Home
207 East Charlton Street
Savannah, GA 31401
(912) 233-6014
Annual literary events—October-May

Louisiana

Tennessee Williams/New Orleans Literary Festival
New Orleans, LA
(504) 286-6680
Last weekend in March; offers theater, walking tours, book fair, panel discussions

Mississippi

Oxford Pilgrimage
Center for the Study of Southern Culture
Barnard Observatory
University of Mississippi
Oxford, MS
(601) 232-5993
Annual event—April

Faulkner and Yoknapatawpha Conference
Center for the Study of Southern Culture
Barnard Observatory
University of Mississippi
Oxford, MS
Annual event—August
(601) 232-5993

North Carolina

The World of Carl Sandburg and
Rootabaga Stories
Asheville, NC
(704) 693-4178
Annual performance—summer months
Daily, 9 a.m. to 5 p.m.; $2 admission

Thomas Wolfe Festival
Thomas Wolfe Memorial
P. O. Box 714
Asheville, NC 28802
(704) 253-8304
Last weekend in September

The Lost Colony
Waterside Theatre
Roanoke Island
Roanoke, NC
1-800-488-5012
Annual performance—June-August

South Carolina

Hampton Plantation Spring Festival
1950 Rutledge Road
McClellanville, SC 29458
(803) 546-9361
Last Saturday in March

Tennessee

Alex Haley Memorial Picnic
Circle Park
Knoxville, TN
Annual event—September

Texas

O. Henry Pun Off World Championship
409 East 5th Street
Austin, TX 78767
(512) 472-1903
Annual event—May

Virginia

June Tolliver Playhouse
Big Stone Gap, VA
1-800-362-0149/(504) 523-1235
Musical adaptation of *The Trail of the
Lonesome Pine* by John Fox, Jr.—mid-
June-Labor Day

West Virginia

Pearl Buck Writer's Festival
Pearl Buck Birthplace Museum
Hillsboro, WV 24946
(304) 653-4430
Annual celebration—August

Cemeteries

Alabama

Knesseth Israel-Beth-El Cemetery
320 11th Court, North
Birmingham, AL
Samuel Ullman

Maple Cemetery
Huntsville, AL
Maria Howard Weeden

Roman Catholic Cemetery
1700 Stone Avenue
Mobile, AL
Father Joseph Abram Ryan

Magnolia Cemetery
Virginia Street
Mobile, AL
August Jane Evans Wilson

Tuskegee Institute Cemetery
Tuskegee Institute
Tuskegee, AL
Booker T. Washington

Evergreen Cemetery
Tuscaloosa, AL
William March [Campbell]

Greenwood Cemetery
Tuscaloosa, AL
Samuel Mintern Peck

Florida

Antioch Cemetery
Route 325
Island Grove, FL
Marjorie Kinnan Rawlings

Garden of the Heavenly Rest
Fort Pierce, FL
Zora Neale Hurston

Rollins College Campus
Winter Park, FL
Rex Beach

Georgia

Westview Cemetery
1679 Westview Drive, SW
Atlanta, GA
Joel Chandler Harris

Oakland Cemetery
248 Oakland Avenue, SE
Atlanta, GA
Margaret Mitchell

Magnolia Cemetery
702 Third Street
Augusta, GA
Paul Hamilton Hayne
James Ryder Randall
Richard Henry Wilde

Rosehill Cemetery
Macon, GA
Harry Stillwell Edwards

Memory Hill Cemetery
Milledgeville, GA
Flannery O'Connor

Oak Hill Cemetery
Rome, GA
Charles Henry Smith [Bill Arp]

Presbyterian Cemetery
Route 19
Roswell, GA
Francis Robert Goulding

Bonaventure Cemetery
Bonaventure Road
Savannah, GA
Conrad Porter Aiken

Kentucky

Plum Grove Cemetery
Greenup County, Kentucky
Jesse Stuart

Lexington Cemetery
Lexington, KY
James Lane Allen

Oak Grove Cemetery
Paducah, KY
Irvin Shrewsbury Cobb

Cemetery Hill
Springfield, KY
Elizabeth Madox Roberts

Louisiana

Magnolia Cemetery
300-20 19th Street
Baton Rouge, LA
Lyle Chambers Saxon

Maryland

Greenmount Cemetery
Greenmount and Oliver Streets
Baltimore, MD
John Pendleton Kennedy
Sidney Lanier

Loudon Park Cemetery
Baltimore, MD
H. L. Mencken

Westminster Church Cemetery
West Fayette Street
Baltimore, MD
Edgar Allan Poe

Mt. Olivet Cemetery
South Harbor Street
Frederick, MD
Francis Scott Key

St. Mary's Catholic Church Cemetery
520 Viers Mill Road
Rockville, MD
F. Scott Fitzgerald
Zelda Sayer Fitzgerald

St. John's Episcopal Church Cemetery
Waverly, MD
Lizette Woodworth Reese

Mississippi

Friendship Cemetery
Como, MS
Stark Young

Greenville Cemetery
1000 South Main Street
Greenville, MS
William Hodding Carter, Jr.
William Alexander Percy

Hill Crest Cemetery
Holly Springs, MS
Sherwood Bonner (grave unmarked)

St. Peter's Cemetery
Jefferson Avenue
Oxford, MS
William Faulkner

North Carolina

Riverside Cemetery
53 Birch Street
Asheville, NC
Thomas Wolfe
O. Henry

New Garden Friends Cemetery
Greensboro, NC
Randall Jarrell

St. James Church
Wilmington, NC
Thomas Godfrey

Wilmington National Cemetery
Wilmington, NC
Inglis Fletcher

Old Chapel Hill Cemetery
Hwy. 54 and Country Club Drive
Chapel Hill, NC
Paul Green

South Carolina

Knight's Hill
Camden, SC
Mary Boykin Miller Chesnut

St. Philip's Protestant Episcopal Church
142 Church Street
Charleston, SC
DuBose Heyward

Magnolia Cemetery
Route 61
Charleston, SC
William Gilmore Simms
Josephine Lyons Scott Pinckney

Trinity Episcopal Churchyard
1100 Sumter Street
Columbia, SC
Henry Timrod

Peterkin Cemetery
Fort Motte, SC
Julia Peterkin

Hampton Plantation State Park
McClellanville, SC
Archibald Hamilton Rutledge

Tennessee

Clifton City Cemetery
Clifton, TN
T.S. Stribling

Texas

Texas State Cemetery
901 Navasta Street
Austin, TX
J. Frank Dobie

Sparkman-Hillcrest Memorial Park
Dallas, TX
Grace Noll Crowell

Indian Creek Cemetery
Indian Creek, TX
Katherine Anne Porter

Oakwood Cemetery
Waco, TX
William Cowper Brann

Austin Memorial Cemetery
Hancock Drive & Bull Creek Rd.
James Michener

Virginia

Arlington National Cemetery
Arlington, VA
William Hervey Allen

Round Hill Cemetery
Marion, VA
Sherwood Anderson

Hollywood Cemetery
4121 South Cherry Street
Richmond, VA
James Branch Cabell
Ellen Glasgow
Mary Johnston
John Ruben Thompson

Southern Prize Winners

A number of authors included in this book have been the recipients of the Nobel Prize for literature and the Pulitzer Prize for different areas of writing.

Nobel Prize in Literature

Pearl S. Buck, 1938
William Faulkner, 1949
Ernest Hemingway, 1954
Isaac Singer, 1978

Pulitzer Prize

Journalism
Hodding Carter, Greenville, MS *Delta Democrat-Times*, 1946 (Editorial Writing)
Alex Haley, *Roots: The Saga of an American Family*, 1977 (Special Citation)

Letters—Fiction
Julia Peterkin, *Scarlet Sister Mary*, 1929
Pearl S. Buck, *The Good Earth*, 1932
T. S. Stribling, *The Store*, 1933
Margaret Mitchell, *Gone with the Wind*, 1937
Marjorie Kinnan Rawlings, *The Yearling*, 1939
Ellen Glasgow, *In This Our Life*, 1942
John Hersey, *A Bell for Adano*, 1945
Robert Penn Warren, *All the King's Men*, 1947
Ernest Hemingway, *The Old Man and the Sea*, 1953
William Faulkner, *A Fable*, 1955
James Agee, *A Death in the Family*, 1958
Harper Lee, *To Kill a Mockingbird*, 1961
William Faulkner, *The Reivers*, 1963
Katherine Anne Porter, *Collected Stories*, 1966
William Styron, *The Confessions of Nat Turner*, 1968

Eudora Welty, *The Optimist's Daughter*, 1973
John Kennedy Toole, *Confederacy of Dunces*, 1981 (posthumously)
Larry McMurtry, *Lonesome Dove*, 1986
Peter Taylor, *A Summons to Memphis*, 1987

Drama
Paul Green, *In Abraham's Bosom*, 1927
Tennessee Williams, *A Streetcar Named Desire*, 1948
John Patrick [Goggan], *The Teahouse of the August Moon*, 1953
Tennessee Williams, *Cat on a Hot Tin Roof*, 1955

History
Carl Sandburg, *Abraham Lincoln: The War Years*, 1940

Biography or Autobiography
Edward Bok, *The Americanization of Edward Bok*, 1921

American Poetry
Before this category was established, Carl Sandburg was honored in 1919 with an award by the Poetry Society of America for his poem *Corn Huskers*.

Robert Frost, *New Hampshire*, 1924
Conrad Aiken, *Selected Poems*, 1930
Robert Frost, *Collected Poems*, 1931
Robert Frost, *A Further Range*, 1937
Robert Frost, *A Witness Tree*, 1943
Carl Sandburg, *Complete Poems*, 1951
Wallace Stevens, *Collected Poems*, 1955
Elizabeth Bishop, *Poems: North & South A Cold Spring*, 1956
Robert Penn Warren, *Promises*, 1958
Robert Penn Warren, *Now and Then*, 1979

Friends of Libraries U.S.A.

Begun in 1982, Friends of Libraries U.S.A. provides support, information, and programs for people interested in promoting their local libraries. National campaigns include Books for Babies, English Literary Tours, Baker & Taylor Awards for outstanding library friends groups, and Literary Landmark dedications.

The Literary Landmark Register, which began in 1987, encourages communities to recognize local literary sites that are connected with authors. During a community ceremony, identifying plaques are placed on the historical property.

The following Southern literary sites honoring authors have been recognized by Friends of Libraries U.S.A.

*Marjorie Kinnan Rawlings house, Cross Creek, FL—1988
*Tennessee Williams house, New Orleans, LA—1988
Walter Farley Wing, Venice Area Public Library, Venice, FL—1989
Stephen Crane house, Daytona Beach, FL—1989
W.E.B. DuBois, Robert W. Woodruff Library, Clark Atlanta University, GA—1991
Ernest Lyons house, Stuart, FL—1992
Elizabeth Bishop house, Key West, FL—1993
*William Faulkner, Rowan Oak, Oxford, MS—1993
*William Faulkner house/now a bookstore, New Orleans, LA—1993
Jose Marti, San Carlos Institute, Key West, FL—1994
*Robert Penn Warren Center, Western Kentucky Univ., Bowling Green, KY—1994
Isaac Bashevis Singer apartment house, Miami, FL—1994
John Hersey house, Key West, FL—1995

Laura Riding Jackson cottage, Vero Beach, FL—1995
Robert Frost cottage, Key West, FL—1995
Wallace Stevens, Key West, FL—1996
*Sherwood Anderson salon, Pontalba Apartments, New Orleans, LA—1998

*Biographical information on these authors is included previously in this book.

Other sites outside the South have also been recognized. More information is available about the Friends of Libraries U.S.A. by calling 1-800-9FOLUSA. Information about authors included in Literary Landmark dedications who are not included elsewhere in this book (included in chronological order based on when the landmark dedication was made):

Walter Farley (1915-1989)

Friends of Libraries U.S.A. honored Walter Farley with a commemorative plaque at the Venice Public Library, Venice, Florida, in 1989.

Creator of the novel, *The Black Stallion* (1941), Walter Farley was born on June 26, 1915, in Syracuse, New York. For over 40 years, Farley entertained children, youth, and young adults with adventure stories featuring his greatest love—horses. His works include *Larry and the Undersea Raider* (1942), *The Island Stallion* (1948), *The Black Stallion Ghost* (1969), and *The Black Stallion Legend* (1983).

Farley died on October 16, 1989, in Sarasota, Florida.

Stephen Crane (1871-1900)

Friends of Libraries U.S.A. placed a commemorative marker in 1989 in Daytona Beach, Florida, marking a house where Stephen Crane lived for a short while and where he wrote "The Open Boat."

Best remembered for the Civil War novel, *The Red Badge of Courage*, Stephen Crane began his writing career as a journalist. In addition to numerous newspaper articles, he wrote novels, short stories, and poems before dying at the age of 28.

Born on November 1, 1871, in Newark, New Jersey, Crane spent most of his childhood in New York. He attended Lafayette College and Syracuse University.

In 1892, he accepted a position with the *New York Herald*, writing about the street people of New York. This provided him with firsthand knowledge that rendered a realistic depiction of the Bowery in his first novel, *Maggie: A Girl of the Streets* (1893), first published under the pseudonym Johnston Smith.

Crane quickly produced poems, sometimes five or six in one day. The *Black Riders* (1895) is a collection of many of Crane's early poems. He received critical praise for employing a unique form to convey the skepticism with which he viewed his early religious teachings; however, many were reluctant to acknowledge his "blasphemy."

The *Red Badge of Courage* was also published in 1895. Criticism about the novel focused around the fact that Crane had no knowledge of real battles. He sought to remedy this fact by accepting a position as war correspondent to cover the revolution between Cuba and Spain. In Florida, awaiting transport to Cuba, he met Cora Stewart who became his companion and common-law wife.

In attempting to sail to Cuba, Crane became shipwrecked off the Florida coast, near Daytona Beach. This frightening experience led to his masterpiece, *The Open Boat*, published first as a short story and then in book form as *The Open Boat and Other Stories* (1898).

A few months after Crane's shipwreck, he and Stewart sailed for Europe to cover the impending war between Greece and Turkey. Writing under the pseudonym of Imogene Carter, Stewart became the first female war correspondent.

For almost three years, Crane traveled from one country to the next in search of battles and publishing his experiences. Feeling the effects of tuberculosis and malaria in early 1899, Crane wrote at an even more feverish pace. Before his death he had produced over 50 short stories, sketches, and newspaper articles and completed the last half of *Active Service* (1899) and nearly two-thirds of *The O'Ruddy* (1903).

Crane died June 5, 1900, in Badenweiler, Germany. He is buried in Evergreen Cemetery, Hillside, New Jersey.

W.E.B. DuBois (1868-1963)

Friends of Libraries U.S.A. honored W.E.B. DuBois with a commemorative plaque at Clark Atlanta University in 1991.

Co-founder of the National Negro Committee, which later became the National Association of the Advancement of Colored People (NAACP), DuBois taught history and economics at Atlanta University in Atlanta, Georgia, from 1897 until 1910 and again from 1932 until 1944. DuBois was the first editor of the NAACP magazine *Crisis*. He wrote *The Souls of Black Folk* (1903), *John Brown* (1909), and *The Black Flame* (1957-61). His *Autobiography* was published posthumously in 1968.

Ernest Lyons

Friends of Libraries U.S.A. honored Ernest Lyons, author of My Florida *(1969), with a commemorative plaque at his home in Stuart, Florida, in 1992.*

Elizabeth Bishop (1911-1979)

Pulitzer Prize—*Poems: North & South A Cold Spring*, 1956

Friends of Libraries U.S.A. placed a commemorative marker in 1993 in Key West, Florida, marking a house where Bishop once lived.

A poet and artist, Elizabeth Bishop painted images of sight, sound, and emotions with pen and paper as well as paintbrush and canvas. Since she was passed from family member to family member during her childhood, Bishop seemed predestined to live the life of a wanderer. When she received notice that she had received the Pulitzer Prize in 1956, she was living in Brazil. She celebrated her success by eating cookies with a local grocer.

Elizabeth Bishop was born on February 8, 1911, in Worcester, Massachusetts. Her father died when she was eight months old; consequently, her mother was hospitalized in sanitariums for the rest of her life. Entering Vassar College 1930, Bishop was on her own. She began her studies as a music major but turned to writing poetry when she realized the stresses of public

performance. She graduated from Vassar in 1934. She never married.

After completing her education, Bishop moved to Florida. She settled in Key West in 1937, where she lived for almost ten years. She purchased a house on White Street and lived a comfortable life writing, painting, swimming, and biking to pay her bills. She planted palms and tropical shrubs in her yard and listened to the neighbors' roosters. The sights and sounds with which she surrounded herself found their way into her writing.

In 1946, her first collection of poetry, *North & South*, was published. It contained allegorical poems such as "The Map," "The Man-Moth," and "The Weed." A year later, in 1947, Bishop received a Guggenheim Fellowship. She served as consultant in poetry to the Library of Congress from 1949 until 1950.

Her second collection of poems, was actually a dual volume. It included poems from her first collection and 17 new poems. *Poems: North & South A Cold Spring*, was published in 1955 and received a Pulitzer Prize in 1956. By this time she was living in Brazil. She had traveled there for a visit, but when she became ill, she settled in to recover. Her recovery period lasted almost 20 years.

While in Brazil, Bishop translated *Minha Vida de Menina*, the diary of "Helena Morley," wrote a Time-Life book about Brazil, and published *Questions of Travel* (1965), her third volume of poetry which includes a brief autobiographical short story.

Bishop left Brazil at the end of the 1960s and began a teaching career at Harvard. She published *Geography III* in 1976 and received the Neustadt International Prize for Literature, marking the first time an American had won the award and the first time a woman had won the award.

Bishop died on October 6, 1979, in Boston, Massachusetts.

Jose Marti (1853-1895)

A commemorative plaque honoring Jose Marti was placed by Friends of Libraries U.S.A. at the San Carlos Institute in Key West, Florida, in 1994.

Born in 1853 in Cuba, the poet and essayist Jose Marti is said to have been one of the most influential Latin American writers. He died in a revolutionary skirmish at Dos Rios, Cuba, in 1895. His works include *Ismaelillo* (1882) and *Verso sencillos* (1891).

Isaac Singer (1904-1991)

Nobel Prize for Literature—1978

Friends of Libraries U.S.A. honored Isaac Singer in 1994 with a commemorative plaque at a Miami apartment building where he lived for some time.

Born in Radzymin, Poland, on July 14, 1904, Singer was the author of "Yentl, the Yeshiva Boy" and *Enemies: A Love Story*, both of which were made into motion pictures. Singer wrote most of his works in Yiddish, the language of the Jewish ghettos. He received the Nobel Prize for literature in 1978.

Singer died on July 24, 1991, in Surfside, Florida.

John Richard Hersey (1914-1993)

Pulitzer Prize—*A Bell for Adano*, 1945

*John Hersey established his retirement home in Key West, Florida, in 1976, while also maintaining a home in Massachusetts. He published four books—*Blues *(1987),* Life Sketches *(1989),* Fling *(1990), and* Antonietta *(1991) after moving to Key West. The house he lived in on Windsor Lane is privately owned. It was recognized by the Friends of Libraries U.S.A. with a commemorative plaque in 1995.*

As a journalist, essayist, novelist, and historian, John Hersey wrote about the events of his day and their effects on the people who lived through them. His works captured the attention of the nation.

Born on June 17, 1914, in Tientsin, China, John Hersey spent the first ten years of his life outside the United States. In 1924, his father became seriously ill, and the family moved to New York. There Hersey attended public and private schools and graduated from Yale University in 1936. He also attended Clare College in Cambridge, Massachusetts, in 1936-37.

He married Frances Ann Cannon on April 27, 1940; they had four children. Their marriage ended in divorce in 1958. Hersey later married Barbara Day Addams Kaufman; they had one child.

In 1937, Hersey accepted a summer job working as secretary and driver for novelist Sinclair Lewis. He then became writer, editor, and correspondent for *Time* magazine, a job he kept for seven years. From 1939 until 1945, he served as an overseas correspondent in Japan, China, the South Pacific, and the Soviet Union. Hersey also worked for *Life* magazine as an editor and correspondent and for the *New Yorker* as a writer.

A Bell for Adano (1944), Hersey's first novel, received the Pulitzer Prize in 1945. This story of an attempt to introduce democracy to a small Italian village was adapted for stage and screen in 1945.

In his next major work, *Hiroshima*, Hersey allowed six fictional survivors to tell about their experiences resulting from the dropping of the bomb. This "nonfiction novel" first appeared as the entire issue of the August 31, 1946, *New Yorker*. The magnitude of Hersey's message captured the nation. When it was published in book form, Albert Einstein ordered 1,000 copies; Book-of-the-Month Club distributed free copies; and ABC (American Broadcasting Company) had it read on radio stations.

Hersey went on to publish over 20 more books during his lifetime, shedding light on national and world events. Included in these books are *The Wall* (1950), about the Holocaust, and *The Child Buyer*. In 1973, Hersey edited *Ralph Ellison: A Collection of Critical Essays* and in 1974 *The Writer's Craft*. His last book, *Antonietta*, was published in 1991.

Hersey died on March 24,1993, while living in Key West, Florida.

Laura Jackson (1901-1991)

Friends of Libraries U.S.A. honored Laura Jackson in 1995 with a commemorative plaque at her cottage in Vero Beach, Florida.

Poet, critic, and short story writer, Laura Jackson was born on January 16, 1901, in New York City. She was a member of "The Fugitives" and wrote commentaries such as "Anarchism is Not Enough" and "Lives with Wives," her most successful work. Jackson died on September 2,

1991, in Sebastian, Florida. She was the author of more than a dozen collections of poetry including *The Telling* (1973) and *How a Poem Comes to Be* (1980).

Robert Frost (1874-1963)

Pulitzer Prizes—*New Hampshire* (1924), *Collected Poems* (1931), *A Further Range* (1937), and *A Witness Tree* (1943)

Frost often vacationed in Key West, Florida. The cottage that he stayed in was recognized by a commemorative plaque by the Friends of Libraries U.S.A. in 1995. The cottage, not open to public tours, is occasionally rented to writers-in-residence.

Tourists can receive information about Frost's Key West days when touring the adjacent Heritage House Museum (410 Caroline Street) which is open for public tours 10 a.m. to 5 p.m. Monday through Saturday and noon until 5 p.m. Sunday.

Frost influenced the nation with his poetry and affected the lives of everyone who came to know him. His poems often dealt with rural life and old-fashioned values.

Born on March 26, 1874, in San Francisco, California, Frost was named Robert Lee after the Confederate general Robert E. Lee. However, he dropped his middle name when he established himself as a writer. When Frost's father died in 1885, he moved with his mother and baby sister to Lawrence, Massachusetts. There, while attending Lawrence High School, Frost became interested in writing poetry. His first poem, "La Noche Triste," was published in his high school newspaper. He attended Dartmouth in 1892 and

Harvard in 1898, but did not receive a degree from either school.

Frost married Elinor White on December 28, 1895; they had six children. Frost and his wife both taught school until 1912 when they moved to England. In 1913, Frost's first collection of poetry, *A Boy's Will*, was published. It was followed in 1914 with *North of Boston*. His poetry had crossed the ocean and received the approval of an admiring North American audience.

When Frost returned to the United States in 1915, much of his time was spent lecturing and teaching. However, he found time to continue writing and was awarded the Pulitzer Prize four times for *New Hampshire* (1924); for *Collected Poems* (1931); for *A Further Range* (1937); and *A Witness Tree* (1943). He was poetry consultant to the Library of Congress from 1958 until 1961.

In 1961, Frost read "Dedication" and "The Gift Outright" at the presidential inauguration of John F. Kennedy. His last collection of poetry, *In the Clearing*, was published in 1962.

Frost died on January 29, 1963, two months before his 89th birthday, in Boston, Massachusetts. He was cremated at Mount Auburn Cemetery.

Wallace Stevens (1879-1955)

Pulitzer Prize—*Collected Poems*, 1955

Friends of Libraries U.S.A. honored Wallace Stevens in 1996 with a commemorative plaque at a Key West hotel where he stayed.

Wallace Stevens was born on October 2, 1879, in Reading, Pennsylvania. An accomplished insurance man, Stevens wrote poetry in his spare time. His first collection of poetry, *Harmonium*, was published in 1923, when Stevens was in his 40s. He is also the author of *Ideas of Order* (1935) and *Notes Toward a Supreme Fiction* (1942).

Stevens died on August 2, 1955, in Hartford, Connecticut. He received the Pulitzer Prize for Poetry in 1955 for *Collected Poems*.

Index of Authors